Created and Directed by Hans Höfer

INSIGHT GUIDES
Venice

Produced by Eva Ambros
Edited by Dr. Heinz Vestner
Photographed by Benjamin W.G. Legde and others
Translated by Cherry Wilder

HOUGHTON MIFFLIN COMPANY

APA PUBLICATIONS

Venice

Second Edition (3rd Reprint)
© **1995 APA PUBLICATIONS (HK) LTD**
All Rights Reserved
Printed in Singapore by Höfer Press Pte. Ltd

Distributed in the United States by:	Distributed in Canada by:	Distributed in the UK & Ireland by:	Worldwide distribution enquiries:
Houghton Mifflin Company	**Thomas Allen & Son**	**GeoCenter International UK Ltd**	**Höfer Communications Pte Ltd**
222 Berkeley Street	390 Steelcase Road East	The Viables Center, Harrow Way	38 Joo Koon Road
Boston, Massachusetts 02116-3764	Markham, Ontario L3R 1G2	Basingstoke, Hampshire RG22 4BJ	Singapore 2262
ISBN: 0-395-66289-3	ISBN: 0-395-66289-3	ISBN: 9-62421-069-1	ISBN: 9-62421-069-1

ABOUT THIS BOOK

The greatest compliment to Venice is the number of other cities that want to be compared with it. Around the world, Copenhagen, St. Petersburg, Bangkok and a small city in California, all seek to be compared to the ancient city-state sitting on foundations in the waters of its own lagoon. This is the city of Marco Polo, an entire school of painters and millions of visitors who keep it alive while at the same time endanger its survival.

With this remarkable history and cultural atmosphere to go with its remarkable beauty, Venice was an absolute must to be included in the Insight Guide series from Apa Publications, whose books now cover more than 180 destinations.

Insight Guides take travellers beyond the usual tourist locations and give readers a greater sense of the entire atmosphere of their destinations. Along the canals and quiet side streets, *Insight Guide: Venice* is the informative companion one needs to fully appreciate this living museum.

All of the Apa books reflect the publishing concepts of Hans Höfer who founded the firm with his first volume, *Insight Guide: Bali*. Each book reflects the training Höfer received in the Bauhaus tradition of book design, typography and photography - marked by fine writing, great photographs and fresh, frank journalism.

Local Team

As with other guides Höfer assigned a single project editor to take charge of this project, enlisting the services of the best available local writers and photographers. For this book, he designated **Eva Ambros** as project editor. She is a Munich native who prefers to live in Italy where she pursues her special areas of interests including Egyptology, Semitic studies and Christian oriental languages. In addition to editing the entire text of this guide, Ambros translated material written originally in Italian.

Claudia Fathy studied Drama in Munich with special emphasis on baroque music-drama and the Commedia dell' Arte. She gives readers a glimpse of the world of theater in her articles on the Teatro La Fenice and Vivaldi and the Venetian Musical Tradition. She also contributed the articles on The Art of the Glass Blowers, The Doge, Venetian Masquerade as well as the detailed Travel Tips at the end of the book.

Ima Agustoni and **Umberto Troni**, husband and wife are "our Venetians". Agustoni is a scriptwriter, moderator and author known and loved by television viewers in German speaking countries for many years. Her articles on Cafés, Bars and Restaurants provides an appetizing guide to Venetian cuisine.

Troni has lectured and wrote about his native city for many years. Our book profited from his authoritative articles over the gradual decline of the Queen of the Adriatic and the city's more recent history.

Journalist **Christine Metzger** provided three of the most important articles in the book: the chapters on The Piazza San Marco, The Cathedral of St. Mark and The Grand Canal.

After graduating in History, Education and German Studies, Metzger worked as an editor in a publishing house in Cologne; today she is a freelance journalist living in Munich.

We were especially fortunate in obtaining the services of the busy author **Dr. Bene**

Fathy

Augustoni

Troni

Metzger

Ambros

Benedikt for the article on the Doge's Palace. The deputy chief editor of the distinguished magazine *Traveller's World* has written guides on Southern Italy, Sicily and Sardinia.

Inge Klostermeier did the important article on the Ghetto and the history of the Jews in Venice. She was born in Munich and completed her studies first in Education and Communication, Political Science and Modern History in Munich and in Berlin.

Hannerl Neumann wrote the chapters on The Great Painters of the Serenissima, and I Frari: The Friar's Church. He also gathered first-hand information for the article on Gondolas and Gondoliers. She studied Communication and Art History and has worked for the *Münchner Merkur* and for Bavarian Television.

Georg Weindl, a trained industrial engineer, has written for *Traveller's World* and other journals. He made a long stay in Venice to prepare his four articles on expeditions through the city. Weindl is not adverse to good food, as we learn from his accounts of the delicious things to be found in the byways of Venice.

Annette Tohak and **Alfred Horn** both come from Bonn. Some years ago Tohak found her way to Burano, which she regards as the most beautiful island in the lagoon. Together with the committed ecologist Horn, Tohak wrote the article about the environmental problems of Venice. A freelance journalist, she lovingly describes the islands Murano, Torvello and Burano. In the chapter Around San Zanipolo, Horn gives an interesting and amusing account of the great Dominican Church and the Condottiere Colleoni.

Nicola Schmitz, author of the articles on the Film Festival and the Biennale Art Exhibition, has also made her home in Italy.

Schmitz is an Art Historian who took the Fine Arts Course at Christie's during a student year in London and completed her studies with a Master of Arts in Venice doing research for her doctorate on the Biennale.

The observations of **Gerhard Sasse** over the literary legends of Venice end the book on a harmonious note. Sasse is a freelance writer in Berlin, working on scripts, radio reports and children's stories.

Most of the photographs in this book were taken by **Benjamin W.G. Legde**. He captures the play of colors and reflections in her shimmering canals. He shows us the splendor of the city - its palaces and churches as well as the daily life of the people and the fabulous masks of carnival. Legde spent many months in Venice preparing the photographs for *Insight Guide: Venice*.

Insight Guide Photographers

Other photographs found in this book are by **Albano Guatti** of New York, **Gerd Pfeiffer**, **Joachim Chwaszeza** and **Alfred Horn** of Munich, **Frederike Fritz** of Col–ogne and **Günter Schneider** of Berlin. The lion's share of archive photographs are from **Archive für Kunst und Geschiechte** (Art and History Archives Berlin).

Our special thanks to the Italian National Tourist Agency in Munich, Sigorina Christina of PROMOVE in Venice, and above all to signor Cesare of the Piazza San Marco branch of the local Provincial Tourist Office (E.P.T.) in Venice.

A very special acknowledgement must be extended to New Zealand-born translator-writer **Cherry Wilder** for her ability to meet with demanding deadlines.

Klostermeier

Neumann

Weindl

Schmitz

Legde

CONTENTS

TRAVEL TIPS

LA SERENISSIMA

"Venice is a city so unreal that one cannot have any idea of what she is like unless one has actually beheld her. Maps, plans, models and travelers' tales are not enough. You must see her!" Carlo Goldoni, the Venetian dramatist, wrote these words about his beloved city in the 18th century.

They are still true today. The special charm of the city in which nothing is quite the same as in other cities has always drawn visitors from all over the world. Her houses, palaces and churches are built on 118 islands in a lagoon. More than 400 bridges span the shimmering network of canals which criss-cross the city. Boats, large and small, gondolas and barges remain the only form of transport, even in the 20th century. Apart from electricity and motor-boats the industrial age seems to have stopped at the Railway Station. A city without automobiles: this is an anachronism which makes Venice a model for future town-planning.

La Serenissima—the most illustrious, the most sublime. This was the proud title worn by the Roman Emperors, and with which the Venetian Republic chose to adorn herself. Through trade with the Orient, Venice rose from a small island state to a world power and maintained this position for centuries. Venice's star began to set in the Age of Discovery. When Napoleon entered the city in the lagoon with his troops in 1797, Venice, where the Doges had ruled for 1000 years, fell to the invaders without a shot being fired.

The unique quality of Venice has been captured in the work of countless poets and writers. Like no other city Venice has become a place of myth and legend, a literary *Fata Morgana*. In the 19th century especially one dwelt upon the approaching decline and fall of the once mighty Queen of the Adriatic; the very signs of this decay possessed a melancholy charm. The Romantic spirit found a perfect setting in Venice, among winding alleyways and edifices of oriental splendor rising from the sea. Romantic literature was enriched by sorrowful meditation on the passing of beauty.

The disastrous floods of 1966 led to a major change. National and international relief campaigns began, funds were set up for rebuilding and for research projects to save the city. Venice, the vast art museum, overflowing with the works of great painters and builders, such as Titian, Tintoretto and Palladio, changed once again into a city pulsing with new life; the city's splendid past blends harmoniously with the flair of a modern metropolis. Now Venice has taken her place as an international congress center, a meeting place for the trade summit talks, and as a patron of modern art.

THE CITY IN THE LAGOON

Its place in the midst of a lagoon gives Venice the unique charm of a castle surrounded by water. This special geographical situation brought about the formation of Venice and its development into one of the richest and most powerful cities in the world.

The word lagoon, which comes from the Latin *lacuna* and can conjure up romantic visions, meant simply 'pool' or 'pond'. A marshy landscape with ponds lay originally between Ravenna and Triest in the curve of the Adriatic coast, and in outlying districts it looks the same to this day. We would now refer to the lagoons in their original state as a biotope or ecological system: salty stretches of water, rich in fish, studded with islands of reeds and banks of silt, the habitat of waterbirds. A narrow island barrier protects the lagoons from the Adriatic, with its occasional storms and rough weather. Natural openings between these tongues of land allow the tides to stream in so that part of the lagoon, the *laguna viva*, is washed clean. Those areas of the lagoon which lie between present-day Venice and the mainland, the *laguna morta*, were always filled with shallow, stagnant water.

In the course of centuries the forces of nature have worked upon the lagoon landscape: some islands have risen up, others have sunken from view. For human beings this is always a difficult inaccessible terrain: for a long time it offered little inducement to settlers. It was this very inaccessibility which led the Veneti, the people of the coast, into the island of the lagoons. Here they found refuge from the waves of invading tribes who attacked the Roman Empire.

The Legendary Foundation

The actual beginnings of the city of Venice may remain obscure forever. The Venetians themselves, however, have shed light on the problem in the simplest possible way. They recorded in their chronicles that the city was founded on March 25, AD 421. This date was worked out by Sabellico, a chronicler of the 15th century. Two things may have influenced his calculations. Firstly, a foundation date lying in the distant past not only laid emphasis on its great age but also increased respect for the city and its traditions. Secondly, Venice must be set forth in the chronicles as the successor to Rome and needed a precise foundation date that lay, not by chance, perhaps, shortly after the conquest of Rome by Alaric the Visigoth.

Although Venice was in fact not yet founded in the 5th century, the region was by no means uninhabited or without a history. The Veneti, a people of Illyrian stock, lived inland from the lagoons from at least 1000 BC. They reckoned their descent from the Eneti who fought against the Greeks on the side of the Trojans and withdrew to the Adriatic coast after the fall of Troy. First they were allied with the Etruscans, then with the Romans. The Veneti fought side by side with the Romans against Hannibal and received imperial citizenship soon after their land became a province of the Empire. Already in the 1st century BC there were flourishing cities such as Aquileia, Verona and Padua in the province of Venetia. The capital, Padua, was one of the richest cities in the empire. The Veneti were traders; they also farmed the land, raised cattle and won salt from the sea. All the larger towns had wharves and harbors and on the islands in those days there lived fishermen, market gardeners and salt workers.

When the Roman Empire was divided in AD 395 the province of Venetia began to play a more important role in world politics for the Emperor Honorius chose Ravenna as the capital of the Western Roman Empire. The province was caught up in the events that would lead not only to the decline of the Western Roman Empire but also to the founding of the city of Venice.

In the course of their migrations Germanic tribes constantly invaded Italy. Many Veneti took refuge on the islands in the lagoons but when danger had passed they used to return to their homes on the mainland. The first true settlement was brought about in AD 452 by the invasion of Attila the Hun. Inhabitants of the mainland who fled before his hordes decided to remain in the safety of the islands.

The form of life which these settlers developed was described a hundred years later by Cassiodorus. This high official of the Ostrogoth court in Ravenna was arranging for the lagoon-dwellers to transport cargo from Istria to Ravenna. "Since you have such numbers of ships," he wrote, "you must come the shallows and currents of these difficult waterways by building special flat-bottomed boats. Already they were in demand as traders.

The basis of their economy was one of the most important mediums of exchange at that time, namely salt. "Instead of plow and sickle," wrote Cassiodorus, "you make great use of the cauldron, to obtain salt, your main source of income…" The dwelling places of the lagoon folk he describes as "Nests of wa-

be responsible for transport. Take the way that one could call your 'streets'... your keel-boats have no need to fear rough ground. In the distance, when the canals which carry your ships cannot be seen it looks for all the world as if you are sailing over the meadows." This shows how well the former refugees had mastered their new environment, the world of the lagoons. They had over-

Previous page: *The State Barge of the Doge* **(painting by Canaletto). Above,** *The First Settlements* **(Drawing by Sabbadino in the 16th century).**

terbirds", lying in places "around which the sea and land meet and struggle together".

The kingdom of the Ostrogoths, whom Cassiodorus served, was set up in 493 by Theodoric the Great. This ruler had been raised at the Byzantine court and was true to the Eastern Roman Emperor. For this reason he was sent against the German prince Odoacer who caused the fall of the last Western Roman Emperor in AD 476 in order to rule in Ravenna himself. The Emperor at Byzantium demanded that, after the fall of the Western Empire, his supremacy should now be acknowledged over the whole of the

Roman Empire. This demand decided the fate of Italy and thus of the province of Venetia. A later change of policy in Byzantium, caused the Ostrogoths to be driven from Italy soon after the death of Theodoric. A governor with the title Exarch of Ravenna ruled the province for the Eastern Roman Emperor in Byzantium.

Already a new danger was to be seen on the horizon: the Lombards (meaning 'longbeards') were moving down from the plains of the Danube in search of land. In AD 568 these cruel and ferocious invaders fell

upon Italy and founded a new kingdom with its capital at Pavia. Even more people from the mainland fled to the safety of the islands. Small settlements such as Murano, Burano Grado or Malamocco grew into flourishing towns. Torcello was a rich trading center, the forerunner of Venice. However the islands round the Rialto, later to be the heart of *La Serenissima*, were still uninhabited.

For the next hundred years while the Lombards continued to expand their kingdom the Sea-Venetians profited from their border position in the lagoon. They were under the rule of the Exarch of Ravenna and

enjoyed the protection of the Byzantine fleet. The towns were administered by tribunes and the regional leader was, as the situation required, a general with the title *Magister Militum*. According to Venetian records one such *Magister Militum* was voted the higher military title of *Dux*. Of this first Doge—as he was called in Venetian speech—nothing is known except his name, Paoluccio Anafesto.

The first hundred years of rule by the Doges were filled with internal unrest; hardly one Doge died a natural death. The individual towns did not form a community but struggled for power in bloody local wars. The pro-Byzantine faction and the separatists were mortal enemies. A leading role in these disputes was played by the noble families of the tribunes, the same clans who would later dictate the policies of the Venetian Republic. Their wealth and influence were based upon their great land holdings on the mainland. They still retained these possessions in spite of the Lombard overlords and doubtless were able to come to terms with the Salian Franks who arrived next on the scene.

When Emperor Leon III of Byzantium forbade the worship of icons, a wave of anti-Byzantine sentiment engulfed the Empire and caused a rising in 726 that was sanctioned by the Pope. This began a complete alteration of the power structure in Italy. The decline of Byzantine rule made itself plain and the Lombards seized the opportunity to conquer Ravenna. Now the Pope, fearing that he would fall into the hands of the Lombards, turned for help to the Carolingian Franks. Charlemagne, King of the Franks, can be seen as the founder of Venice.

The Birth of Venice

The Frankish army, summoned by the Pope, finally conquered the Kingdom of the Lombards in 774. The important role that Charlemagne played in Italian politics from this time reached its high point when he was crowned Holy Roman Emperor on Christmas Day of the year 800. This was a public affront to the Emperor in Byzantium. The inevitable conflict that followed was fought partly for the possession of the towns of Sea-Venetia. The Veneti themselves wavered between the Byzantines and the Franks: there was no unity in their own ranks.

In 809 Pippin, the son of Charlemagne, conquered the lagoons. This event inspired the Venetian chroniclers of later days to flights of fancy. Pippin, they wrote, must watch while his army drowned before the invincible Rialto island and then creep away defeated. In fact, Pippin destroyed many of

The year 812 brought at last the Peace of Aaachen. The recognition of his imperial title was worth so much to Charlemagne that he was ready to part with the Venetian towns in the lagoon and the east Adriatic region in order to keep this honor. In this situation Byzantine rule was not unwelcome to Rialto-Venice: a distant overlord allowed them much more elbow room. Moreover their valuable trading contacts to the east were now secure.

Agnello Partecipazio (811-827) was the first Doge who ruled from the new residence

the towns in the lagoons including the seat of the Doge, Heracliana, and his new residence at Malamocco.

The *Rialtine*—a group of 118 islands on both sides of the Grand Canal—would now become the new center of the lagoon. *Rialto* (from the latin *rivus altus* which means deep channel) was the name for the new residence of the Doges; the name *Venezia* for the city first appeared in the 10th century.

Left, Charlemagne (painting by Albrecht Dürer). Above, island in the lagoon—the same yesterday as today.

on the Rialto. On the site of the present Palace of the Doges he built his first official residence, still of wood in those days and surrounded by a garden. The center of the city, from the Piazza San Marco to the Rialto bridge, and the west bank of the Grand Canal, were already settled. A vigorous campaign was carried out against the natural dangers of the lagoon: the islands were built up and reinforced, and as a protection against the floods, canals were dug and rivers were diverted. A branch of the river Brenta, however, still flows through Venice: the Grand Canal.

UNDER THE WINGED LION

On feast days, besides the Italian flag, a banner in medieval style bearing the device of a winged lion flies before the Basilica San Marco. This symbol of St. Mark the Evangelist remains the hallmark of the city of Venice.

Around the Piazza San Marco the lion stands proudly on all the buildings. He is golden, before a star-studded background of midnight blue; he is carved in stone with a grim and awe-inspiring expression; sometimes he has a drawn sword, sometimes an open book bearing the words '*Pax tibi Marce, evangelista meus*' (Peace be with you, O Marcus my evangelist). In the most out of the way corners of the city one meets the golden lion.

The True Ruler

Like scarcely any other city, Venice has maintained the cult of its patron saint through the centuries. He is at once the protector of the Venetians and part of that ideology which made them a great power. St. Mark was the true ruler of the city: coins were minted bearing his image; Venice was to go down in history as the Republic of St. Mark. The banner of St. Mark waved over the whole empire of maritime trade; the lion kept watch before the citadel, over portals and fortress walls, encouraging the Venetians in their ascendency. His patronage turned them into a chosen people and gave wings to their political aspiration and achievement. To this day the Venetians have a great love for St. Mark.

At the entrance to St. Mark's Church stands a shield which tells us that the Evangelist lies buried here and on the facade there are mosaics which show how he was brought to Venice. Nowhere does one hear the story that in 1968, by order of Pope Paul VI, the saint's remains were to have been flown to the new St. Mark's Cathedral in Cairo. Every Venetian one asks laughs gently at such a notion. Is this return journey a modern legend or have the Venetians been deceived as they deceived the Egyptians in the 9th century?

In those days—it was the year 827—the two merchants Buono and Rustico traveled with 10 ships to Alexandria, probably under orders from the Doge Giustiniano Partecipazio. Their mission was to obtain the relics of the saint for Venice. Today it is hard for us to grasp the importance of the role played by the cult of relics in the middle ages. In the presence of a saint one was sure of God's grace and favor even in worldly things.

The higher a saint was ranked in the Christian hierarchy during his lifetime the more efficacious were his mortal remains in raising the status of his last resting place.

The two Venetians obtained the bones of St. Mark by a trick. They made use of a rumor that the Caliph planned to pull down the Church of St. Mark in Alexandria and use the stone to build a palace. Fearing that the relics could be destroyed two monks were willing to let the Venetians have them for a paltry sum. There are sources which describe this transaction as pure robbery, especially in view of the secrecy with which the relics were carried off. Since the customs officials, as Moslems, found pork an abomination the precious relics were smuggled out of the country hidden in a basket under quantities of pork and ham.

In order to hide the fact that the body of St. Mark, the founder of the Christian church in Egypt, had been stolen, the remains of St. Claudia were laid in his silken mummy case. Perhaps this is the reason that many Egyptian Christians insist that St. Mark has never left Egypt.

After a stormy voyage which all survived under the protection of the saint the ship arrived in the city on the lagoon and was given a joyous welcome. Soon afterwards work began, next to the Doge's residence, on a splendid memorial church to house the precious relics. When the church was destroyed by fire in 976 the bones of the saint are said to have remained unharmed. The story goes that, much earlier, they were walled up inside a pillar for protection. For more than a hundred years this remained a secret even from the Venetians. First in the year 1094, on the occasion of the second consecration of the present Basilica, this pillar miraculously opened and the arm of St. Mark stretched forth. An eternal flame burns upon this spot and June 25, the day on which the saint's bones were found again, is a festival.

After the crypt of the Basilica had served as the burial place of the relics for 700 years they were reinforced under the high altar in 1811. And there they should still be resting. Who can tell?

Right, *The Arrival of the Relics of St. Mark in Venice,* **a 13th-century mosaic, which forms the west facade of St. Mark's Church (Porta di San Alippio).**

THE LION OF ST. MARK

Rialto-Venice, now the new seat of government of the Venetian towns in the lagoons, was systematically built into a center of power. A new saint was meant to replace the former patron of the city, the Byzantine St. Theodor. The choice of St. Mark the Evangelist was made on political as well as religious grounds. The young city wished to be the seat of a Patriarch. The importance of the title of Patriarch can be judged from the fact that in the 9th century only five bishops

Rialto-Venice, however, could claim the presence of the saint himself, since his sacred relics had been stolen from Alexandria. Aquileia won this struggle for the patriarchal title but Venice, with the possession of the relics of St. Mark had laid foundation of a powerful state religion. Under the protection of St. Mark and in the shadow of his banner with the device of a winged lion Venice, La Serenissima, would rise to the greatest heights.

of the Catholic church held this honor: the Pope and the Patriarchs of Byzantium, Antioch, Jerusalem and Aquileia. The criterion for the bestowal of this title was that a city could call upon an apostolic succession. Aquileia, on the Venetian mainland, chose as its patron Mark, the Evangelist and pupil of Peter, who was believed to have preached in the town before his missionary journey to Egypt. The Bishop of Grado, another city of the lagoons, felt that the right to the title was his, since the Patriarch of Aquileia had fled before the Lombards to Grado and brought the patriarchate with him.

In the 9th and 10th centuries Venice still did not play a large part in international affairs but she maneuvered with much diplomatic skill between the two great empires that were her neighbors. Her goals included independence from Byzantium, free trade routes and stable export markets. Through treaties Venice secured her commercial freedom on all sides, so that even the Pope and the Saracens, who held Sicily since 827, were her trading partners. Great prestige was won by the building of her own fleet which could offer its services to Byzantium or to the Frankish Emperor.

In Byzantium it was soon recognized that the dominion over the Venetian sea towns had a more and more nominal character. Trading treaties and state gifts showed that both parties understood the situation. Actual independence was reached in AD 840 when the Doge Pietro Tradonico made a treaty with Lothar I, a grandson of Charlemagne, without obtaining permission from Byzantium. The Doge of Venice was now the equal partner of the Holy Roman Emperor.

subdue the whole coast and lay the foundations of Venetian supremacy in the Adriatic.

To commemorate this event the Doges celebrated every year on Ascension Day the *Festa della Sensa*, the Wedding with the Sea. In this ceremony, which has recently been revived, the Doge was borne out to the sea in his magnificent ship of state, the *Bucintoro*, and with stately gestures cast into the waves a golden ring. He uttered these words: *"Desponsamus te mare in signum*

The Venetian trading vessels were caused great hardship by the attacks of pirates in the Adriatic sea. Slavic tribes, who had been driven right to the sea coast during the time of the great migrations, now made the seaways unsafe. Venetian military expeditions to the Istrian and Dalmatian coasts were not always successful and gave no lasting solution to the problem. It was not until the year 1000 that Doge Pietro Orseolo II managed to

Left, the Lion of St. Mark (15th century, Museum of St. Mark's Church). Above, the Arsenal (old sketch).

veri perpetuique dominii—We wed thee, O sea, in token of our true and lasting dominion." The Venetians made their pact with the sea in the form of a marriage ceremony, a magic oath of fealty that was renewed every year in token of their enduring dominion over the Adriatic.

On the Way to Republic

The commercial spirit was the essential element in Venice and the merchants were the driving force in the state. So it was the rich patrician families who brought about in

Venice a republican form of government which existed in none of the other Italian city states of the Middle Ages. They were determined not to be dictated to by any one man, especially when it did not serve their financial interests, and they continually rose up in bloody rebellions. During an uprising against the Doge Pietro Candiano IV in the year 976, a fire destroyed the city center, including the Doge's palace, with the city archives, and the first Church of St. Mark.

Hereditary rule by the Doges, as practised in the earlier centuries, gradually had to

Book. The *Signoria*, the heads of government, consisted of the Doge, his six Councillors, the *Consiglieri*, and three speakers from the *Quarantia,* the 40 members of the supreme court. The basic principle of this patrician oligarchy, the Venetian Republic, was to reduce the number of government posts so that complete control was possible.

The notorious Council of Ten, an organization resembling a secret state police, was first introduced in 1310 as a reaction to the uprising of Bajamonte Tiepolo against the Closure of the Great Council. Another at-

weaken in order to preserve internal peace. The power of the Doge was deliberately limited and at his side there grew a controlling state apparatus recruited from the great families and watching their interests. Since 1172 their most important body was the Great Council, the *Maggior Consiglio*, which also elected the Doge. This council grew in numbers from 35 to almost 2000 members.

With the 'Closure of the Great Council' in the year 1297 places on the Council became hereditary. The names of the noble families entitled to a place were written in the Golden

tempt at a coup d'état, directed by the Doge himself, was discovered by the *Dieci* (the Ten) in 1355. Marin Faliero had also attempted to seize power from the privileged patrician families of the Great Council.

Commerce with the Crusaders

"...the Venetians provided them (the Crusaders) with a rich market containing everything necessary for men and their horses. The fleet that Venice had made available was so rich and fine that no Christian man had ever seen one finer..." So writes the

French chronicler de Villehardouin in his account of the Fourth Crusade. This crusade, which set sail from Venice in autumn 1202, was meant to sail to Egypt but Enrico Dandolo, the only Doge who ever led a crusade, steered it towards Byzantium, against Venice's own liege lords.

The crusading movement, summoned up by Pope Urban II in 1095 to protect Byzantium and free the Holy Land, became an interesting source of income for Venice. After showing some initial concern for the Moslem trading partners the Venetians took part in the lucrative business of transporting troops to the Holy Land. Stung by the success of their commercial rivals Genoa and Pisa, they also took an active part in the military operations. A third part of the ports of Tyre and Askalon fell into their hands and they were able to extend their trading colonies considerably.

The mighty army of the Fourth Crusade was more or less forced to place itself under the supreme command of the Doge, for it was unable to raise the sum of 85,000 silver marks agreed upon for transport and the provisioning of the troops. Enrico Dandolo—at this time far gone in years and, it is said, almost blind—led the Crusaders first to Zara. When the unruly Dalmatian coastal towns had been subdued the army settled into winter quarters. Then, instead of taking themselves off to Egypt, the Crusaders proceeded to Constantinople (Byzantium).

The moral justification for the attack on Christian Byzantium was supposed to be the unification of the Roman Church with the Greek-Orthodox Church which had declared itself independent of the Pope in 1054. In fact this was a last blow struck by Venice at her overlords. In 1203 Constantinople fell to the Crusaders. In 1204, when the city was stormed a second time the crusading armies raged through the streets with unbelievable savagery and plundered even the churches. The Icon of the Ni-

copeian Madonna and the superb bronze horses are two of the most famous pieces of booty seized by the Venetians.

Chroniclers and historians have always found the Venetians deeply implicated in the destruction of Constantinople and the decline of Byzantine culture. For the Venetians themselves, however, this was the step towards complete autonomy and their development into a world power.

The fall of Constantinople laid the foundations for the mighty commercial empire that the Venetians called their 'Stato da

Mar' or Sea State. The Byzantine Empire was divided among the victors and Venice received three-eighths of the city on the Golden Horn, most of the Aegean islands, bases in the Peloponnese, the island of Corfu and the island of Crete—all important for trade with the Levant. Later the Sea State was able to secure the Istrian and Dalmatian coastal districts that she had attempted to bring under her control for so long.

The so-called Latin Empire, consisting of part of the former Byzantine domain, was ruled by Balduin of Flanders, set up by the Doge Dandolo. Now that the balance of

Left, *The Sack of Byzantium* (painting by Tintoretto, the Doges Palace). Right, Enrico Dandolo (the Doges Palace).

27

power had been reversed it was a dependency of Venice. Dandolo himself, had refused the title of Emperor on grounds of age but the Doge was able to call himself 'Lord of a quarter and an eighth of the Roman Empire'.

The Sea State of the Venetians actually consisted of a chain of strategically important strongholds along their trade routes. Through these bases they ensured themselves free passage and lines of supply. They were not much interested in the possession of large tracts of land.

After the fall of Constantinople there began for Venice an age of splendor which lasted for 300 years; she could regard herself as a great international power and her trade enjoyed an incomparable expansion. Of course even this era was not free from crisis; there was a multitude of foreign and domestic difficulties. One of the most serious conflicts arose with her trade rival Genoa; they waged a continual battle for supremacy in the Mediterranean.

When Michael Paleologus seized the Latin Empire in 1261 and set up a new Byzantine Empire, Genoa gave him military aid.

The Venetian merchants were driven out of Constantinople. The hostility that flared up between La Serenissima and Genoa, La Superba, (the proud one) as a result of this was to last a hundred years. One of the best known incidents of this time is the capture of Marco Polo during the sea battle of Curzola in 1298. In prison he dictated to Rusticiano of Pisa the story of his travels to the land of Kublai Khan.

After the Black Death, the great outbreak of plague in the middle of the 14th century which carried off a third of the population of Europe, the two opponents Venice and Genoa, clashed as fiercely as ever. In 1378 the Genoans fought their way right into the lagoons but they were forced to withdraw from the seige of Chiogga in 1380. While the Peace of Turin did not bring Venice any important advantage Genoa had been so weakened by the fighting that she no longer played an important role in trade with the Levant.

The Condottieri

After the war with Genoa, Venice enjoyed a longer period of comparative peace. Trade flourished; profitable local industries expanded from the silk-weaving and glass-blowing to the sugar refinery, printing and shipbuilding. The Arsenal, the state dockyard founded in 1104, had grown into the largest industrial complex in Europe.

Slowly new dangers began to appear on the horizon. Since the middle of the 14th century the Ottoman Turks, a nomadic people from the steppes of Asia pressed ever closer to Europe. It was clear that it would be disastrous for Venice to concentrate only on trade with the east. Her attention turned more and more towards terra firma, the Italian mainland. What had began modestly enough in 1340 with the capture of Treviso had gone on in great style since the beginning of the 15th century. The greatest rival of Venice was Milan which expanded steadily under the dynasty of the Visconti.

Since they lacked standing armies the hostile city states used to hire the services of

Condottieri. Although these mercenaries changed sides according to their wages they were highly regarded and often rewarded by their employers with land and princely titles. Condottieri such as Caramagnola, Gattamelata and Colleoni fought in the service of La Serenissima.

In these years Venice was ruled by one of the most famous of the Doges, Tommaso Mocenigo (1413-1423). Because of his keen interest in the expansion of Venetian territory on the mainland he tried to keep a balance of power between Venice and the

3000 smaller trading vessels, sailed by 17,000 men, and 300 great ships with crews totalling 8000. Besides this we have 45 galleys with not fewer than 11,000 men abroad."

'Mistress of Gold'

In spite of all warnings Foscari was elected Doge and during his reign (1423-1457), the longest in Venetian history, Venice reached her greatest territorial expansion. The Venetian domain reached from the Alps to the river Po and as far as Bergamo

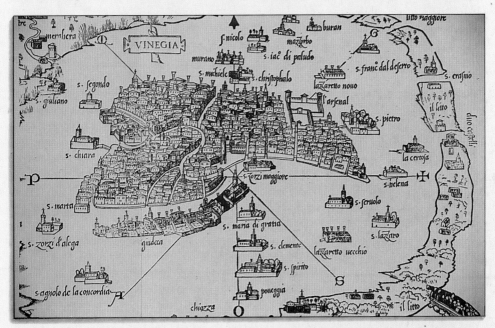

other states of northern Italy. As he felt the approach of death he appealed to the Great Council: they should on no account choose Francesco Foscari as his successor. This man would lead the city into an inglorious war.

Much of his great speech to the Council is an impressive summing up of Venetian commercial achievement. "*The turnover of our foreign trade has reached ten million ducats a year, profit is 40%. Venice owns*

Left, Colleoni (statue by Verrochio). Above, perspective plan of Venice, early 16th century.

in the west. La Serenissima was at the height of her power: she was "*Mistress of all the gold in Christendom*"; as the Doge Tomaso Mocenigo had prophesied in his speech.

The Turks had taken Constantinople in 1453 but Venice was still able to cope with this threat. In fact the Sea State even acquired the island of Cyprus. Through a shrewd gambit the patrician's daughter Caterina Cornaro was made Queen of Cyprus. When her husband, King Jacob II died soon afterwards Catarina ruled until 1489 then abdicated in favor of the true regent: Venice, the Serenissima.

Das ist der edel Ritter · Marcho polo von Swnedig der groſt landtfarer · der vns beſchreibt die groſſen wunder der welt die er ſelbſt geſehen hat · Von aim ain aufgang biſ zu dem nidergāg der ſunnē · der gleychē vor nicht meer gehort ſeyn

30

A Trading Nation
Between Orient and Occident

"Every market place is surrounded by high houses. In the lower stories there are shops where all kinds of wares are stored and sold. Spices and all kinds of baubles and beads. I learned from a customs official that the daily consumption of pepper runs to 43 tons and every ton is 243 pounds. In this way one can attempt to grasp the amounts of meat, wine, spices and such things that are used every day by the people of Qinsay."

These figures over the seat of the Sung dynasty, Hangchou (Qinsay) comes from the famous book of his travels by the Venetian Marco Polo. In 1271, together with his father Niccolo Polo and his uncle Maffeo, he set out for the court of the Great Khan of the Mongols in Cathay or China. After a three year journey through Baghdad, Persia and right across central Asia, they reached Peking in 1275. Marco, who was now 21 years old, found favor with the Emperor, Kublai Khan, who entrusted him with high offices of state.

As he returned to his native town in 1295, loaded with gifts, he was able to tell his countrymen remarkable stories. Only a few of them believed his description of a city as large as Hangchou, which, with a population of 2 million, was the biggest and richest city in the world; at that time, this sounded like pure fantasy. A convincing detail was the fabulous amount of pepper used there in a single day. Pepper, in the Middle Ages, was weighed out a peppercorn at a time, and was as precious as gold.

The accuracy of Marco Polo's information was first recognized years later and his Book of Wonders awoke some unexpected echoes. The novelties from China included the ingredients for making porcelain and the use, in cooking, of 'pasta' hitherto unknown in Europe. Marco Polo was also the first European who reported the use of paper money and gave an account of coal mining.

Left, Marco Polo (woodcut from the German edition of his book, 15th century).

His description of the Lands of Spices, their geography and the sea-routes that led to them, fascinated and influenced generations of merchants and sea-farers, including the Genoese, Christopher Columbus.

The Spice Trade

Spices! For centuries this was the magic word that made the hearts of merchants beat faster. For unimaginable riches were to be gained with spices. The everyday use of spices was a hundred times higher than it is today and the prices of these precious substances were astronomical. Already in Roman times spices were a valued medium of exchange and since the Crusades the spice trade had reached new heights of prosperity.

The outlandish use of spices which soldiers and pilgrims had learnt in the Orient now found their way into the kitchens of ordinary people. Exotic seasonings were enjoyed for their pungent aroma but the fact that they came from fabled lands increased their attraction. The cultivation of local herbs was not highly developed.

The Venetians controlled the spice trade right into the 16th century. Their warehouses were filled with pepper, cinnamon, cloves, ginger, tumeric, nutmeg and cardamom. Already at the beginning of the 15th century the trade in spices had an annual turnover of 540,000 ducats which would mean about 30 million dollars today. Spices were only a part of the Venetian imports from the East; other luxury goods included silk, furs, velvets, precious stones, pearls and perfumery.

Their exposed position in the lagoon made the island dwellers into skilful traders from earliest times; they did not have enough land for intensive cultivation. Already in the year AD 750 Venetian traders came to the marketplace in Pavia, the Lombard capital, with velvets and silks, feathers from peacocks and golden pheasants, tyrian purple and valuable furs.

Their most important medium of exchange was still in those days salt and salted fish. The great importance of salt in the produce markets of the Middle Ages can scarcely be appreciated today. Cassiodorus called it "edible money" and its value can be compared with petroleum today.

Sea Trade

Oriental goods first reached Venice in Byzantine ships but soon the Venetians were able to send ships of their own. Sea voyages were a dangerous undertaking. Attacks by

lay in their swiftness and their fighting power. They controlled the trade in luxury goods and served on the trade routes which had regular time tables.

At the beginning of the 15th century 3000 trading vessels sailed under the Venetian flag. Most of them were in the coastal trade, delivering wood, stone or grain, or were part of the fishing fleet. Overseas trade was carried out by about 300 ships which traveled on their own or with the heavily armed convoys organized by the state, the *Mude*. The municipal trading ventures had the

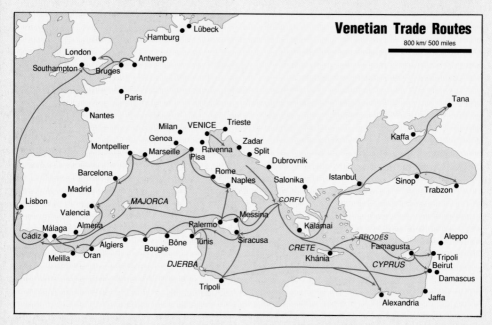

pirates were just as much feared as stormy weather. It was not until the end of the 13th century when simple, accurate charts and the compass assisted navigation, that mariners were no longer at the mercy of bad weather or forced to seek an anchorage every night.

The development of ship-building techniques meant that ships had increasing cargo space and were faster and more easily manageable. Two types of ship were used in international trade: the long low galley, with sails and oars, and the cog, a roomy round-bellied sailing ship. The advantage of the galleys, which were actually ships of war,

advantage of being relatively safe and La Serenissima charged high prices for cargo space in the galleys and for the protective convoy. On account of these high costs there were always private ship owners who traveled at their own risk and were rewarded with appreciably higher profits.

The sea voyage was always the most dangerous part of overseas trade. A way of reducing the business risk was the formation of a partnership, the *colleganza*. As a rule this was made between two merchants; one remained in Venice and put up three quarters of the capital, while the other, who went on the voyage, put up the remaining quarter. The profit, after deduction of costs, was divided between the two.

The standard route taken by the Mude or convoys reached from England to Tana and Trebizond on the Black Sea. The most important trading partner of the Venetians, however, was Egypt. Other important harbors of the near east were Beirut and Byzantium. As well as luxury goods, cotton and sugar were brought in the Levant and in the plantations of Cyprus. Wax, honey, wheat, oil and wine came from the Greek Islands.

In all larger cities the Venetians had trading establishments where they did business and exercised considerable political influence in many countries. Although Venetians were regarded as hard businessmen they were held in high esteem for their fair dealing, and even their lively participation in the slave trade did not alter this.

The Slave Trade

Although the slave trade had been officially forbidden since the 9th century it was nonetheless still a good source of income. The slaves were mostly obtained in Tana where the convoys sailed on from Byzantium. Circassians and Georgians, of Greek-Orthodox faith, who were resold, in Egypt and North Africa, could be treated in good conscience as 'non-Christians' because they did not belong to the Catholic church. Trade with heathen slaves was not forbidden.

A wrecked ship, found on the coast of Yugoslavia in 1967, showed what trade goods were popular in the east in the 16th century. The "Gagiana", which according to the Venetian insurance lists, went down on the way to the east in 1583, contained the following cargo: 2000 glass articles from Murano, copper ornaments, damask, English woolen cloth, ceramic objets d'art, gold, silver and precious stones. Iron, lead, tin, copper, amber and timber were also desir-

able commodities in the Orient. Much of this freight was obtained by the Venetians in England and Flanders with the western convoy.

A profitable enterprise that was combined with the Levantine trade was the organization of pilgrimages. For an estimated $2500 in modern currency the Venetians offered the pilgrims a package tour. This included the return fare, a donkey ride to Jerusalem and the various customs duties which Christians must pay in the Holy Land.

The first cloud arose in the clear sky of the

Venetian trading empire when the Turks conquered Byzantium and entered the sphere of influence of the Serenissima. The greater danger came from Portugal, where Prince Henry the Navigator, (1415-1461) was encouraging voyages of exploration. The attempts to find a sea route to the Indies were an attack on the monopoly of the spice trade. Christopher Columbus, born in Genoa, received support for his voyage in 1492 from Ferdinand and Isabella, proud rulers of Spain. In 1499 as Vasco da Gama sailed home to Portugal, from India, the decline of Venice had begun.

Left, the trade routes of the Venetians. Right, a cog (copper engraving, 15th century).

33

IOANNES BELLINVS

THE QUEEN OF THE ADRIATIC IN DECLINE

At the beginning of the 16th century despite the first signs of her approaching decline, Venice had reached glorious heights. Now a serious danger threatened the proud Republic from Europe: the League of Cambrai had been formed by the great continental powers to make war on Venice. The states which had agreed upon a partition of the Venetian territories were France under Louis XII, Spain, Hungary and not least the German Emperor Maximilian and the Pope. In 1509 the European offensive at Agnadello defeated the armies of Venice and seized her territory.

The city was able to save herself once again: Doge Leonardo Loredan (1501-1521) used skilful diplomacy to play off the allies against each other and break the League. A loss of territory on the mainland had to be endured but the Republic kept its independence.

Passing Glory

After Cambrai, however, Venice's position as a great power was lost; she never again played a leading role in international politics. For the moment it seemed wise to be careful and in doubtful situations to adopt a neutral position. The sharpest attacks on the Venetian monopolies came from the Portuguese, the English, the Flemings and the Dutch, while the Turks were in the act of seizing for themselves Venice's colonial territories.

Although sea trade was moving into the Atlantic Ocean as a result of the Age of Discovery, Venice was able to play the role of a trade clearing house between Europe and Asia.

In the middle of the 16th century the Venetians were plagued by new anxieties which included the lower freight charges of the Spanish, Portuguese and English, and the improvement in shipbuilding techniques

Left, *Leonardo Loredan* (painting of Giovanni Bellini, London National Gallery).

and commercial organization, particularly among the Dutch.

There were also pirate attacks: not only Moslem sea-robbers but Genoese, Maltese and Catalans attacked Venetian ships. Among the solutions to this problem one suggestion was a canal through the Isthmus of Suez. This scheme which would first be carried out in the middle of the 19th century, was doomed to failure in the 16th century because of political changes in the near east. The greatness of Venice had passed; the new spice capitals of Europe were Lisbon and Antwerp.

An economic problem faced by Venice began at home: her wealthy merchant class began to invest more of their capital on the mainland. The villas in Brenta bear witness to the enormous wealth of these Venetian patricians. The policy of Venice when she took over the mainland towns was the same as it had been in her Aegean and Adriatic colonies; it depended upon a firm bilateral agreement.

The local provincial government enjoyed a good measure of autonomy in their decisions but they were controlled by a state trustee, the Rector. This system of 'enforced federation' proved so stable that it lasted until the end of the Republic.

Venice and the Turks

The Ottoman Turks were a moslem people from the mountains of Bithynia. Their Sultans organized a powerful fighting force of kidnapped Christian boys, the Janissaries, and had territorial ambitions in Asia Minor, Greece and the Balkans. After a notable set-back at the hands of Tamburlaine, the ageing Mongol conqueror, in 1400, the Ottomans recovered their strength. At last, in 1453, for the second time, they turned their attention to the ancient city on the Golden Horn known as Constantinople, formerly Byzantium. The conquering Turks gave it a new name: *Istanbul*. The Venetian Republic had to weigh her strategy with the

Turks most carefully. According to the needs of the moment they made use of two policies, one peaceful, one military.

A policy of appeasement with Istanbul was necessary in order to guarantee sea-traffic and trade. The Venetian Ambassador to the High Port enjoyed privileges extended to no other European. An advantage for the Venetians was that the Turks depended upon them for their only access to European markets. In spite of this Venice must always be prepared to resist Ottoman expansion. For this reason the Sea State erected massive

fortresses in Corfu, Candia (Crete) Cyprus, on the Greek mainland, and in Dalmatia. Since 1545 the Venetian galleys were reinforced with armed galley slaves. The mightiest fighting ships, the Galeasses or great galleys, were equipped on both sides, above the banks of oars, with a row of cannon. In the Battle of Lepanto they brought victory for the first time.

The Battle of Lepanto

Soon there were grounds for war; Sultan Selim II laid claim to the island of Cyprus which had been in Venetian hands since 1489. A Turkish fleet of 350 ships and a force of 100,000 men beseiged Famagusta and after five months the stronghold fell. The Venetian commander, Marcantonio Bragadin died an agonizing death at the hands of the Turks: he was flayed alive.

The horrible death of Bragadin outraged the whole of Europe. Pope Paul IV was among the first to demand the immediate formation of a "Holy League". Under the supreme command of Don John of Austria, a brother of the Spanish king, Philip II, the armies of Venice, Spain and the Holy See gathered to do battle with the Turks.

In summer 1571 the combined Christian forces, with 26,000 men reached Messina. Half of the fleet consisted of Venetian ships, under the command of the aged admiral Sebastian Venier and of Agostino Barbarigo. The Turkish fleet, which had gathered off Lepanto, near Paras in the Gulf of Corinth, consisted of 200 galleys and a swarm of smaller vessels under the command of Ali Pasha. The engagement began on Oct. 5, 1571 and after a bloody battle the Christian allies gained the victory.

The Venetians, who amazed Europe with their technology, celebrated this victory as a great event. Pictures in the Doge's palace bear impressive witness to the Battle of Lepanto. In spite of all this Lepanto gave the Venetians no lasting advantage. The divergent interests of her allies forced Venice to sign a separate peace treaty with the Turks and give up Cyprus forever.

Venice and the Church

Since Martin Luther with his thesis attacking Indulgences had unleashed a wave of protest against Rome and the Papacy, the Reformation spread throughout Europe. The time had come for a basic alteration in the relationship between church and state. The Catholic clergy were forced to find ways of internal reform and enlightenment. The Council of Trent (1545-1563) was summoned to deal with religious disputes. It led to a strengthening of the Catholic church but it also deepened the schism between the Church and the Reformers.

In disputes with the pope Venice had always taken a stand as an independent sovereign state. '*Siamo Veneziani, por Christiani*' 'We are first Venetians, then Christians'. This saying showed the self-willed Venetians attitude only too clearly. The tension between Rome and Venice finally led to a breach during the reign of Pope Paul V (1605-1621). This Pope, who watched jealously over the rights of the church came into conflict with the Doge developed the telescope with which he was able to begin intensive research on the heavenly bodies. His assistant was the monk Paolo Sarpi. Although he was a cleric, Sarpi defended state independence from the church.

The dispute between Venice and the Pope was kindled by the arrest of two priests from the Veneto who were charged by the Council of Ten with a secular offence. Pope Paul gave orders for the priests to be sentenced by a Roman court but the Venetian government refused to obey. Their legal adviser was

Leonardo Donato. Donato, Doge since 1606, was a free-thinker, inspired by humanism and the ideas of the Renaissance.

During Donato's term of office, scientific research at the University of Padua reached a high point: Galileo Galilei held the post of Professor of Mathematics from 1592-1610. There the great physicist and astronomer

Paolo Sarpi. Paul V laid the clergy of Venice under an Interdict (they were forbidden to perform any church services) and excommunicated the government. The Republic refused to recognize both the excommunication and the Interdict; the priests were forced to perform their offices.

Venice endured this test of strength with Rome with the help of Paolo Sarpi, a scholar and an independant thinker. Sir Henry Wotton, the English Ambassador, believed Sarpi might turn Protestant. But Venice made peace with Rome and Sarpi remained in the service of his beloved city.

Left, *Sultan Mohammed II* (painting by Gentile Bellini). Above, *The Battle of Lepanto* (painting by Vincento, Doges Palace).

The Plague in 1630

The 17th century brought the Venetians little good fortune. The once flourishing merchant empire fell more and more into decay and rivals were close at hand. The Hapsburgs developed the harbor of Triest and thought nothing of employing pirates to get rid of the ships of the Republic.

When Venice supported the French in their war with the Austrians for possession of Mantua fate struck them a heavy blow: the war brought plague to the city. In 16 months 50,000 inhabitants died, a third of the population. In thanksgiving for the end of the epidemic the church of Santa Maria della Salute was founded.

The Advance of the Turks

The long awaited Turkish attack occurred at a time when Venice had scarcely recovered from the effects of the Plague. In the middle of the year 1645 the Turkish army landed in Crete. The Venetians tried to halt their advance by cutting off their supplies. After some initial success they were forced at last in 1669, to cede Crete, one of their most important strongholds in the Aegean to the Turkish invader.

The fortunes of Venice improved once more in 1683. That year, John III Sobieski of Poland, whose chief foreign policy objective was to compensate for Poland's earlier territorial losses to the Turks, concluded a treaty with the Holy Roman emperor. In accordance with that treaty, he defended and defeated Vienna from the Turks later that year. This put an end to a hundred years of Ottoman expansion. Venice knew how to turn this situation to her advantage and made alliances with Austria and Russia. Already in 1684 the Doge Francesco Morosini landed in Morea (the Peloponnese) and in three years recaptured the peninsula from the Turks. This last great Venetian victory was recognized at the Peace of Carlowitz in 1699 but even this success was not long lasting.

Hostilities flared up again within a few years. Although Venice was able to hold Corfu the real victor was Austria, whose troops under Prince Eugene destroyed the Turkish forces. At the Peace of Passowitz (1718) Austria received much new territory. Venice, however, was forced to give up Morea and her last possessions in the Aegean.

The End of Republic

The 18th century was a time in which the former Queen of the Adriatic withdrew completely from the stage of world history. The wars against the Turks had cost the Republic the lives of many of her sons; now she attempted to remain neutral and not to become involved in the wars of the French, Spanish and Austrian succession. The Rialto was no longer a center of overseas trade, the great clearing houses were now Genoa, Leghorn, the Hapsburg city of Triest and the harbors of northern Europe.

The last great project for the Venetians was the building of the Murazzi, massive breakwaters of Istrian stone, to protect the city from the sea. They are nine miles long, 46 feet wide and 49.5 feet high.

Repeated attempts to reform the system of government failed; in 1789, the year that Ludovico Manin was elected as Doge, the French Revolution broke out and Venice remained neutral. In 1796 the 26-year-old Napoleon Bonaparte arrived in Italy. Freedom for the people against the rule of the aristocrat—that was his promise. He marched into Venetian territories without meeting any resistance; on the first day of May 1797 the French army stood at the edge of the lagoon.

In this same month the Great Council, in a tumultuous sitting, declared the abolition of the Republic and gave way to a provisory government. This body, which in itself had too few members present to come to a legal decision, voted with 512 to only 20 votes for the end of the Venetian Republic.

Right, removal of the Horses of St. Mark (old engraving).

THE GREAT PAINTERS OF THE SERENISSIMA

The Venetian school which produced such famous painters as Giorgione, Titian and Tintoretto, has a special place in the rich annals of Italian art. Florence is known as the cradle of Renaissance painting, the Baroque style reached its climax in Rome but in a certain sense Venice is famous as the city of painting in general, the essence of all the Italian schools. The painters of Venice, however, did not play a leading role in the discovery of new forms of artistic expression.

During the early Renaissance (in the 15th century) while artists elsewhere tried to depict men and nature more realistically and studied perspective, the Venetians continued to place stiff figures of saints before a plain gold background. The prototypes for this style were the mosaics of St. Mark's Church and the icon paintings of the Byzantine masters. Even the techniques of oil painting, first fully developed by Titian, were by no means a Venetian invention.

It was Antonella da Messina, a Sicilian, who brought the new technique to Venice. He himself had learned it from the Flemish artists. Up to this time tempera colors, bound with an emulsion of egg water and oil, had been used. Tempera dried very quickly and possessed little luminosity but colors bound only with oil and thus slow drying allowed the artist to experiment on the canvas during the actual painting. These experiments with colors are the secret of the Venetian painters. Their brother artists in other Italian cities strove for realism and exact drawing but the Venetian painters let the colors speak.

Another advantage which the artists of La Serenissima had over their colleagues in the rest of Italy is that they never allowed themselves be governed by one particular style. They accepted new ideas and new developments in their painting but each painter formed his own unmistakable personal style. In Venice one does not speak of Renaissance painters or Mannerists but of Titian, Tintoretto or Veronese. The painter as self confident artist, emancipated from the control of his patron—the painter was born in Venice.

The Bellinis: A Family Business

Jacopo Bellini (c. 1424-1470) learned the basic lessons of Renaissance painting from his teacher Gentile da Fabriano in Florence. His most brilliant pupils were his sons. The older son Gentile Bellini (1429-1507) quickly received recognition and fame and rose to be official State Painter of the Republic. In this post he did many historical pictures in which he reproduced festive occasions with an almost photographic accuracy against the background of his native city.

In 1479 Venice sent him for a year to the court of the Sultan Mohammed II at Constantinople. The Sultan was so delighted by his portraits that he presented the artist with a special letter of thanks to take home to La Serenissima. This document brought Gentile an annual income of 200 scudi for life.

The real genius of the family was the younger brother Giovanni (1430-1516). Giovanni Bellini tended more than his brother towards realistic and life-like paintings of people and landscape. One of his best-known works is the portrait of Doge Leonardo Loredan in the National Portrait Gallery, London.

In spite of Giovanni's talent the older brother was very often given preference over the younger. There was never any conflict between the two brothers; this was due to their mutual admiration and love and to Giovanni's great modesty. Possibly the prejudice against Giovanni can be traced back to the fact that he was illegitimate. He did not live under the same roof as his father and brother although he worked very closely with them and was remembered in the will of Anna da Pesaro, Jacopo's rich wife. Another reason for his lack of worldly success might lie in his deep artistic understanding. It was more important for him to develop as a painter than to fulfill the wishes of a patron.

His work in the Great Council Chamber, for example, went so slowly that the authorities had to send over an official from the justice department every day to see that Giovanni got on with the job. "Giambellino", as he was called, turned down a commission from the Duchess of Mantua Isabella D'Este, because he didn't want to stick to her strict schedule.

In later years, however, he too became State Painter, the successor to his brother. After his death he was laid to rest in the Church of St. John and St. Paul, like his brother Gentile. It was indeed a high honor, for this Dominican church was, since the middle of the 14th century, the chosen resting place of the Doges.

Vittore Carpaccio: Realism and Detail in the 16th century

He was born about 1400 as the son of the Scarpa family but later chose the better-sounding name of Carpaccio. He is counted

Left, Gentile Bellini (self portrait). Right, Giovanni Bellini (self portrait).

as a pupil of the Bellinis. His speciality was great cycles of pictures with religious or historical themes, before the background of contemporary Venice. His commissions came mainly from the Fraternities, the *Scuole*. His most famous work, an eight part cycle on the life and death of St. Ursula, was painted for the Chambers of the Fraternity of Santa Orsola, near the Church of St. John and St. Paul. (Today it is shown in the Academy.) The paintings of Carpaccio are

notable for a love of detail, great narrative talent and a sensitive use of color.

Giorgione: the Enigma

He came from Castelfranco, near Treviso, and entered the workshop of the Bellinis when he was 10 years old. Because of his imposing build, he was called Giorgione which means 'Big George'. His unique talent and his lovable personality made him the darling of courtly society and one of the most beloved painters of Venice. Together with Titian he was given the commission for the frescoes in the German Trading House, the *Fondaco dei Tedeschi*. He was allowed to work according to his own ideas and without any pre-arranged subject matter, which was most unusual for the time. Vasari, "the father of art history", wrote in the 16th century, concerning Giorgione's frescoes: "…I have never understood the meaning of the complete work and have never found anyone who could explain this meaning to me." To this day the contents of Giorgione's pictures are puzzling to art historians. Giorgione died of plague at the age of 34 and became a

legend to his admiring colleagues. Many of them modeled their style on his; Giorgione's way of depicting the landscape was especially influential. This and the fact that unfinished pictures by Giorgione were finished by other painters makes a complete survey of all his works difficult. Many pictures have been ascribed to him and at least 30 are certainly by his hand.

Titian: Genius with a Business Sense

Tiziano Vecellio (1477-1576) came to the atelier of Giovanni Bellini from Pieve di Cadore, a small village on the southern slopes of the Alps, when he was barely 15 years old. No-one could guess that in years to come he would be the most famous artist in Europe, a prince among painters. His greatest model was at first Giorgione but after this painter's early death Titian freed himself from the introverted and mysterious manner of his master and developed his own style. There followed the works on which his fame is based: large single canvases in strong, glowing colors, with men and women as the central theme. Like no other painter before him, Titian made color and contrasts of light and shade the essential elements of his art.

Already, two years before the death of Giovanni Bellini, the ambitious Titian had replaced his former teacher as State Painter. He received commissions not only from the city of Venice but also from the church, the Venetian aristocracy and the princely houses of Italy, such as the Gonzage in Mantua, the Este in Ferrara, and the Della Rovere in Urbino. At the high point of his career he received commissions from the pope, the Emperor Charles V and from his son, Philip II of Spain. Charles V made Titian his court painter, the only artist who did his portraits.

Among his contemporaries Titian was reputed to have a keen business sense. In order to carry out his many commissions he kept as many as 10 assistants and pupils busy in the workshop of his great house, completing large parts of his paintings. As Titian died of the plague, aged almost one hundred, he left behind an enormous body of work.

Tintoretto: A Passion for Painting

Jacopo Robusti (1518-1594), as the painter was really called, received his nickname Tintoretto 'the little dyer' from his father's occupation as a dyer of cloth. In contrast to Titian who liked to move in social circles, Tintoretto lived with his wife and seven children in a house on the edge of the city and devoted himself to painting. He was assisted by two sons and a daughter whom he trained to paint. His commissions came chiefly from the church, the Fraternities and the Venetian government.

His pictures are larger than life, full of floating, plunging figures in dramatic attitudes, with contrasts of light and shade. A picture of this kind is for example *The Last Judgment* in the Doge's Palace, 72 feet wide and 23 feet high, possibly the largest single canvas in the world and one which shows the largest number of human figures. Tintoretto was devoted to his art but could not manage his financial affairs and was often in difficulties. He often painted for the cost of materials or made no charge for his paintings at all. He died penniless although in 1574 he was made official painter to the Doge and received a pension.

Veronese: the Society Portrait Painter

Paolo Caliari (1528-1588) was called Veronese after his native city of Verona. The self-taught painter was brought to Venice at the age of 27 by the Giustiniani family. With his glowing colors in pictures that were carefree and full of the joy of living he captured the taste of the times and was chosen to work on the decoration of the Doge's Palace. He himself directed and carried out the painting in the church of San Sebastiano. His painting was so admired that in 1556, with the agreement of Titian and Sansovino, he received the golden chain of the Procurator of San Marco, one of the city's highest honors.

His works show a broad spectrum of religious, historical and mythological motifs. In his pictures of festive occasions, even those drawn from the Bible, he included portraits of high society in the Venice of his day. After the death of Veronese over a hundred years passed before the Serenissima produced another great painter.

Tiepolo: Wizard of Scenic Illusion

Giovanni Battista Tiepolo (1696-1770), son of a Venetian ship-broker, learned paint-

Left, Tintoretto (self portrait). Right, Titian (self portrait).

ing from his uncle Gregorio Lazzarini. He was especially interested in the old masters Tintoretto and Veronese. Unlike them, however, Tiepolo's palette consisted of pastel tones; delicate airy colors make the space within his pictures shine with an unearthly radiance. The celebrated artist was heaped with commissions in his home city. His fame spread quickly beyond Venice into other Italian cities and he received commissions in other countries. From 1750-53 he worked with his sons on the Imperial hall and the staircase of the Würzburg Residence.

For all his love of art Tiepolo, like Titian, was a clear-headed businessman. He turned down a commission from King Frederick of Sweden to work on his castle in Stockholm, for example, because the payment offered was too low. In 1762 King Charles III of Spain brought him to the court at Madrid where he died in 1770 at the age of 74.

With the great Rococo painter Tiepolo the era of fascinating artists which had lasted for 350 years came to an end. Now, only a few years before the fall of the Republic, the city in the lagoon was no longer important as a patron of famous painters.

VENICE IS NO LONGER AN ISLAND

Napoleon regarded Venice as his property, as indeed he regarded the whole of Italy. His soldiers plundered many churches and monasteries, the Horses of St. Mark and the treasures of the Basilica were taken to Paris. The loss of independence was compensated for a little when the French authorities chose Venetians to form a communal government. This government, which planned great reforms, lasted only a short time. Already in autumn 1797 at the end of the second coalition, France handed Venice and the Veneto over to Austria.

At last the time had come when the former Serenissima ceased to be a sovereign power and became a subject state. The trade links to the mainland were cut and the once flourishing harbor was now only a branch of the Hapsburg city of Triest. When the Arsenal, once the greatest shipbuilding center in the world, was reduced to a repair dock for ships, many tradesmen, from carpenters to carriers, were affected. Economic crises did not stop Venice from attracting international interest once again: in the year 1880 the Roman Catholic Conclave met on the island of San Giorgio Maggiore and elected Pope Pius VII.

Napoleon's victorious march through Europe brought a change of government in Venice. After the Austrians were defeated at the battle of Austerlitz on Dec. 2, 1805, the army of the French Emperor reoccupied the Veneto. Now the ruler over the city in the lagoon was Eugène de Beauharnais, Napoleon's stepson, the Viceroy of Italy. At this time the Napoleonic wing was built on the Piazza San Marco and the Giardini Pubblici, the large park on the Basin of St. Mark, was laid out. The Basilica San Marco became in 1807 the seat of the Patriarch who had lived since the 15th century in the episcopal church of San Pietro di Castello.

The second period of French rule lasted only eight years but increased the economic misery of the Venetians so much that they cheered when the Austrians returned.

After the Congress of Vienna

The powers which had formed a victorious alliance against Napoleon met in the autumn of the year 1815 in Vienna to settle the new political situation in Europe. In the final decree of June 9, 1815, the Emperor of

Austria was promised, among other things, the territories of Lombardy and Venice.

The new Austrian overlords had two faces. One moment the Venetians were treated well, the next they were politically and economically oppressed. The harbor, once regarded as 'free' was so laden with indirect tolls and taxes that wares from Venice could hardly be sold profitably. Products from the Veneto had to pass a customs barrier at Murano. On the other hand the Austrian government encouraged agricultural improvements such as the planting of mulberry trees.

Left, portrait of Victor Emanuel II standing on the Riva della Schiavoni. Right, the Garibaldi Brigade.

Venice slowly began to win back importance as a cultural center that attracted tourists. The Emperor Franz II and many members of the Imperial family often visited the city on the lagoon and contributed to its romantic legend. This aura of romance came in the wake of writers such as Lord Byron, George Sand and Alfred de Musset or the composer Felix Mendelssohn. The Teatro La Fenice was the scene of important premières, at which Venetian and Austrian aristocrats spoke to each other in French.

This apparently comforting picture was in

New industries including tobacco manufacture were set up in Venice and the glass industry on the island of Murano was reintroduced. The greatest event of the Austrian era was, however, the opening of the railway from Milan to Venice in the year 1846. Venice was connected to the mainland by a bridge almost two-and-a-half miles long. This was a symbolic gesture—the very situation that had led to the foundation of the city and had made it rich and powerful had now changed.

Venice was no longer an island.

marked contrast to the growing misery of the people of Venice. In only a few years the population had fallen from 136,000 in the year 1800 to 100,000, a third of whom were classed as poor.

When Franz II died in the year 1835 he was followed by Ferdinand I, an enlightened ruler who had thoughts of reform. In his time a number of public institutions were set up which still exist, for example the *Museo Correr*, a museum for the art and history of Venice. It was a spectacular experience when the Piazzo San Marco was lit with gas lamps for the first time in 1843.

The Revolt against Austria

Eighteen forty-eight was the year in which liberal forces gathered even in Vienna against the absolutist government and demanded in a revolutionary uprising the introduction of a constitution. Ferdinand I abdicated in favor of his nephew Franz Joseph and the almighty Chancellor Metternich was forced to resign. The wave of unrest spread to Italy and gave the Italian nationalists the chance to strike a blow for freedom. The resistance of Venice against her Austrian rulers lasted a year and was led by Daniele

Manin and Niccolo Tommaso. The Austrians were only able to put down the uprising when a cholera epidemic broke out in the city. Another 17 years must pass before Venice finally managed to throw off Austrian rule.

Those fighting for an independent Italy had years of great success. With the military support of France they forced Austria to return Lombardy in 1859 and through a plebiscite in 1860 Tuscany, the Romagna, Parma and Modena voted to join a united Italy. In 1861 the Sardinian King, Victor

Italian Venice

Through its affiliation with Italy, Venice became the capital of a small province and finally lost the role of a great metropolis that she played for centuries. This loss of identity is still an unsolved problem and will remain a decisive one. Every political decision in Venice is now subject to the slow Roman bureaucracy and the interests of the local officials.

It must be said, however, that the first 10 years after 1866 brought a remarkable up-

Emmanuel II, on whom the freedom fighters placed all their hopes, took on the title of King of Italy. At last in 1866, after the united Italians and Prussians had defeated Austria, Venice and the Veneto voted to join Victor Emanuel's young kingdom. A new era began, full of hope but with many problems waiting to be solved.

Left, the Railway bridge links Venice with the mainland. Above, the industrial district of Mestre, seen from Venice.

surge of prosperity to Venice. A new harbor, the *Stazione Marittima*, was built. Venice was connected to the interior Italian and the transalpine railway systems and there was an increase in Mediterranean trade as a result of the Suez Canal. This meant that within about 15 years Venice had not only caught up with Triest but had advanced to the second largest harbor in Italy after Genoa.

Throughout the 19th century English visitors flocked to Venice to admire its legendary beauty. J.M. Turner, the great painter made watercolors of a city which exactly suited his atmospheric use of color. In the

1840s John Ruskin, the art historian, began his long love/hate relationaship with Venice and in 1889 the poet, Robert Browning, died in the Ca' Rezzonico.

The city itself at the end of the 19th century was a relatively quiet tourist center. New streets were built and canals were filled in to make pedestrian traffic easier. Beautiful ships set out from the *Stazione Marittima* to cruise romantically on the Mediterranean. Rich European society yielded to the fascination of Venice. The first *vaporetti*, built by a Paris firm, arrived and the gondoliers went on strike to protect against their motorized rivals.

Every year famous painters such as Manet and Renoir visited Venice. In 1883 Richard Wagner died in his marvelous Palazzo Vendramin-Calergi. In 1895 the famous international art exhibition, the biennial, was first introduced. A turbulent century was ending for Venice, a new century had begun.

Venizia Nuova: the New Venice

In fact the 20th century began with a crash! In the year 1902 the thousand-year-old Campanile of San Marco fell down and was, in 10 years, rebuilt in its original form. In 1917 the first industrial zone, Marghera, brought with it ironworks, chemical factories and wharves. The harbor, which was necessary for the building project, because the *Stazione Marittima* could no longer accommodate all the necessary supplies, brought Venice even more economic growth. Those responsible for this prosperity were three Venetian managers: Volpi, later Mussolini's Minister of Finance, Gaggia, the President of the Employers' Association, and Cini who restored the buildings on the island of San Giorgio Maggiore and erected an international study and congress center.

In 1926 Mestre, which had increased greatly in population because of the nearby industries, was made into a separate community. The thirties, when Italy fought in Abyssinia, and also the years of the Second World War made Porto Marghera into an important center of the Italian armament industry and led to further prosperity in the region. Fortunately the city of Venice did not suffer bomb damage during the course of the war.

The building up of the industrial zone of Marghera between 1960 and 1964 shifted the bulk of the population of the Venetian community finally to Mestre. The city in the lagoon became more and more *centro storico*, the historical city center, which attracts so many visitors with its inimitable atmosphere, but which has little to offer its own citizens.

The exodus of the population from the city is worrying; in 1951 there were 174,000 inhabitants, today there are about half that number. The city authorities face grave problems. There are few jobs for those who wish to remain in Venice. One has a chance in administration, tourism, arts and crafts, and in the glass factory at Murano which employs about 6000 people.

A continual nightmare for the inhabitants of the island city is high water. A terrible flood took place in 1966 when the water level rose by nearly two meters. The catastrophe brought some improvements in its wake: the world was made aware of the precarious situation of Venice. Rome too recognized the need for emergency measures and special legislation made funds available for repairs. The warnings of the ecologists over damage caused in the lagoon by the petro-chemical industry were heard at last. Industrial plants began to install filtration systems to reduce pollution.

There is still much to be done even if some of the problems are being solved. One thing is certain; Venice must fall back on her natural hinterland and must have more autonomy. Only in this way will it be possible for La Serenissima to meet the problems of the year 2000 as a modern city.

Right, The Fall of the Campanile of San Marco (photo, A. Zaghis).

49

VENICE AND THE VENETIANS

The palace of the Doges was once the residence of La Serenissima, the glorious republic of Venice. Today Venice is the capital of the region Veneto and the seat of government is Ca'Balbi, a handsome building on the Grand Canal. Only a step or two from the Rialto bridge lies the city hall, its official rooms spreading between the Farsetti and Loredan Palazzi. The community government controls Venice and Mestre, two fundamentally different worlds joined by a two-and-a-half-mile bridge. Venice, together with the nearby islands Lido, Murano, Burano and Torcello (population 1985: 126,118) forms the natural 'floating world', the largest pedestrian zone on earth.

On the mainland lies Mestre, expanding every year; its 251,000 inhabitants live at the hectic tempo of a motorized industrial city. The two cities cannot come together. On the contrary frustration and tension are growing between them. The role of the Dominante, the ruler, which Venice played on the mainland for centuries was lost in 1797 with the fall of the Republic, along with her power and glory as a great trade metropolis. Today's managers are at the head of high-turnover firms on the mainland; the Veneto region is one of the four richest in Italy. These managers visit Venice to entertain a business partner or to battle with red tape.

The harbor of Venice now takes second place to Porto Marghera. Public transport to and from the Veneto is slow and dear. No real estate is available in the island city for a modern commercial enterprise. Venice can offer jobs mainly in the tourist industry and in administration. Many Venetians who don't want to live on the city's glorious memories and who want to start their own business move to the mainland '*di là dall 'aqua*' over the water. Fourteen thousand people commute daily, others come to their home city as tourists. In the last 15 years over 40,000 middle income Venetians have made the sad decision to leave the city because of housing difficulties. When they go a living part of the unique Venetian quality of Venice is lost. For this is the secret of the city: the people and the inimitable rhythm of their lives.

The New Face of Venice

One must learn to walk slowly. This is the Venetian philosophy out of which managers and stockbrockers want to make capital. Suddenly Venice is 'in' again. Since one knows that the island is not sinking and that the floods will be kept at bay with a high-cost project Venice has a future once again. Venice is becoming the best run city center for culture and congresses. Big money flows into Venice, a great deal from private sources, less from the state.

Restoration is going on everywhere; every morning teams of bricklayers with laden boats and floating cranes stream into Venice. They clamber busily on to the scaffolding. Their banging and hammering is music to the ears of the Venetians. A fresh breeze is blowing everywhere, over the marble facades, through the palaces, in every hidden corner. The new motto is "Drink in the culture of Venice…find inner serenity in the Serenissima."

This may not be possible for the mass of tourists (12 million visitors a year); it is meant for an elite who meet to the sound of Vivaldi's music at the fireside of a newly gilded salon. Now is the time for politicians to set Venice on the best course. It is time to come to grips with the housing program which so far exists only on paper. The Venetians do not want to live in a museum but in a living city with its own old endearing customs.

The Venetian

The Venetian travels a great deal but wherever he may be he feels homesick for his own city and its rhythm. Only in the alleyways and squares of Venice, far from the traffic's roar, can he really show his open, sociable nature. How enjoyable it is to stretch out a quick greeting in passing into a longer chat. Friends don't lose touch, you hear the talk of the town every day, you're in the know about everything! The Venetian loves company, he is ironic, self-confident and at the same time touchy. It is not always easy to get along with the native Venetian. It is best to use a friendly and sympathetic approach so as to break through the proud

ders, in the evening it is a *Valentino* jacket embroidered with paillettes. All Venetian women are well turned out with chic coiffures; the aristocratic ladies are discreetly made up, ordinary women are painted in many colors. Who knows how much time a housewife from Cannaregio or Castello spends at her dressing table?

The Venetian Mamma

Early every morning she sets out as soon as her husband and children are out of the

Venetian's shell and so as not to provoke his sarcasm which is sometimes hurtful.

And the Venetian Woman?

Everything that one can say about Venetians in general can be said about the woman of Venice. She is poised, proud, lovable, full of curiosity. Perhaps she tends to spend too much time at her toilette. She seldom goes out to work, although one meets women of the upper class more and more in leading cultural posts. During the day she slips a *Missoni* pullover around her shoul-

house. She pulls her typical wheeled shopping basket up and down the bridges to the Rialto market to buy fresh fish and vegetables. She is all dressed up with a fresh hairdo, bright make up and so much gold jewelry she might be going to an Opera première at La Fenice. She has been up cleaning and polishing since the crack of dawn: one must always be ready for visitors.

Murano glass and crystal sparkle in the china cabinet, on the sofa cushions there is freshly starched Burano lace. A whiff of lavender and the setting is perfect. A housewife has a lot to do. Husbands and children come home to eat at midday and always expect her to whip up a number of special dishes.

Venetians are lovers of good food: rice dishes, fish and a variety of vegetables are on the menu every day. The Venetian Mamma is kept busy by her children: one must keep an eye on the little ones when they play on the canal bank to see that they don't fall into the water. The older children are always having friends over and they love freshly baked cakes and fragrant hot chocolate while they're doing their homework. The

in Cortina. The lovely hillsides near Abano, Asolo or Conegliano are inviting places for a long walk to the Palladio villas and rustic wine taverns. A true Venetian family owns a car and a boat.

Since the 'green revolution' the Venetian have declared war on the diesel motorboats. Their choppy wake, their noise and smell must all disappear. Rowing and sailing regattas are all the rage. One has to learn how to row standing up—how often beginners fall into the water! A course with the famous rowing clubs *Querini* and *Bucintoro* is not

mothers sit in the cozy parlor knitting and planning the Sunday outing.

Leisure Attractions

Venice has much to offer because of its unique situation. The sea at its door is in fact that elegant bathing beach, the Lido, which is the second home of the Venetians in summer. The Dolomites are only an hour away by car. Many Venetians have a winter place

Left, she has lots to tell. Above, anti-wrinkle cream for anyone?

expensive. Perhaps one will have the chance to take part in a competition called the *Disdotona* (18 rowers) at the *Regatta Storica*.

The water festivals of the Venetians are rich in tradition…moments of living cultural history. The palaces on the Grand Canal hung with silk, radiate the elegance and pomp of other days. '*Alza remi*! Oars up' is the cry and the 16-foot (four-meter) long oars are proudly hoisted straight up, to the wild applause of the spectators.

The Venetian is a keen sportsman, in the water in summer and in the snow in winter. He always has a tan which is very chic in

Venice today…quite the opposite from the days of the Republic. When the high-born Venetian ladies sat on the *altana* (typical Venetian roof terraces) letting their hennaed hair bleach in the sun they took care to preserve their aristocratic pallor. Noblesse oblige. These days one must have a fur coat to go with one's suntan. In the evening mist, at the cocktail hour, a gorgeous parade of fashionable furs goes swinging gently through the narrow lanes to the Palazzo San Marco.

One passes the time of day, pauses for a

monument of Carlo Goldoni who wrote so many delightful comedies in Venetian dialect. Every evening they stream along in jeans and joggers to the Campo San Bartolomeo near the Rialto bridge and spend a couple of hours together. Their demands for discotheques and sports centers are getting louder but the Mayor is rather hard of hearing. Goldoni, on his pedestal, gives a sly laugh as if he takes pleasure in their gestures and their talk and recognizes many of his Harlequins and Columbines again.

"Pronti!" cries the garbage man (*Spazzin*)

moment, goes to the Caffè Florian or into a bar. Standing at the counter one drinks an *ombretta* (a small glass of wine) and takes a *cicchetto* (a bite to eat, a savory). The choice of wine and the variety of the *cicchetti* depend on the flair of the hostess. A stranger watching this picture might think that Venice is provincial.

This is not true—Venice is a cosmopolitan city where human characteristics are served up for all to see. Nothing is hidden; one walks along, one steps on the stage to see and be seen—just for the fun of it.

The meeting place for young people is the

in the early morning—today is collection day. He goes calling and whistling from door to door and collects the sacks of garbage. A heap of sacks grows on the canal bank and is carried away by ship to be burnt.

"*Posta!*" shouts the mailman. "*Siora Maria na letera de so fio*, Signora Maria, a letter from your son." A window opens in the upper story, Siora Maria lets down a basket on a string and pulls it up again with her letter. This saves a trip up and down the stairs; there are not many elevators in the tall houses. If someone must be rushed to hospital the water ambulance speeds along with blue lights flashing and a siren. A passing gondola rocks violently in the water. The sick are transported in carrying chairs, there are no stretchers.

Only the police, the fire bridge and the ambulance are allowed to travel fast; the speed limit on the canals is five miles (eight km) an hour. Only a few people keep to this speed limit hence the continual fight against the dangerous waves made by the motor boats. The Gondolieri demonstrate more and more wildly in front of the city hall but it doesn't do a bit of good.

the sirocco hasn't put him in a bad mood it sometimes happens that he sings his favorite song: "*La biondina in gondoeta*".

The sirocco is a warm, moist wind that oppresses everyone in summer. The ladies keep cool with the aid of an elegant fan, the men fan themselves with their newspapers. When stormy sirocco winds blow in winter the high water siren sounds. The Venetians quickly don their tall gumboots. Shopkeepers pile their wares on higher shelves. In the alleys and on the plazas the duck-boards are put down. Normally no-one lives on the

What are the gondoliers called in Venetian dialect? *Pope*. "*Pope*" is what one shouts when wanting to cross the Grand Canal. The gondolier picks up his passenger and makes the crossing for 250 lire. Venetians stand up during short trips in a gondola but anyone who can't balance so well is advised to sit down. This comfortable and cheap service is called "Traghetto". There are six traghetti on the Grand Canal. When the gondolier has nice passengers and

Left, gondoliers. Right, feeding the pigeons. Above, meeting in the marketplace.

ground floor in Venice—or else he would have to take a gondola to go to bed during high water.

Of course there are no automobiles in Venice but in all the alleyways, on the bridges and in the squares there are the indispensable *carretto* or push carts. "*Attention! Attention!*" is the warning cry of the delivery boys who must try to find a way through the crowded streets. The Venetians scatter at once, the tourists remain stubbornly standing in the way and are often run over! It is an amusing sight to see the delivery boys carrying stacks of lighter things—

flower pots, leaning towers of pizzas—on their heads. Many Venetians have their own push-carts which are available at the iron-mongers in every size. Since water taxis are terribly dear they push the carretto to the family car in its garage and bring home their trunks and suitcases this way.

Venetians like to use the *vaporetto*, literally the little steamer. Line I is the slowest and most popular because it stops at every mooring place on the Grand Canal. The Captains of the vaporetti take pride in keeping up with the timetable to the second even

in winter when they have to find their way through the fog with radar.

Venice is a labyrinth; on-one can find their way without a plan of the city and a compass. A Venetian, when asked the way, says: "*Sempre diritto, cinque-minute.*" "*Sempre diritto*" means straight ahead but often "straight ahead as the crows flies" and the Venetian can get a long way in five minutes because he knows all the short cuts. "*Andar per le sconte*" means to take a short cut.

The Festival of Cats is a happy event first held in 1987 and the Venetians have responded to it whole-heartedly. The spotlight

is not on pampered pure-bred pussies but on '*il gatto di laguna*' the alley cat. During the Festival of Cats Micio and Micia, as they are called, were given extra food and a round of applause.

The Venetians are great cat lovers. Over 200,000 cats wander free in Venice, that is at least two cats per person. They are regularly fed by old women, restaurant owners donate food. Micio and Micia are so well fed that they don't hunt rats any more.

The architecture students who organized the Festival of Cats had a marvelous idea. They gave away cats, each one with its own basket, plus vaccination and health certificates from a vet, valid throughout Europe. Lo and behold the tourists were queuing up at San Giovanni Evagelista, eager to take home such a typical souvenir of Venice. If you fancy one of the pigeons from the Piazza San Marco or one of the elegant sea gulls from the Grand Canal nothing stands in your way…but you must catch it yourself. An animal that the Venetians are particularly proud of and which cannot be caught or carried away, is of course the Lion of St. Mark.

Do you want to take part in the most beautiful festival in Venice? Then come to St. Mark's Church on April 25, when the Venetians honor their patron saint. Once one of the most important feast days of the Serenissima, the *Festa di San Marco* is still a great event. The tradition of giving one's sweetheart a rosebud, *il bocolo*, on this day, goes back to a sentimental legend. In a battle against the Turks a young Venetian was sorely wounded. He sank down to die beside a white rosebush and plucked for his beloved, far away in Venice, a single bud, dyed red with his heart's blood. The flower miraculously came to the maiden in Venice after his death. Today, because the Venetians still need the protection of St. Mark, the Venetian girls bring the rosebuds they had received to the saint's grave, in love and gratitude.

Right and left, beautiful Venetian girls.

IS VENICE SINKING?

High water in Venice! The Piazza San Marco four feet under water, the water in Venice almost six-and-a-half feet above sea level. The entrances of the palazzi along the Grand Canal are under water…electricity and telephone services have broken down. Italy and the rest of the world are full of anxiety for their unique city. These were the reports as the great flood disaster struck Venice on Nov. 4, 1966. The ecological problems of Venice and the lagoon had not been treated seriously—now it was the day of reckoning.

As is often the case a disaster was necessary to make those responsible in the government and the community react with definite plans and financial support. In fact Venice had been threatened by high water (*aqua alta*) throughout its long history. The reedy islands in the lagoon, where early settlers first sought refuge from the Huns and other invaders, were always subject to flooding of biblical proportions.

No-one could deny, however, that flooding now occurred more frequently, earlier in the year and was more damaging. What are the reasons for this increasing threat to Venice and the lagoon?

The Geographical Situation

We must take account of the geographical situation of Venice. Its lagoon lies at the northern end of the Adriatic Sea and is divided from the open sea by a row of narrow islands. Twice a day the lagoon is washed by the tides and filled with new salt water.

Between the islands in the lagoon are three large openings (*bocche*) which form Venice's only outlets to the sea and which carry the whole of the maritime tanker traffic. These three waterways are the Lido channel (2950 feet wide, 36 feet deep), the Malamocca channel (1540 feet wide, 49 feet deep) and the passage at Chiogga (1640 feet wide, 23 feet deep). Through these three openings the winter winds (sirocco) drive huge tidal waves into the lagoon, causing enormously high water pressure, partly because of the narrowness of the Adriatic at this point. The water which rushes in in this way must be able to spread out and drain away as quickly as possible to prevent a dramatic rise in the water level. This quick draining of the lagoon is no longer possible because of high industrial pollution, so that floods cannot be avoided.

The Effects of Industry

In 1917 as the Arsenal (where weapons and ships were built) had to close down, a thousand families were out of work. New economic perspectives were necessary; Venice, forced to industrialize, built Industrial Zone I on the edge of the lagoon at Porto Marghera. In order to build this industrial complex a large area of land was reclaimed from the lagoon. This development intensified after World War II with the building of Industrial Zone II. The large airport at Mestre was built and many fish-ponds (*valle*) in the lagoon were dammed. Large areas of the lagoon were used for all these projects, the lagoon was drastically narrowed and this led to an increased number of floods.

Another problem has arisen because the floor of the lagoon sunk markedly. This has been caused by the draining away of underground water reserves for domestic and industrial use and by the pumping of natural gas from under the lagoon.

During the nineteen-twenties and the thirties, decades that were not noted for awareness of environmental problems, the industrialization along the edges of the lagoon continued. Porto Marghera became the center of Mussolini's armament industry in wartime. Later this development was greatly intensified.

Learning from the Past

A glance at her history shows that the old Republic of Venice was much more careful of her environment than she is today. There were attempts to cope with the recurring problem of high water—according to 13th-century witnesses—by many arrangements for stablizing the water in the lagoon. All larger ships, for example, had to transfer their cargo to smaller boats for the entry into the lagoon. From the 16th century the course of the rivers Brenta, Sile and Piave were changed by large earthworks because the lagoon was silting up.

lagoon brought heavy penalties including the death sentence.

After the floods of 1966

Even after the disaster of 1966 there was much pollution of the lagoon. In 1969, for example, a new canal (Canale dei Petroli) was dug for oil refineries. Through this new excavation and the straightening of the waterway there were further disruptions to the

The city fathers of the old Republic set great store by the experience of fishermen which was based on careful observation of nature. They were consulted when the building of a new canal could influence the bottom of the lagoon and the movement of currents, for example. In the 18th century the building of the walls (*murazzi*) on the Lido was begun in order to stop a flood. Infringements against the laws for protection of the

Above, the Piazzo San Marco under water.

delicate system of currents in the lagoon. The experiences of 1966 could not prevent the draining of 10,000 acres (4000 hectares) of the lagoon to form Industrial Zone III at Porto Marghera. There were so many protests against this project that it was stopped in 1968 but the preparatory work had already done irreparable damage.

The large scale restoration of historical buildings has been celebrated as one of the positive measures that followed the disaster of 1966. This was accomplished with a great deal of voluntary concern and international support, from UNESCO, for example. Another important measure was the capping of the artesian wells of Porto Marghera which had supplied Venice with water and also the shutting down of the projects for extracting natural gas from the bottom of the lagoon (Val Padana). Thanks to these measures Venice has apparently not sunken any further since 1983.

Today the water supplies for the city of Venice and the industrial zones is drawn from the foothills of the Alps with pipelines. Old Venice supplied her citizens from many cisterns which mainly held surface water;

through improperly filtered industrial fumes. Sulfur attacks the walls of the buildings and eats into their very substance.

An equally pressing problem is the heavy pollution of the water with industrial and household waste. Whoever has experienced the stink of the canals in the middle of summer knows about this problem. Once the lagoon teemed with fish, now there are only a tenth of the usual number.

In spite of this, artificial fertilizer still pours into the lagoon from the 625,000 acres (250,000 hectares) of agricultural land

these fine old wells can still be seen in the city squares.

The poor quality of the water, the air and the soil in Venice and the lagoon is a result of industrial pollution. There was always discussion about the preservation of the priceless buildings of the city but not over general environmental problems. Now everyone is aware of the connection between pollution and the need for restoration. Costly repairs to historic buildings make no sense so long as the cause of their decay is not dealt with. One immediate cause of this decay is the increased sulfur content of the air

nearby and pollutes the water even more.

A great threat to the buildings in the historical city center are the motorboats which chug in hordes through the canals. The waves they cause beat continually against the decaying foundations of the palazzi and erode them dangerously. One radical demand is for the prohibition of all motorboats. Since the whole economic traffic of Venice depends upon boat transport and a return to the gondola is not possible, this problem will be hard to solve.

Above, not everyone needs gumboots.

Political Measures to Save Venice

All these ecological problems have been taken into account on a political level. In the years 1973 and 1984 special laws were passed and finance was made readily available for the restoration of Venice. These plans include:

* The restoration of the hydro-geological balance;

* The prevention of further subsidence of the lagoon basin;

* The restoration and the raising of buildings on the islands and in the historical city center;

* Protective measures against flooding, including work on the three entrances to the lagoon with mobile blockades.

It has been stated explicitly that these are experimental plans to be made step by step and stopped if necessary.

High Technology or a More Natural Solution?

A widely publicized technological project to solve the problem of flooding has pushed aside other environmental problems. This large project includes plans for solid dykes of stone and concrete each 5,550 feet (16,182 meters) long to be erected at the entrances to the lagoon. Openings between these dykes will be fitted with movable flood gates, to be shut during high water.

Because the project comes to grips with only one aspect of the ecological calamity in the lagoon it has caused great controversy. Ecologists and fishermen declare that this 'high-tech' solution will disturb the ground structure and the water balance of the lagoon too gravely. The voices of those who favor a more natural solution of all the environmental problems are becoming more insistent. Their suggestions are:

* The waterways between the three lagoon entrances should be flattened and given a more natural curvature, with earthworks.

* Heavy tankers should not enter the lagoon.

* The industrial zones should be supplied with raw materials by pipelines over land, not by ship.

* The many smaller canals and streams of the lagoon should be dredged and deepened so that, in case of flooding, the water can drain off quickly.

* The elevation of the buildings of Venice by half a meter with the aid of steel supports anchored in the floor of the lagoon is also recommended.

Plans exist for the removal of the whole industrial zone away from the lagoon into the hinterland. Both the employers and the unions have protested against this.

Other suggestions include the prohibition of artificial fertilizers and phosphate washing powders, as well as a more effective use of the existing purification plants for waste from industries, private households, glass factories and hospitals. On the Lido, for example, only 30 percent of the households are connected to the drainage system.

There is an urgent need for measures to force the industries to reduce air pollution by filter systems. The polluted areas of the lagoon can also be cleaned by removal of the dirt on the surface. Heavy metals on the floor of the lagoon can be cleared by dredging. It is also important to forbid the dumping of warm cooler-water from power plants into the lagoon. The rise in temperature together with the pollution of the water can lead to the heavy growth of algae which is known to disturb the oxygen content of the water.

Is Venice sinking into the sea? Will it be an island in a sewer? Let us hope that the people and the authorities can be far sighted as they begin the work to keep Venice what it is: one of the most beautiful cities in the world.

VENICE: ADMISSION BY TICKET ONLY?

On a lovely day in May 1987 as the number of visitors reached the 120,000 mark again the Mayor brought up a plan that had been discussed for years, a quota system for tourists. An entry fee of 10,000 lire per person and the closing of the city when the numbers became too high...this must stem the tide of visitors. In September 1987, after much discussion, it was announced that Venice would remain an open city. Pilgrims and travelers had always contributed to its vitality and its cosmopolitan atmosphere. In fact with a fantastic array of cultural activities, Venice was attracting a big international audience.

Those who already love the beautiful Serenissima and those who long to visit her will have plenty of opportunity even at the height of the season to discover Venice for themselves. The labyrinth of winding alleyways invites us to lose ourselves, to set off on an unplanned voyage of discovery. No need to worry...sooner or later a shield will show the way to some well-known square.

The following pages will guide you through the maze of the magic city. The beginning must be at the heart of the Serenissima: the Piazza San Marco, the Basilica San Marco and the Doge's Palace. In other days as the visitor could approach Venice only from the sea the mighty edifices of the city's best known facade made an indelible impression. Today one mainly enters through the back door, at the railway station or the parking lot at the Piazzale Roma. One can still give everyday reality the slip and arrange one's own classical entry into Venice by taking from here the Vaporetto No 5. After crossing the Canale della Guidecca the water bus steers from the island of San Giorgio Maggiore right at that legendary panorama of the city in the lagoon. Another approach, just as splendid, is a trip through Venice's most magnificent street, the Grand Canal, to which three chapters of this book are dedicated. The descriptions of the palazzi and their history is oriented to a trip on the Vaporetto No I, from whose mooring places one can get the best view of the beautiful palaces. Another chapter deals with the Rialto bridge and the Venetian markets as well as the church of Santa Maria della Salute whose splendid dome marks the end of the Grand Canal.

Five round trips through the six city districts, the *Sestieri* will lead you not only to the most important sights and the most beautiful spots in the heart of the city but also into the fringes of 'another Venice' where fewer visitors find their way. The great churches in Venetian gothic style, San Zanipolo and I Frari, as well as the most important art work of the great Venetian painters in the Scuola San Rocco and the Accademia, are brought to you in another exciting chapter. At the end of the book is a guide to Venice complete in itself. This gives plenty of practical advice plus a short description of all the most important things to see.

MESTRE

to Airport Marco Polo

Camping Rialto

Canale Osellino

Barene di Tessera

Ponte di Pietra

PASSO

Porto di Campalto

Camping Venezia

Barene del Passo

Camping
Barche

Can. Salso

Scaricatore alle Fiotte

Seno della Seppa

Canale di Campalto

Ramo di Griola

Can. di S. Giuliano

P S. GIULIANO

I.DI S. GIULIANO

I.CAMPALTO

Canale

Canale Torrolo

PORTO
MARGHERA

Can. Ind. Brentella

Canale Industriale Nord

Canale di S. Secondo

n. 11
Ponte della Libertà

Zeniole

I.S.SECONDO
(EX FORTE)

Can. d. Sacche

Canale delle Tresse

Canale

Canale

I.NUOVA DEL
TRONCHETTO

P

CANN

Stazione Ferrov.
S. Lucia
(Station)

Canal Gra

S. CF

Vittorio

Canale Dorena

Ca
Sa

Emanuele III

I.DELLE
TRESSE

P

Piazzale
Roma

S.
d.

Malamocco

Molo di Ponente

Molo di Levante

S. POLO

DORSODUR(

Stazione Marittima

SACCA
FISOLA

Canale

Canale Vecchio di Fusina

Can. di Fusina

SACCA
S.BIAGIO

LA GIUDECC/

FUSINA

I.S.GIORGIO
IN ALGA

Canale Nuovo

Canale Fasiol

P

Camping Fusina

C.Buso

Canale Nuovo di Fusina

Canale Contorta S. Angelo

Marghera

ex Forte S.Angelo
della Polvere

SACCA SESSOLA

74

MADONNA DEL MONTE

Can. di S. Francesco

S.FRANCESCO
DEL DESERTO

Coa della Latte

Canale Carbonera

Ramo del Sorze

Canale Scomenzera

DI

S. GIACOMO

CA LA VELA

Can. Passaora

Il Perer

I.DI TESSERA
(EX BATTERIA)

la di Tessera

S. GIACOMO
IN PALUDE

S.ERASMO

Canale Bisatto

PALUDE

Canale di Tresso

Angeli

Canale degli Angeli

Can. S. Maria

Canale di S. Erasmo

C.Castagna

Can. Ondello

MURANO

Ca. Carara

Litorale di Sant' Erasmo

Canale dei

Marani

Can. S. Cristoforo

Ch. di San Michele
(Church)

Can. d. Bissal

Torre Massimiliano
(ex Forte s.Erasmo)

S.MICHELE

LE VIGNOLE

VENEZIA
(VENICE)

Canale delle Fondamente Nuove

ex Idroscalo
S.Andrea

Ponte di
Rialto
(Bridge)

Canale delle Navi

Porto di Lido

S.PIETRO

Piazza
n Marco

Pal. Ducale
(Doge´s Palace)

CASTELLO

Canale di S. Nicolo

Aeroporto
G.Nicelli
(Airport)

CO

Canale di S. Marco

LA CERTOSA

P.D.Salute
S. Maria
d. Salute

Can.

S.GIORGIO
MAGGIORE

Teatro Verde

Grazia

Ortanello

S.ELENA

decca

Canale la

Grazia

Ortano

S.SERVOLO

Osp. al Mare

LA GRAZIA

Can. Lazzaretto

Bagni Comunali
(Swimming Baths)

Canale

S.Maria
Elisabetta

Hôtel des Bains

S.CLEMENTE

S. LAZZARO
DEGLI ARMENI

LIDO

le di S. Spirito

LAZZARETTO
VECCHIO

Casino Municipale

Albergo Excelsior

Venice and Mestre

800 m/ 0,5 miles

75

THE PIAZZA SAN MARCO

Squares in Venice are called "Campo": Campo dei Mori, Campo San Bartolomeo, Campo San Stefano… Squares are small in Venice, little more than a widening out of a narrow alley, just enough room for a couple of tables and chairs, a memorial or a stunted tree. The site in the lagoon forced the Venetians to build in the same way as the architects of modern apartments using every inch of space. Squares were a luxury, but in one particular square the pride and self-confidence of the Venetians are set forth for all to see! It is 580 feet (175 meters) in length, 270 feet (82 meters) across on the wider side, 190 feet (57.5 meters) wide on the narrower side. This is not a "Campo", not a cramped little square, this is a Piazza, worthy of a cosmopolitan city,

Previous pages: View of Giudecca; gondola; reflections in the lagoon; The Piazzetta; a water gate.

a center of commerce; this is *the* Piazza, *Piazza San Marco*.

On the one hand it is the embodiment of Venice—at least 90 percent of all tourists visit the Piazza San Marco—on the other hand it is a caricature of the city dominated by the tourists and pigeons which add nothing to its historic beauty. Some find it symptomatic of the destiny of Venice that, where once mariners and merchants from all over the world took their ease, today sandwich-chewing tourists, dropping cokecans, line up to be photographed with bedraggled pigeons.

However critically one regards the Piazza San Marco one cannot escape from its enchantment. Even the fastidious visitor pays the incredible price for a cup of coffee at Florian's or the Quadri with gritted teeth and, surrounded by pigeons and tourists, enjoys the view of the domes of St. Mark's, the Campanile and the Loggetta and—depending on the coffee-house—of the Procuratie Vecchie or the Procuratie Nuove. Groups pass by on guided tours and if one sits long enough one will hear a guide utter that inevitable if rather inexpressive sentence of Napoleon's that the Piazza San Marco is "the finest drawing-room in Europe".

Napoleon, the conqueror of Venice, managed to give this *salon* its ugliest corner, the *Ala Napoleonica*. It joins the Procuratie Vecchie and the Procuratie Nuove, a junction that was never intended by the Venetians and which, today more than ever, works as a limitation and a restriction of the spacious piazza rather than an improvement. Until 1807 a church stood in this position; it was torn down because the Emperor of the French who resided in the Procuratie Nuove required a more impressive portal to his chambers.

In order to enjoy the spatial qualities of the Piazza San Marco without being disturbed by Napoleon, the visitor should approach the square from the

MARKET PLACE

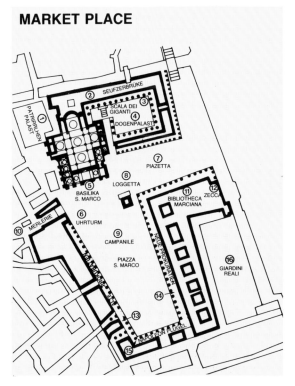

west, entering through the arcade of the *Ala Napoleonica*. With the Napoleonic wing at one's back the old and new Procuration buildings stretch diagonally away from each other to left and right and the Piazza lies open right to the Basilica San Marco.

The Procuratie were the offices of the Procurators who were responsible for all public buildings. The old chambers, a work of the early renaissance, were built at the beginning of the 16th century. Fifty arcades form the lower storey—today there are shops here and the famous **Caffè Quadri**—and there are hundred arches in each of the two upper stories.

The Procuratie Nuove was built at the end of the 15th and beginning of the 17th century as an extension of the administration buildings. The medieval building on this site, replaced by the Procuratie Nuove, stood up against the Campanile, but the new building was set back and intended as a continuation of St. Mark's Library which borders the Piazzetta. Today the Procuratie Nuove houses the **Museo Correr** (entry through the Napoleonic Wing); it contains exhibitions on the history of Venice and a picture gallery (including Carpaccio's famous "Two Courtesans"). In the same building there is a section of the **Museo del Risorgimento** commemorating the unification of Italy and the resistance against Austrian rule. On the ground floor of the Procuratie Nuove is the oldest café in Italy, the **Caffè Florian**, opened in 1720. (The interior is 19th century.) Mark Twain and Hemingway, as well as Goethe and Proust drank their coffee here and spread the reputation of the Caffè Florian throughout the world.

The Procuratie Nuove was completed in 1640 by Longhena, the older building was built from plans by Mauro Codussi, who completed the building

Piazza San Marco.

with a flourish in the east—the **Clock Tower**, erected at the end of the 15th century. The upper story with the lion of St. Mark against a background of stars and shining blue mosaic was added in the 18th century.

People crowd on to the roof terrace of the Procuratie Nuove in fine weather to look under the robes of the two moors who strike the great bell every hour. Like the clock, which also shows the phases of the moon and the position of the sun in the zodiac, the moors are from the 15th century.

To the left of St. Mark's Church lies a small square—it is probably called a piazzetta rather than a 'campo' because it is so close to the Piazza San Marco. Two lions of red marble give it the rest of its name, hence it was named **Piazzetta dei Leoncini**. To the east lies the palace of the Patriarchs, built during the first half of the 19th century when the Bishop's seat was moved from San Pietro di Castello to San Marco.

The side of the Basilica that faces the Piazzetta dei Leoncini (see the chapter on St. Mark's Church) is interesting for its many strange and obscure designs from the orient. The **Porta dei Fiori**, the gate of flowers, stands in the fourth arcade and has a relief of the Nativity, a masterpiece of Venetian romanesque. In the first arch there is a relief from the 7th and the 8th century showing the empty throne of Christ with twelve lambs who symbolize the Disciples.

From the three flagpoles which stand on the Piazza before the church there once flew the banners of the kingdoms of Morea, Candia and Cyprus, conquests of Venice. The Piazza San Marco was always the political center of the Republic, representing the power of Venice and her claims to sovereignty. Commerce and government were divided in the 9th century when the Doge changes his place of resi-

The Piazzetta with a view of the Clock Tower.

dence. St. Mark's, the church of the Doges, was always the State church, the expression of worldly power. Already in the 12th century the present dimensions of the Piazza San Marco were laid down; it was paved for the first time in 1260. The gray paving stones are, however, from the 18th century.

The key patterns which decorate the tiles of the Piazza and the Piazzetta also date from this time. They can be seen best from the belfry of the **Campanile**, which can be reached by an elevator. This famous landmark is 310 feet (93 meters) high, the trademark of Venice and the oldest building on the Piazza San Marco. Work on it was begun in the 9th century, the belfry with its pointed roof was built in the 16th century.

The **Loggetta**, at the foot of the Campanile, is the work of the Renaissance architect Sansovino. In the small elegant marble hall the palace guard gathered during sittings of the Great Council. In the plan of the city the Loggetta leads into the St. Mark's Library, also a work of Sansovino.

As the Campanile collapsed in 1902 the Loggetta was also destroyed; it was carefully rebuilt exactly like the original. The Venetians have always been suspicious of changes to the Piazza; not even the Doge was allowed to make alterations without consulting the Council—the high-handed intrusion of Napoleon must have hit the democratically inclined Venetians very hard.

Personal publicity and too much accent on the individual were never a Venetian weakness. In the whole of the Piazza San Marco there is not one personal monument. The Condottiere Colleoni who was determined to have his memorial on the Piazza San Marco, was a victim of Venetian diplomacy. The city fathers accepted the money he left them at his death in 1475 and placed his equestrian statue, as agreed, on St.

Souvenir seller before the Procuratie Vecchio.

Mark's square. It happened to be on the *Campo* San Marco in front of the Church of St. John and St. Paul but after all campo *does* mean square...

The pedestal that stands at the corner of the south facade of St. Mark's Church does suggest that someone has been taken down but in fact it never carried a statue: proclamations were made from this platform.

The **South Facade of St. Mark's Church**, the side of the Basilica which faces the Piazzetta and the Molo, is magnificently designed and emphasizes the effect both of the Piazzetta and of the Doge's Palace. Two pillars, wonderfully decorated with oriental reliefs, trophies of conquest probably made in 6th-century Syria, stand here as symbols of power. Embedded in the wall of the church there is an exquisite group of porphyry figures, also late antique trophies, who may represent the four **Tetrarchs:** Diocletian, Val-

erius, Maximian and Constantius, Roman Emperors of the 3rd century.

The Piazzetta, the small L-shaped square that joins on to the Piazza San Marco, was originally a harbor basin filled in during the 12th century. The occasion for the wave of building activity at this time which altered both the Piazza and the Piazzetta was Venice's entry into world politics. The Serenissima arbitrated in a dispute between the Emperor Frederick Barbarossa and Pope Alexander III and in 1177 the two opponents were expected in Venice.

The city wished to look its best for the reconciliation between these two leaders. The city's 'best room', the Piazza San Marco, with the Piazzetta, as antechamber to the Doge's Palace and mooring place for ships, was redecorated and a new palace of the Doges was built on the east side of the Piazzetta. The redecoration went on for 400 years; the final touch was Sansovino's **Li-**

Waiting for customers. Café on the Piazza San Marco.

brary of St. Mark opposite the Doge's Palace, which is regarded as his masterpiece.

Jakob Burckhardt called it "the most splendid secular building in Italy". With this work, begun in 1537, Sansovino introduced a new architectural style that spread throughout Europe. He was directed by classical ideals...the influence of the Roman antique is to be seen in the pillars bearing the archways of the lower story. He went on to develop his own style, combining elements of the high renaissance in Rome with much that was typically Venetian.

The interior of the library is also well worth seeing. There is fine white and gold plasterwork on the staircase and the entrance hall has a 'perspective' ceiling showing the figure of *Wisdom* painted by Titian. The Golden Chamber, also decorated under his direction, has 21 allegorical figures on the ceiling, three of them by Veronese. Portraits of philosophers decorate the walls, some painted by Tintoretto.

Many of the books in St. Mark's Library were transported in 1905 to the Zecca, but the most precious pieces in the collection are still on display in the library which also houses the **Archeological Museum**.

The **Zecca**, which reaches from the Molo to St. Mark's Library, is also a work from Sansovino and was begun in the same year as the Library. The Zecca looks heavy, far less elegant than its neighbor; square windows line the two upper stories and there is a row of arches on the lower story. Perhaps Sansovino intended this massive look—the building was not meant to contain spiritual treasures such as precious books, it was meant to serve Mammon. Until 1870 this was the city mint.

Money, intellect, the power of church and state. The Piazza San Marco represents and reconciles everything that was important for the community, the commonwealth of the mighty city-state of Venice.

Visitors who used to come by sea could tell from afar whose realm they were approaching. At the entry to the Piazzetta, on the **Molo**, two huge monoliths were set up in 1172...more booty, of course, and stemming from the orient like nearly all the wealth of Venice. On these two symbols of power are enthroned those from whom the young city claimed her titles; St. Theodor, the first patron saint, riding on a mythical beast that may be a crocodile, and on the other pedestal the winged lion as symbol of St. Mark. With the seizure of this saint the Venetians begin their real history, a tale of success and riches, a story that tells of worldly power and of destruction by Napoleon. It is the story of a city that was once a bridge between east and west but is now only a tourist attraction. Perhaps the Piazza San Marco is just the right place for us to let all this pass in review.

Left, the Tetrarchs. Right, bronze statuette in the Loggetta.

THE CATHEDRAL OF ST. MARK

"From the outside, as is often observed, St Mark's looks like an Oriental pavilion half pleasure-house, half war-tent, belonging to some great satrap. Inside, glittering with jewels and gold, faced with precious Eastern marbles, jasper and alabaster, porphyry and verd-antique, sustained by Byzantine columns in the same materials, of varying sizes and epochs, scarcely a pair alike, this dark cruciform cave has the look of a robber's den."

Mary McCarthy 'Venice Observed'

The history of St. Mark's Church began with a theft. It was no ordinary crime, the loot was not gold or jewels or costly stuff—all these things the merchants from Rivus Altus obtained more or less legally—the Venetians stole bones. Not just any old bones, perish the thought. To raise the confidence of the young city, to give the new bishopric a worthy patron, for all this the mortal remains of a very extraordinary man were required, an Evangelist, no less. One of these Gospel-Makers, St. Mark, lay buried in Alexandria; there was only one thing to do—send over a little expedition and snatch that skeleton from its sarcophagus. The bones were then smuggled out in a vat of pork, unclean meat, which the Moslem customs officials could not touch. Packed in this way St. Mark began his triumphal journey to Venice. A suitable legend was soon invented; the saint had been wrecked on an island in the lagoon where an angel appeared to him and greeted him with these words '*Pax tibi, Marce evangelista meus*' 'Peace be with thee, O Mark, my evangelist.'

On his arrival the saint was first presented to the Doge, not the Bishop. His

Previous pages: The Horses of St. Mark. Below, the domes of St. Mark.

permanent resting place was not in the Episcopal church but in the state church, the Doge's chapel, right next to his palace. The theft of the relics occurred for reasons of state, it was meant to strengthen the position of the Doge in Rome. "First we are Venetians, then Christians. *Siamo Veneziani, poi Cristiani.*" This attitude divided Rome and Venice during the whole history of the Republic.

At first, and we are in the year 828, Venice had a precious relic but no church worthy of it. So began the building of the first Basilica San Marco which was consecrated in 832. It burned down in 976 when the Doge's Palace also went up in flames and in the same place a second building was consecrated in 978.

The church which we admire today had its foundations laid in the 11th century; the church was consecrated for the third time in 1094. It was modeled upon the Church of the Apostles in Constantinople and its ground plan was a Greek cross; the vestibule or narthex had a two-story facade with five arcades in each one. In the following centuries as Venice's power and wealth developed the church was greatly altered. Its present appearance dates from the late 15th and early 16th centuries, a time when the star of Venice was just beginning to set as a result of the discovery of new trade routes. Burckhardt writes "The island state, unique in world history, shows here what, in the time of its finest flowering, it held for beautiful, sublime and holy."

Beautiful, sublime and holy—but a most unholy event, the sack of Constantinople, brought about the first redecoration of St. Mark's. Unimaginable treasures came the way of the Venetians through this act of conquest; the Serenissima won new territories and became a world power. This pros-

The south facade of St. Mark.

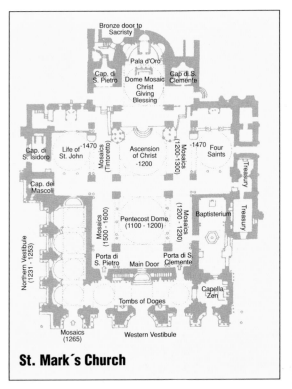

St. Mark's Church

perity had to be displayed: St. Mark's received new domes, the narthex was widened, marble was used and mosaics were laid down. The baptistry and the Chapel of St. Isidore were built; the plain, sober facades were enriched by double pillars in the lower arcades.

The arcades of the upper story received in the first half of the 15th century their most distinctive alteration. The round archways were made pointed; turrets and figures decorated the roof. So the building of the Basilica, one of the most astonishing architectural monuments in Europe, was complete. It is a treasury of styles, a symbol of worldly power and an expression of the Venetian state as a European phenomenon; the traditions of late antiquity have been carried on first by Byzantium, then by Venice.

Five archways divide the front of the building and in the central arch, specially emphasized is the main portal with the bronze doors which came from Byzantium in the 11th century. The side entries are rich with mosaics; the oldest, on the **Porta di San Alippio**, shows the relics of St. Mark's being placed in the church that had been built for him, and we can see what the church looked like in the middle of the 13th century. Next to the widened domes we can see the horses which stand over the main doors. They came from Byzantium in 1204, one of the city's most valuable trophies, always the envy of the rivals of Venice. "To capture the horses of St. Mark" meant "To conquer Venice."

Napoleon, who ended the Republic, took the hint—he not only looted the treasury of St. Mark's and hauled down the winged lion from its column on the Mole, he captured the horses of St. Mark and carried them off to Paris. There they remained for 20 years before being returned, together with the lions, (slightly damaged). Today the statutes have taken shelter in a museum from another enemy: air pollution. There

was anxiety over the state of the centuries old works of art and copies were installed in the gallery over the main doors. The originals may be seen in the **Museo Marciano**.

The middle entry leads into the vestibule; the original flat ceilings were replaced with vaulting in the course of the 13th-century alterations. At the same time the northern narthex or vestibule was built. The mosaics which were done between 1230 and 1275 show in chronological order scenes from the first two books of the Old Testament, Genesis and Exodus. In the first dome right from the main doors (A) is the story of Creation. The barrel vaults (B and C) show the Flood, the Building of the Ark, and the Tower of Babel. The life of Abraham is shown in the dome (D) left of the main doors.

Three domes of the northern narthex (EFG) show 40 scenes of the life of Joseph and the last dome (H) before the **Domes of the Vestibule**.

side entry to the church, shows scenes from the life of Moses. This Moses cycle was based on the illustrations from the biblical text known as the *Cotton Bible*, made in Alexandria in the 5th century. Directly opposite the side door there is a bronze bust of Pope John XXII. Guiseppe Roncalli was Patriarch of Venice before becoming Pope in 1958. Other former Patriarchs of Venice who became Pope include Albino Luciano who ruled all too briefly as John Paul I and Pope Pius X (1903-1914) who was canonized in 1954, bringing the Venetians yet another saint.

In this narthex one should see the bronze doors, the floor (11th and 12th centuries) and the many pillars with their beautiful capitals.

A first impression of the interior of St. Mark's depends greatly upon the time of day when one comes through the main doors. Come as early as pos-sible! St. Mark's opens at 7 a.m. and there are two or two and a half hours before the buses arrive from the Piazzale Roma. Then thousands of people who have only one day to spend in Venice will storm into the places where they think Venice is to be found: the Piazza San Marco and St. Mark's Church. In a crowd of tourists from all over the world it is difficult to absorb the grandeur and dignity of the church. The observer should have time to appreciate the rise and fall of the domes and the archways, the harmonious balance of serenity and dynamic strength, the play of light and shade.

The quality of the light is another reason why the church should be visited before noon; the only openings that admit light are those in the domes and in the large archways in the south. In former times light also came up from the lower zone but since many windows were bricked up in the 12th century the

Mosaic, 13th century— "*The creation of Eve*".

lower part of the Basilica now lies in darkness and one's gaze is automatically drawn upwards to the domes and the soft golden glow of the mosaics.

They cover an area of about one acre and form the largest mosaic cycle in the west. They stem mainly from the end of the 12th century and from the 13th century; later additions are not to be compared with the medieval work. In the very first dome, the **Pentecost Dome**, is one of the oldest works: at the zenith is the heavenly dove with rays of light reaching out to the 12 apostles. The main dome shows the **Ascension**—Christ is borne aloft by four angels—and in the choir dome is **Christ giving blessing**, with 13 prophets and the Virgin Mary. The mosaics of these three domes are of the greatest artistic importance.

The domes in the northern arm of the cross were decorated in the 12th century and show resemblances to the Pentecost Dome: their theme is **The Life of St. John the Evangelist**. Opposite, in the southern arm of the cross are four saints of whom the Venetians possessed relics: St. Nicholas, St. Clemens, St. Blasius, and St. Leonard.

Not only the domes of St. Mark's but also the arches, pillars and walls are all adorned with mosaics. The church is so laden with pictures and designs that the architecture fades into the background. In this St. Mark's differs from its Byzantine prototype and the presentation of the figures is also typically Venetian. The Byzantine figures are stiff, the persons shown have no relation to one another but the figures in the mosaics of St. Mark's are full of vitality and play out their scenes together.

Other works in the interior include:

Over the main doorway Christ with the Virgin Mary and St. Mark (13th century, restored) and in the arch of the main door scenes from the Apocalypse

Choir stalls and the main choir dome.

(16th century, partly modern).

The barrel vault that divides the Pentecost Dome from the Ascension Dome is called the **Passion Vault** and shows the story of Christ's Passion from the kiss of Judas to the Resurrection (13th century).

Left of the Pentecost Dome, looking from the main doorway, one sees Christ and the Apostles (13th and 16th centuries) and opposite the Passion, the Garden of Gethsemane and Apostles (13th century).

Between the northern and the Ascension Domes are the miracles of Jesus. The designs come from Tintoretto (16th century). Opposite, between the great dome and the south dome there are scenes from the life of Christ.

Between the main dome and the choir dome, which shows Christ giving blessing, there are also scenes from the life of Jesus, designed by Tintoretto.

It is difficult to concentrate on the other beautiful things until one has seen enough of the mosaics. Then we can see the floor, which works in places like a handwoven oriental carpet. The piles on which St Mark's is built have given way in various places; the flooring has sunken and seems to undulate before our eyes.

The screen that divides the choir from the nave should not be missed. It consists of 16 marble archways from the 10th century…unfortunately the lower part of the screen is almost hidden by a wooden platform. Right and left of the screen are two pulpits. On the right hand one, a platform with nine pillars, the Doge showed himself to the people after his election.

The choir is entered through the **Chapel of St. Clement**, right of the screen. In the vestibule to the choir two pulpits for singers catch the eye; their bronze reliefs showing scenes from the life of St. Mark are by Sansovino.

The High Altar stands under a canopy carried by alabaster pillars; they stem either from the 6th century or from the 12 and 13th centuries, the experts cannot agree on this point. If the earlier date is correct they must be of Byzantine origin reworked in the middle ages. The shaft of every pillar is covered with low reliefs which show scenes from the life of the Virgin Mary and of Jesus Christ up to the Crucifixion.

The best known and most costly work is today behind the High Altar: the famous altarpiece, the **Pala D'Oro** is set with pearls, and with precious and semi-precious stones. It measures 11.5 by 5 feet (three meters by one meter) and although it radiates harmony and completeness it was created in four phases in the course of 500 years. The oldest parts are the medallions on the framework. The Doge Pietro Orseolo I had them made by Byzantine goldsmiths in the 10th century. The enamel plates that frame three sides of the lower part—showing scenes from the

A confessional.

New Testament and the life of St. Mark—are Venetian work of the 12th century.

The enamels that have decorated the centerpiece since 1209 were brought as trophies to Venice from Constantinople in 1204. The last craftsman who worked on the Pala D'Oro was the Venetian goldsmith, Gianpaolo Buoninsegna, in 1345. Christ enthroned, surrounded by the Evangelists, prophets, apostles and angels, stems from this period. During religious festivals the Pala D'Oro can be turned to face the High Altar.

In the central niche of the three set into the curve of the apse is a **Tabernacle** with bronze doors, the work of Sansovino, the most important architect and sculptor of the 16th century. He also made the **Sacristy** in the left-hand niche, a wonderful piece of work with relief sculptures of the Burial and Resurrection of Christ. The mosaic in the

apse of Christ giving blessing stems from the year 1505; the figures of the saints, however, are among the oldest mosaics, done in the 11th century when the church was rebuilt.

After leaving the choir the visitor goes left; in the transept crowned by the dome with the pictures of the four saints is the entry to the **Treasury**. This must not be missed: it gives an impression of the incredible riches that the Venetians obtained through conquest and plunder in the course of centuries to honor their stolen saint. The sack of Constantinople formed the solid basis of the Treasury of St. Mark's and it was continually added to in the centuries that followed. Many pieces were lost in 1797 when the Republic ceased to exist.

About 300 pieces still remain including beautiful reliquaries, a lamp or thurible in the shape of a Basilica, wonderful vessels of precious stone and the famous Throne of St. Mark of pale gray alabaster, said to have been a gift from the Emperor of Byzantium to the Patriarch who then lived in Grado. Its transfer into the hands of the Venetians at the beginning of the 9th century had for them enormous symbolic power. Through the person of the Evangelist they sought to legitimate their position as the heirs of the Roman Empire.

Before leaving the church the visitor must see the **Cappella dei Mascoli** (in the northern side aisle, left) a complete late gothic work with mosaics from 1430-1450. Next on the right is the **Cappella di San Isodoro**, with mosaics and altar from the 14th century. Also of interest is the **Baptistry**, a room with two domes carried by pillars, built in the 14th century with mosaics from this time.

When one has left the church through the main doors and stands in the narthex again the **Cappella Zen** is on the left, a massive memorial of Cardinal Zen, a patron of the city who was laid to rest here at about the beginning of the 16th century.

Left, floor mosaics in the narthex under water. Right, at the High Altar.

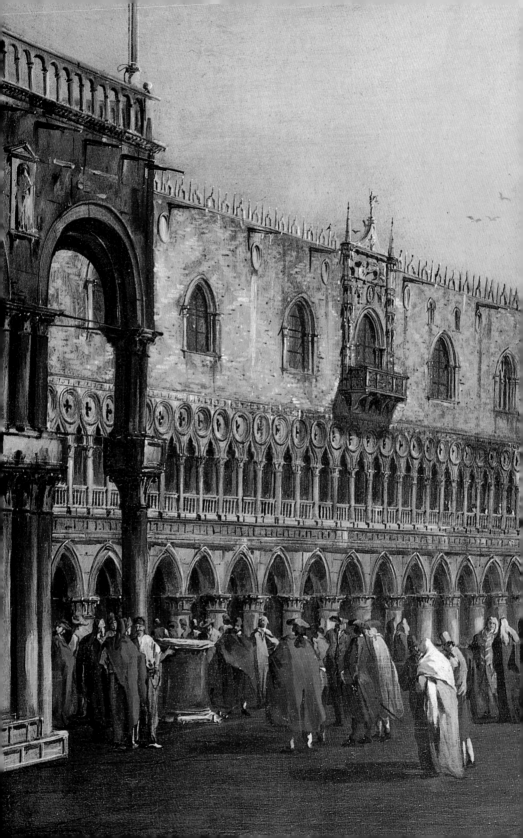

THE DOGE'S PALACE

The Doge's Palace is the emblem of Venice: the great representative building of the Republic, the trademark of Venetian tourism, one of the first association that comes to mind on hearing the word 'Venice'. It is a cliché from a postcard but also the first great impression for the seafarer who came towards the city over the Adriatic sea.

The Doge's Palace was the seat of the Doge and also his home; it was the meeting place of the Council and the Senate; it was the festive stage for all acts of state, the reception hall for friends and enemies. It was the Supreme Court and the nerve center of the Secret Service—it was in fact the head of the city, the Republic, and the great commercial empire. It shows Venice at the height of her power and is a hymn of praise, a swan song and an epitaph, all in one.

Its form is as wilful and puzzling as the Venetian state itself. Art historians and architectural philosophers are alienated and fascinated at once by this building which seems to defy the law of gravity and the rules of statics. Here at the palace we have no firm foundation carrying gables, instead two filigree rows of pillars, like a lace curtain, grow out of the ground to support a massive block, full of elemental power. This story is covered with a delicate network of rhombic marble tiles, yellow-white and pale red, like a carpet, which takes away every trace of heaviness from the building.

These facades are an allegory of Venice itself: the short, sturdy pillars stand for the tree trunks that form the roots of the city and carry its palaces. The fantastic pillars of the second row of arcades tell of the city's wealth; the upper story glows with the delicate ethereal colors of the sky over the Adri-

atic or the lagoon. There is a more down to earth explanation: the facades of the Doge's Palace simply recall the previous wooden building, a standard construction with strong supports in the lower story, finer bearers on the first floor and a hall made of wooden planks as the next story. This model was used for the 246-foot-long and 56-foot-high stone building; this explains the apparently illogical placing of the 'heavy' part on the 'light'.

In 814 the first Doge's Palace was erected as a wooden citadel at the time when the Doges moved their seat of government from Malamocco to Rivus Altus (deep canal, Rialto), that is to an almost inaccessible island in the swamps of the lagoon. In the year 828 divine protection was added to earthly fortifications as the newly chosen Bishopric 'obtained' its patron, St. Mark, from Egypt.

Now the town hall of the rising settle-

Previous pages: the Doge's Palace (painting by Guardi). Left, the Doge's Palace, southwest corner. Right, the Doge's Palace from the lagoon.

ment needed a sign of dominion for all to see. The Doge's Palace became sacred to the patron saint and the state church and from here it controlled the entrance to the Canal Grande and the Rialto like a palisaded fortress, surrounded by water.

After it had been burned to the ground more than once and rebuilt the first stone palace was erected in 1177, the south wing first of all as a suitable setting for the large hall in which the Great Council gathered. In 1340 the foundation stone of the vast room was laid; it was meant to hold all 900 councillors and to be larger than any other hall in Europe.

Deep laid piles and a framework of larch trunks served as the foundation to the palace. It no longer required protective walls, towers or other fortifications; Venice felt safe in the lagoon, protected by its fleet.

The balcony was the festive stage upon which the Doge showed himself to the people surrounded by sculptures which reflected Venice's self-esteem. He made his entry framed by saints with Venezia in the robe of Justice standing in triumph overhead. State guests landed at the Doge's feet. They entered by the Piazzetta, the reception area of the city in the lagoon and were led towards the Campanile, the loggia and the mysterious domes of St. Mark's Church. The Piazzetta is flanked by two massive pillars, right on the quay, antique trophies from Asia Minor. The left, gray pillar, bears St. Theodore on a dragon, the first patron of the city. His successor, St. Mark, is enthroned on a red pillar to the right in the shape of his symbolic beast, the winged lion.

The Doge's Palace was never simply a residence for the Doge. It housed the most important institutes of the Republic: the legislature, the executive and the judiciary, three classic types of civil

Ground plan, 2nd and 3rd stories.

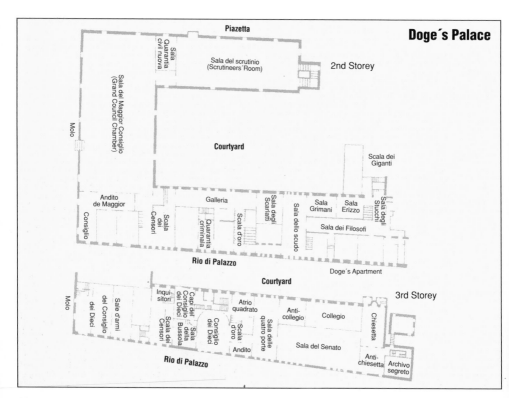

98

power which today come from the people. When elected the Doge must give up all other offices and commercial enterprises and live in the palace—a prisoner in a golden cage.

As the Doge went to his coronation his path was decorated in the course of the centuries, as lavishly as the triumphal path of a roman general. The main entrance, the **Porta della Carta** (1438-42) lies between St. Mark's and the palace and exactly opposite the Campanile, as a bond between secular and sacred rule. At the Porta della Carta laws were proclaimed and petitions presented; the people were forbidden to go past this point.

The Doge entered the inner courtyard through the **Arco Foscari** an arch adorned with sculpture, donated by the Doge Francesco Foscari in 1450. On the **Scala dei Giganti**, the Staircase of the Giants (1484-1501) the newly elected Doge was crowned with the

zoia, the jeweled phrygian cap. He stood beneath a lion of St. Mark, between statues of Neptune and Mars, symbols of Venice's dominion over sea and land and looked at the most impressive aspect of the Arco Foscari. There he beheld Adam and Eve, as representatives of erring mankind, the Virtues, as ideals for his rule, and St. Mark, as the proudest symbol of all.

From the Scala dei Giganti, the **Scala D'Oro**, the Golden Staircase (1538-59), leads to the Doge's apartments and the government chambers. Their original furniture has gone, destroyed or stolen by Napoleon's troops in 1797, but they provide an unusual example of a palace (and a museum) in which every art work is in the exact place for which it was originally made. The theme is repeated so often that it becomes wearying: the glorification of Venice and the Doge in the company of antique gods or Christian saints.

The Doge's Palace and the Riva degli Schiavoni.

The **Atrio Quadrato**, in which excursions begin, shows the Doge Girolamo Priuli being presented with the sword and the balance, symbols of a just government, by Venice, clad as Justitia. Tintoretto did this painting as the centerpiece of the coffered wooden ceiling in 1560.

The next rooms—like most of the palace—were newly done out after a fire in the year 1574; the **Sala della Quattro Porte** (the chamber with four doors) shows an antechamber and vaulting in the style of Palladio, all from that time.

The **Anticollegio** was the antechamber to the Collegio in which noble guests waited for an audience. Tintoretto's wall paintings show scenes from classical mythology always with a Venetian reference. The compositions are full of bold imagination, the effects of light and shade and a sophisticated understanding of human figures. Paolo Veronese's *"Rape of Europa"* is shown as a festive 'genre' picture of the rich city of Venice; Jacopo Bassano shows *"The Return of Joseph from Canaan"* in an ideal rustic landscape.

In the **Sala del Collegio** the Collegium or Council of State met under the leadership of the Doge; it included Ministers and Advisors, the highest judges, the representatives of the Great Council, the provinces and the religious orders. The Collegium received foreign ambassadors, it was the highest court of justice and formulated or controlled Venice's political policy even towards the church.

The room is splendid but harmonious. The coffered ceiling, richly carved and gilded, frames paintings from Paolo Veronese. Over the Doge's throne stands Venezia between Pax and Justitia, peace and justice. In the great wall paintings over the seats of the Collegium the Doge Sebastiano Venier

The Great Council Chamber.

gives thanks for his sea victory over the Turks at Lepanto (1571). Tintoretto shows Venezia and Faith, personified, carrying a chalice, as mediator to Christ, who is the center point of the composition.

The **Sala del Senato**, the Senate, also known as the Smaller Council, met twice a week and was composed of 40, then 60 and finally about 100 members. Representatives of the provinces and the religious orders were also in the outer ranks of this council. The Senate was in existence since 1229 and was more or less the executive of the Republic; it determined Venetian policy. The splendid wooden ceiling (1590) tends towards the baroque. Behind the platform lie the Doge's private chapel and the secret archives.

The excursion continues through the Sala della Quatre Porte into the **Sala dei Consiglio dei Dieci**. The *Council of Ten* was the secret state court set up in 1310 for the security of the Republic after the conspiracy of Bajamonte Tiepolo. It was also the highest constitutional court (the judiciary, so to speak), a tribunal of the Inquisition and the command center of a perfect, wide-reaching Secret Service. The Ten were chosen by the Senate for a year; their names were kept secret; the Doge and his six advisors and an Avvogadore (or state attorney) completed this body. The ceiling of the semi-circular tribunal (1533) shows Zeus casting bolts of lightning at the Vices—a picture of the work of the Council of Ten. The picture is a copy, the original was carried off to the Louvre by Napoleon. It was Veronese's first work in Venice and it made him famous at once.

The **Sala della Bussola** is called after its wooden paneling; it means literally a binnacle, the box that houses a compass. Here witnesses and the accused waited for questioning or sentence. Denunciations could be slipped into the mouth of the lion near the door: it is one of the many post-boxes of this type throughout the city.

In the **Sala dei Tre Capi** there met the three heads of the Council of Ten, who are considered to be the highest judges of the Inquisition. Secret staircases lead to the torture chamber overhead and to the Bridge of Sighs. Through the former Armory, which now houses a collection of weapons, the excursion leads up the **Scala dei Censori**, the staircase of the censors, to the **Sala del Maggior Consiglio**, the Chamber of the Great Council.

From the antechamber (**Audito del Maggior Consiglio**), where the Councillors strolled during pauses in the sessions, we reach the **Sala della Quarantia Civil Vecchia** (Chamber of the Forty), the highest civil court, established in 1179, and the **Sala del Guariento**, named for the painter Guariento. In 1365 he painted the large front wall of the Great Council Chamber with a Crowning of the Virgin in the style of Giotto.

The **Great Council Chamber** is the largest room in the palace (174 by 82 feet, 44 feet high) built in these present dimensions from 1340-1355 and renewed in renaissance style after a fire.

The Great Council was a body of nobles that developed in 1172 from the original assembly of the people. In 1297 the Golden Book, a register of all the noble families, determined who could vote; later this number reached from 1500 to 1800. The Great Council chose the Doge from its own ranks and passed laws; it was the legislative body. The chamber was once filled with rows of benches around a central speaker's rostrum; on the east side the Doge presided with his advisors and the highest officials.

The paintings on the ceiling naturally celebrate Venice, with an Apotheosis painted by Veronese in dramatic perspective. Over a crowd of citizens and a balcony full of the nobility Venezia floats upon a cloud and is crowned by an angel. The giant east wall is covered by an oil painting *Paradise* by Tintoretto which actually shows the *Last Judgment*. This monumental work which replaced a fresco by Guariento, measures 72 feet (21 meters) by 23 feet (six meters) and is painted on smaller pieces of canvas patched together. Hundreds of the blessed, with saints and angels, are ranged in the form of a cross, forming a dynamic group about the throne of Christ (just above the Doge's head). The picture is full of lively color contrasts and spectacular effects of light. In the ceiling a frieze shows portraits of the first 70 Doges and their coats of arms. The portrait of Marin Faliero, convicted of high treason, the second on the west wall, is painted over in black.

The **Sala del Scrutinio** was used during divisions of the Great Council and the choosing of the Doge. The frieze of the Doges' portraits continues here; the Last Judgment on the entry wall was painted by Palma the younger (1587-1594).

The excursion now leads through the reception rooms and living quarters of the Doge and over the Bridge of Sighs to the prison beyond the Rio de Palazzo, then back over the censors' staircase.

The Doge's Palace shows the Republic of Venice at the height of her power, but its decoration suits 'the once triumphant bride of the sea', in the words of Goethe, whose decline had already begun. At the end of the 16th century world trade flourished in America and East Asia; the Mediterranean was provincial, the Adriatic almost forgotten.

The former world power lasted a further 200 years until she dissolved the Republic herself—1797, in the Great Council Chamber, under the eyes of the old Doges who had made Venice great and powerful.

Below: left, statue of Eve on the Arco Foscari; and right, the Bridge of Sighs (old engraving).

THE DOGE

"The Doges who come after him should know that Doges are not gentlemen, not even Dukes, but the glorified slaves of the Republic."

These words were written by Petrarch, the great renaissance poet and humanist, a friend of the Doge Marin Faliero, who was executed for conspiracy in 1355, at a time when the Doge's powers had indeed been greatly reduced. The Venetian head of state was only a figurehead; he lived like a prisoner in a golden cage.

The magnificent robes of the Doge showed his function as Venice's representative. Over a long purple robe he wore a golden cape, the *pallium*, and a white stole. His head was covered by the *corno*, a headgear embroidered with gold and set with precious stones, that resembled a Phrygian cap. There are beautiful examples of the Doge's splendid costumes in the **Museo Correr**.

The title "Doge" is the Venetian dialect form of the Italian *Duce* and comes from the Latin *Dux*, leader or duke. The duties of the Doge included presiding over the Council and controlling the offices of state. At meetings of the Council, the legislative assembly, he had to work for unanimous decisions; only in time of war did the Doge possess absolute powers. Since the 14th century the Doge did not make military decisions but was represented by his generals in the field.

Eroding Power

A catalog of regulations from the year 1600 makes it clear how tightly the Doge was bound by the ties of the state and how few privileges remained to him at this time. Neither he nor any of his family were permitted to take part in any commercial enterprise; none of the members of the Doge's family were permitted to leave the city without the express agreement of the Great Council. The sons of the Doges were forbidden to hold office; from the 16th century onwards the Dogaressa, his wife, was no longer crowned. The Doge himself was watched closely; his letters were censored and he was forbidden private contact with foreign ambassadors. The mistrust felt for individual demands for power was so great that his income was strictly controlled by the Great Council and he was not allowed to accept any gifts except flowers and fragrant herbs.

All these prohibitions grew over the years after bad experiences with Doges who were power-hungry. Since the end of the 12th century the Doges were chosen by the Great Council in a complicated ballot designed to prevent the rise of individual families.

From thirty gold balls a boy chose nine which he handed to nine members of the Council whose faces he could not see. These nine chose

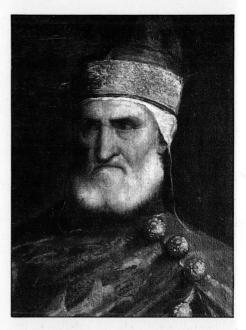

40 electors from the Council from whom 12 men chose 25 electors who were in turn reduced to nine by the use of the golden balls and these nine again chose 40 men. From these 40, 11 were chosen who named 40 final electors. A candidate was elected when he received 25 votes.

In spite of all this the names of the same families often appear in the list of 120 Doges of La Serenissima. The Mocenigo and Partecipazio families alone produced seven Doges each and the Contarini family produced eight.

Above, the Doge Gritti (Titian).

103

THE MERCERIE

Carnivals masks, Murano glass and gondolas of every kind—these are the typical souvenirs of Venice. In the very center of the city round the Piazza San Marco they tempt you on every corner, in colorful show cases.

Shopping in Venice has a special charm. The familiar gondolas etc are available not only as cheap mass-produced souvenirs, but also in artistic and expensive variants. Those interested can find little galleries and dusty antiquarian bookshops where they can discover objets d'art and precious old books. In order to enjoy the excitement of finding something truly old and Venetian you need to have a bit of curiosity and go a few steps further.

A little shopping trip in the city center will show us three different facets of Venice: first of all the **Mercerie**, the classic shopping quarter between the Piazza San Marco and the Rialto, then the down-to-earth little shops between the Campo San Salvador and the Campo San Stefano, and finally the elegant establishments in the **Via Largo XXIV Marzo**, west of the Piazza San Marco, bringing us back to our starting point in front of St. Mark's.

We set out from the Torre dell'Orologio, the clock tower on the Piazza San Marco. Behind it we plunge into the darkness of the narrow alleys of the Mercerie. The word *Mercerie* can be seen elsewhere in Venice but it means simply mercery, a place where fabrics and dress goods are sold. (Italian *Mercerie* = English mercery). The name has been given to this shopping district because it was once a place where textiles were sold.

In the **Mercerie Dell'Orologia** we find mainly small souvenir shops and jewelry stores. It is hard to believe that all the articles of 'Murano glass' are really produced on the island of Murano. Souvenirs with the Venetian look come from all over the world. Traditional quality products can be seen in one of the factories on Murano or in the glass making museum on the island. Visitors who would like to see glassblowers at work don't have to go so far. A little way behind the clock tower there is a shield that tells you how to visit a glass-making workshop.

One comes upon the first elegant boutique in the **Calle Fiubera** that opens into the Mercerie Dell'Orologia. Here is **Gianfranco Ferre**. A word or two about fashion. Naturally fashion is very important in Venice as in every Italian city. Branches of the best known firms and fashion designers are a matter of course. Among the most exclusive addresses we find the Venetian Roberta di Camerino, who designs accessories and **haute couture**, or Franco Zancan—**Franz** for short—whose cus-

tom-made shoes and charming creations have customers all over the world. Fine carnival masks are sold in **La Mona** and the customers can watch them being made.

Turning off into the **Merceria San Zulian** we find all sorts of goods in every price range—from the workshirts in check cotton and the colorful pinks and blues of *Benetton* to the princely offerings at the *Cartier* branch. A watchmaker, also of the luxury class, is the *Gioielleria*, nearby. During a shopping trip through the Mercerie one should cast a glance at the upper stories and note the contrast between the decorative chic of the shop fronts and the old buildings.

We can also see how clearly old and new are clustered together when we take a few steps behind the Church of San Zulian in the direction of the Campo Santa Maria Formosa. On the corner of the **Salizzada San Lio** is a modern supermarket, nothing startling but with a varied range of goods at moderate prices.

Although it is not something that must be seen by visitors to Venice, lovers of the genuine taste of foamy Espresso should visit the big store for household appliances in the **Calle delle Bande**. Coffee machines from *Gaggiu* and *Pavoni* are available at comparatively reasonable prices.

It is fun to look around in the Merceria without any special purchase in mind. You will enjoy the amusing atmosphere, the variety of displays, the bright ideas of the shopkeepers, the way in which things are fitted into every nook and cranny so that every centimeter of space is used.

Back at the Chiesa San Zulian we bear north in the direction of the Rialto. In the **Merceria San Salvatore**, which goes past the church of the same name, there are expensive boutiques with ele-

An antique shop.

gant fashions in leatherware. Exclusive jewelry is sold by *Salvad' ori*, a jeweler making a play on words. (Italian *oro* = gold). Things are just as exclusive at *Rosa Salva*—and delicious: fine pastries, cakes and marzipan figures. There is often a queue before the shop.

On the **Campo San Salvador** we leave the Merceria and turn left into the Calle di Lovo. Here on the way over the **Campo Manin** and the **Campo Sant'Angelo** in the direction of *Campo San Stefano* we find, in comparison with the Merceria, another kind of shop. There are little grocery stores with pump mortadella, imposing hams, spicy salami. Every now and then a nice little bar tempts us with the smell of fresh espresso or we see a pastrycook's full of goodies. Everyday shopping doesn't have to be unexciting; we can enjoy the sight and the enticing aroma of this delicious food.

Masks. Masks can be bought all over Venice not only on the Campo San Stefano. Since the carnival was revived recently the number of mask shops grows from year to year. There is for instance the mask-maker **Gabi Lechner**, in the Salizzada San Lio, or the **Laboratoria Artigiano Maschere**, at the Barbarie delle Tolle, while **Mondonovo**, makers of fantasy masks, are on the Rio Terra Canal, Dorsoduro.

Next to the fantasy creations of papier maché we find the classic masks of the *Commedia dell' Arte*, and next to the pretty miniature china masks for the collector's cabinet we find works of art: classical gods and goddesses from the world of myth and legend.

On the way from Campo San Stefano over the **Campo San Maurizio** to the Via Largo XXII Marzo we can discover another special Venetian craft: marbled paper. It is sold in shops called *legatoria*, meaning simply 'book-bindery'. This old technique which gives paper a

fine marbled veneer came originally from the east. A special mixture is spread on the impregnated paper and with a comb the wavy patterns are formed...they often look like peacock's feathers. Once the marbled paper was popular for binding books and pamphlets and also as a background for documents which gave protection against forgery. Today there is a wide choice of photo albums, writing cases, writing paper greeting cards and notebooks, with matching pencils and other accesssories.

For the Venetians the Mercerie has long been displaced by the district around the **Via Largo XXII Marzo** as the smartest shopping address in town. In streets that are unusually wide for Venice there are exquisite antique shops, antiquarian book-shops, fashion boutiques and jewelry stores near various banks with suitably solid facades.

The gap between the Via Largo XXII

Marzo and the Piazza San Marco is closed by the **Salizzada San Moisé**. In the immediate neighborhood of the luxury hotel **Bauer-Grünwald** there are, of course, luxury shops: leatherware from *Fendi*, luggage from *Louis Vuiton*, shoes from *Magli* and tucked away in the **Calle Vallaresco** that leads to the Vaporetto Station San Marco, we find the high class knitwear of *Missioni*. At the end of the Salizzada, directly opposite the Napoleonic Wing, lie the elegant show rooms of *Roberta di Camerino*.

For those with less money to spend there is a kiosk on the left with an up to date selection of international newspapers and magazines. A British tourist can be seen enjoying *The Guardian*, while a French traveler combs *Le Figaro*, a German looks into *Der Spiegel* and *The Wall Street Journal* is scanned by an American.

Behind the kiosk lies the most important address for letter-writing visitors to Venice: the post office on the **Bocca di Piazza.**

Shopping for Hidden Treasures

We come through the Napoleonic Wing on to the Piazza San Marco again. The arcades surrounding 'the finest drawing-room in Europe' are definitely among the most exclusive addresses found in the city. There are no fashions but the best choice of beautiful Murano glass, gold and jewelry or hand-worked lace; the display rooms for this classic handicraft are in the arcade of the Procuratie Nuove.

Shopping in Venice is not only the elegance of the Piazza San Marco, the Salizzada San Moisé and the Via Larga XXII Marzo, or the busy little shops of the Mercerie. It is always rewarding to leave the main streets and wander off the beaten track looking for something new. The maze of the Venetian streets is full of hidden treasure.

Left, glassware. Right, Masks, a seahorse.

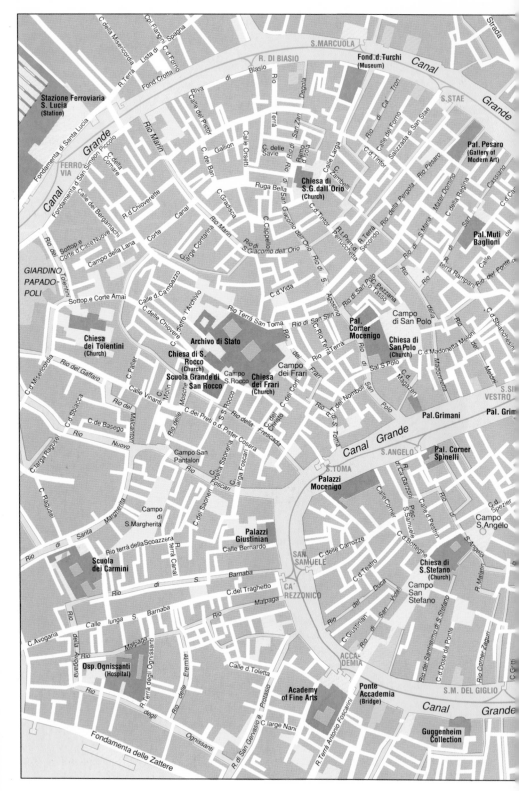

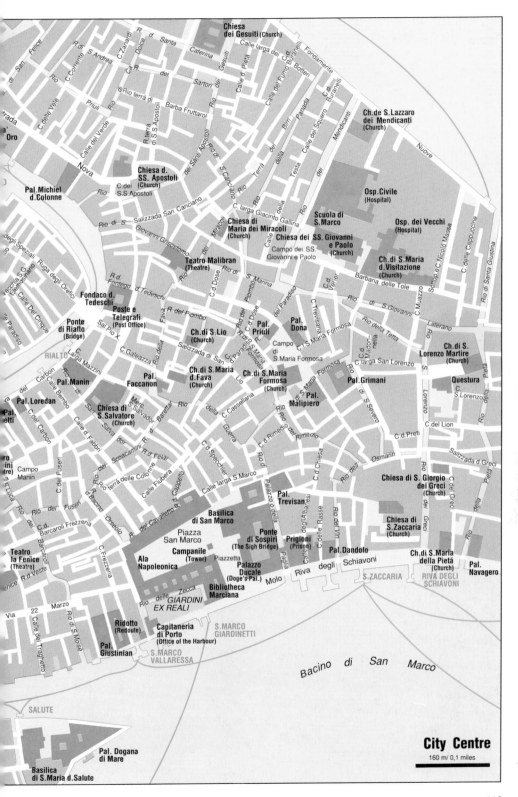

Chiesa
dei Gesuiti (Church)

Ch.de S.Lazzaro
dei Mendicanti
(Church)

Chiesa d.
SS. Apostoli
(Church)

Pal.Michiel
d.Colonne

Osp.Civile
(Hospital)

Scuola di
S.Marco

Osp. dei Vecchi
(Hospital)

Chiesa di
Maria dei Miracoli
(Church)

Chiesa dei SS. Giovanni
e Paolo
(Church)

Teatro Malibran
(Theatre)

Campo dei SS.
Giovanni e Paolo

Ch.di S.Maria
d.Visitazione
(Church)

Nova

Fondaco d.
Tedeschi

Barbaria delle Tole

Poste e
Telegrafi
(Post Office)

Pal.
Priuli

Pal.
Dona

Ch.di S.Lio
(Church)

Ch.di S.
Lorenzo Martire
(Church)

Ponte
di Rialto
(Bridge)

Campo
di
S.Maria Formosa

RIALTO

Ch.di S.Maria
d.Fava
(Church)

Ch.di S.Maria
Formosa
(Church)

Questura

Pal.
Faccanon

Pal.Grimani

Pal.Manin

Pal.
Malipiero

Chiesa di
S.Salvatore
(Church)

Pal.Loredan

Pal.
etti

Chiesa di S. Giorgio
dei Greci
(Church)

Campo
Manin

Chiesa di
S.Zaccaria
(Church)

Pal.
Trevisan

Basilica
di San Marco

Teatro
la Fenice
(Theatre)

Piazza
San Marco

Ponte
di Sospiri
(The Sigh Bridge)

Prigioni
(Prison)

Ch.di S.Maria
della Pietà
(Church)

Campanile
(Tower)

Piazzetta

Pal.Dandolo

Pal.
Navagero

Ala
Napoleonica

Palazzo
Ducale
(Doge's Pal.)

S.ZACCARIA

RIVA DEGLI
SCHIAVONI

Zecca

Bibliotheca
Marciana

Riva   degli   Schiavoni

Via   22   Marzo

GIARDINI
EX REALI

Ridotto
(Redoute)

Capitaneria
di Porto
(Office of the Harbour)

S.MARCO
GIARDINETTI

Pal.
Giustinian

S.MARCO
VALLARESSA

Bacino   di   San   Marco

SALUTE

Pal. Dogana
di Mare

Basilica
di S.Maria d.Salute

City Centre

160 m/ 0,1 miles

113

THE GRAND CANAL

"...and now we go towards that great street that they call the Grand Canal... yes, in my opinion it's the most beautiful street in the whole world, in the finest possible position and running right through the city. The houses are very large and high, the old ones built of good stones and all of them brightly painted. Those built many years ago have facades of shining white marble that comes from Istria, a hundred miles away. They are decorated with great blocks of porphyry and serpentine. Inside they mostly have two large chambers with golden ceilings, carved marble fireplaces, woven gold bed-covers, painted and gilded screens and the most beautiful furniture. And this is the most triumphant city that I have seen in all my days..."

Nearly 500 years have passed since the author of these lines, the Envoy Phillipe de Commynes, traveled down the grand Canal. Not many of the buildings that he saw are still standing—only about 70 of the gothic palaces remain—the gold in the inner chambers has long faded and the marble has turned black. The times when Venice was the most triumphant city began to come to an end and in the lifetime of Phillipe de Commynnes. He is still right about one thing: the Grand Canal is the most beautiful street in the world.

It is 23 miles (38 km) long and winds through the city in the shape of a great question mark from the **Piazzale Roma** in the northwest to the **San Marco Basin** in the southeast, a true 'water street'. Police and fire brigade flit by in their motor boats, the gray customs ships make their rounds—tradesmen, delivery men, wedding and funeral processions, the trash collectors and the movers' men—everything travels by water. Venice stands in water; what this

really means for the daily life of the people is something that is first grasped when one sees the busy traffic on the main street.

The Venetians also call their splendid street "Canalazzo", a word made from canal and palazzo, and this characterizes the Grand Canal very well. It is a string of palaces, wonderfully self-contained, a structure that is important as a unity as well as in detail. It is a reflection of the structure of Venetian society in which the interests of all were closely bound up with the egotistical striving of individuals.

Until the High Renaissance nearly all the palaces were of the same height, with the same ground plan and facade. Characteristic for this time is the division of the facade into three and the central group of windows on the first floor. In the baroque period the palaces were larger and more splendid but kept their typically Venetian features. No

Left, the Grand Canal, view from the Scalzi Bridge at the Station. Right, Ca' d' Oro, the house of gold.

palace was very much finer than the others, no patrician family though of erecting martial towers in Venice as they did in Florence. It was not only technically impossible (the palazzi stand on piles like the rest of the city) but this sort of ostentation was not the way of the Venetians: they were diplomats and democrats. If someone did overstep the mark there were sumptuary laws which regulated the size of the houses and the use of certain types of building and decoration. These luxury laws tried to regulate the everyday life of the well-to-do, laying down what should be eaten, what robes might be worn and even the interior decoration of the patrician houses.

The lack of space in the city and the function that the palaces had to fulfil determined their construction. The palace was a combination of family home and warehouse built by successful patricians, busy in commerce and in the service of the state, two areas that were always closely bound together in Venice. The palaces always faced towards the water; two entries, one on land, one in water led to the *andron* in the lowest storey, a landing from which rooms opened to left and right. Here boats were moored, wares were unloaded and stowed away in the store rooms. Running parallel to the andron on the first floor was the '*piano nobile*' or 'portega'. Like the *andron* it ran the whole width of the house from front to back. The rooms which led off from this hallway served as living rooms. Inside staircases were first used in the 15th century; before that the upper floors were reached by an outside staircase.

The prototype of the Venetian palace is the **Fondaco dei Turchi** which now houses the **Natural History Museum**: The palace was built during the 13th century and is one of the oldest palaces in Venice, stemming from the veneto-

Gondola stop at the Scalzi Bridge railway station.

byzantine epoch. (Typical for this style are the slender pillars and the high round archways.)

From the 13th to the 15th century it was the residence in Venice of the Dukes of Ferrara. Then from 1608 to 1621 it was the official seat of the Imperial Envoy, George Fugger. In 1621 turkish merchants moved in; they altered the building, closed up doors and windows, built a mosque and baths. Their trading center lasted until 1838.

During the second half of the 19th century the palace was thoroughly restored. It is now the **Natural History Museum** and contains a good collection of the marine fauna of the Adriatic as well as a zoological collection and a collection of minerals. On the ground floor there is a display of Venetian fountains.

The Fondaco dei Turchi is the first important palace one sees on a trip through the Grand Canal. One starts off at the railway station and takes the vaporetto, the 'bus service' on the Grand Canal. Numbers 1 and 2 take this route and No. 2, the 'Diretto' is a fast service. For sightseeing it is better to take Line 1, which chugs along comfortably from stop to stop, allowing the visitor to get off and explore some inviting place—a museum, an especially beautiful palace or a sunny restaurant.

The Fondaco Dei Turchi lies on the right hand side of the Canal opposite the Vaporetto station **San Marcuola**. Right next to the Fondaco is the **Deposito del Megio**, a plain castellated brick building from the 15th century, bearing a lion of St. Mark; it served the republic as a granary. Next door is an example of a baroque palace; the Palazzo Belloni-Battagia, built between 1647 and 1663 by Longhena.

Opposite there is a fine example from the Venetian renaissance: the **Palazzo Vendramin Calergi**, built about 1500

Aboard the Vaporetto.

by Mauro Codussi. It rises 72 feet (22 meters) above the water, with three stories, clearly divided horizontally. The windows, with their round arches and small round panes, give a wonderful effect of lightness. The central group of windows is so nicely proportioned that it preserves the group of the whole design. In this house Richard Wagner died. Wagner often visited Venice at the time he was composing words and music for *Tristram and Isolde*. The cry of the gondoliers is supposed to have inspired the shepherd melody at the end of the third act of this opera.

Whoever wants to try his luck at the Casino which operates in the Palazzo Vendramin Calergi in winter should get off the vaporetto at the San Marcuola stop. The visitor who simply wants to enjoy the sight of the palace should get off near the baroque church **San Stae**, at the vaporetto station of the same name. From the square in front of the church

there is a good view of a group of four palaces: Palazzo Barbarigo, Palazzo Zulian, Palazzo Ruoda, (all 17th century) and **Palazzo Gussoni-Grimani**, erected between 1548 and 1556. Its facade was kept very plain because the main feature of the building was to be its frescoes by Tintoretto. Alas, none of the painting has survived.

Back on the ship we pass on the right one of the most ornate palaces on the Canal Grande: the **Palazzo Pesaro**. Which took 58 years to complete; when the architect Longhena died in 1682 the piano nobile had just been finished. His successor Gaspari brought the work to an end in 1710. The Palazzo Pesaro, an example of Venetian baroque architecture, contains the **Museum of Oriental Art** and the **Museum of Modern Art**, which has one of the most important collections in Italy with works by Chagall, Rodin, Stuck, Lembach and Klinger.

Left, the Fondaco dei Turchi. Right, a water gate.

Baroque pomp on one side, gothic lightness on the other: airy and delicate arcades seem to float above the water, their proportions so fine, their pillars so slender that one can hardly trust them to support anything. This is the **Ca'd'Oro**, one of Venice's most famous palaces, unusual in many ways; it has for instance, only one torresello. The owner, Marino Contarini, for whom it was built in the middle of the 15th century, seems to have personally seen to its design.

He insisted, for example, that the open pillared hall in the lower storey should be integrated into the new building although it was out of fashion at the time. He also had the white marble facade painted; details were picked out in ultramarine, red and also in gold. So the palace received its name Ca'd'Oro, the golden house.

Ca' is short for Casa. Until the end of the Republic in 1797 only one building in Venice could be called a 'palazzo': the Doge's palace or Palazzo Ducale. The house of a patrician, however splendid it might be, was referred to simply, with a fine understatement, as 'Casa' or house.

After being closed for 15 years for restoration this masterpiece of late Venetian gothic was reopened in 1984. The Ca'd'Oro now houses the collection of Baron Franchetti, furniture, sculpture and paintings mainly from the 18th and 16th centuries. It includes works from Mantegna, Carpaccio, Bellini, Titian and Van Dyck.

The best view of the Ca'd'Oro is from the **Pescheria**, the Fish Market; one can cross the canal with a traghetto. Right of the Ca'd'Oro one sees two gothic palazzi, **Palazzi Pesaro** and **Sagredo**. Also, on the other bank there stands left of the Rio dei SS Apostoli the **Palazzo Mangilli-Valmarana** from the 18th century.

Street on the banks of the Canal, opposite the Palazzo Bembo.

On the left hand side before the Rialto Bridge there are long undecorated functional buildings, the **Fabbriche Nuove**, from the middle of the 16th century and the **Fabbriche Vecchio**, from a few decades earlier. The **Palazzo dei Camerlenghi** is the last building.

On the left hand side one sees opposite the Fabbriche the *Ca' da Mosto*, one of the oldest buildings on the Grand Canal. (Lower floor 13th century, upper floors completed in the 17th century) with the original Byzantine decorative patterns. Until the end of the Republic this was one of the best known and most exclusive hotels, patronised by the Austrian Emperor Joseph II among others. Last building before the bridge is the **Fondaco dei Tedeschi**. (See chapter Around the Rialto)

At the Rialto the Canal Grande is at its narrowest, 99 ft (30 meters) wide. A visitor can get off the Vaporetto, wander through the Rialto market, where vegetables, meat and cheese are sold every morning, and explore part of the Canal on foot. It is best to go along the right or western side because the most interesting buildings are to be seen on the east side. The **Palazzo Dolfin-Manin** can be recognized by its open arcades on the ground floor; it was begun in 1538 by Sansovino, the most important Venetian architect.

Sansovino was something of a state architect, the master builder who planned the St. Mark's Library, the Mint and the Loggetta at the foot of the Campanile. The Palazzo Dolfin-Manin is a simple building: the decorative elements are limited to doric pilasters and ionic and corinthian half-pillars. The palace has gone down in history as the home of the last Doge, Ludovico Manin, who was driven out of office by Napoleon in 1797.

Next comes a wider building, the late gothic **Palazzo Bembo**, in which the

The Palazzi Loredan and Farsetti.

andron and the protega are doubled.

The **Palazzo Loredan** and the **Palazzo Farsetti** are as alike as twins. Loredan is considered one of the best preserved palaces from the Veneto-Byzantine era. Its lower storey—like that of the Palazzo Farsetti— stems from the 13th century. The rows of round arches on the water in the Palazzo Farsetti are especially fine. Today the city administration is housed in these two buildings.

Opposite the vaporetto station **San Silvestro**, at the mouth of the Rio San Luca one sees the **Palazzo Grimani**. This massive renaissance building seems too monumental at first but a closer look shows that it was put together with surprising clarity and logic. It shows clearly the work of several builders: the two lower floors are regarded as the masterwork of Michele Sanmichelis, who died in 1546, leaving the building unfinished. Grigi added

the upper storey and Rusconi completed the building. The Grimani were an extremely rich family. The son of Marino Grimani, builder of the palace, was elected Doge in 1595. Following Venetian tradition the coronation was very simple but his lady wife put on such a show with her sumptuous clothes and her entertainments that it caused a scandal throughout Italy.

Diagonally opposite the Palazzo Grimani stands another renaissance building, the **Palazzo Padadopoli**, a much more conservative and less pretentious affair than what Sanmichelis built. Giangiacomo Grigi, who added the third storey to the Palazzo Grimani, was the architect.

On the left the **Palazzo Martinengro** is of some interest because it is two-storied, which was unusual at the beginning of the 16th century.

On the right stands the **Palazzo Bernardo** a gothic building from about

A view of the Volta dei Canal with Ca' Foscari straight ahead, Palazzo Balbi right with pointed turrets.

1442 which recalls the Ca'd'Oro and especially the Doge's Palace: the second piano nobile has exactly the same dimensions as the Loggia. Its two doors lead to separate courtyards from which outside staircases lead to the upper floors.

At the vaporetto station **Sant' Angelo** there is another work of the early renaissance architect Mauro Codussi, the **Palazzo Corner-Spinelli**. It was built at the end of the 15th century and is noticeably more conservative and more traditionally put together than Codussi's Palazzo Vendramin-Calergi.

Shortly before the Canal makes its wide curve to the left four palaces catch the eye on the left bank that were once in the possession of a single family. These are the Mocenigo palaces: from left to right the **Palazzo Mocenigo-Nero** (late 16th century), the **Mocenigo Double Palace**, from the 18th century, and the **Palazzo Mocenigo Vecchio**

which was renovated in the 17th century but was originally gothic.

The Mocenigos were a rich and influential family which produced seven Doges. Great historical events are associated with the name Mocenigo and great personages enjoyed their hospitality...more or less. Giordano Bruno, for instance, who accepted an invitation from Giovanni Mocenigo in 1591 could not have been the happiest of guests when his hosts denounced him and delivered him to the Roman Inquisition. Nine years later Bruno was burnt in Rome for his belief in the infinity of the world and in the existence of many universes.

Things went better for Lord Byron. He lived in the double palace from 1818 to 1819. "*I intend to stay in Venice for the winter.*" he wrote. "*It has not disappointed me although to be sure its decay, which is everywhere apparent, might have this effect on others. I have*

Left, a lion in the garden of the Palazzo Cavelli Franchetti. Right, taking a gondola ride.

been too long accustomed to ruins to be displeased by devastation."

The romantic poet certainly didn't seem to be affected by the devastation and decay of Venice. Love affairs, sporting achievements to impress the Venetians—for example his famous swim down the Grand Canal to the Lido—helped him to pass the time pleasantly. Fourteen servants, a valet, a gondolier, a coach and a billiard table helped Lord Byron keep disappointment at bay.

Venetian themes appear in Byron's work: the tragedy *The Two Foscari* tells the story of the Doge Francesco Foscari whose term of office was plagued by the intrigues, envy and malice of a rival candidate. In the end he was forced to resign his office and died a broken man in the palace he had built in the middle of the 15th century as a sign of his power and dignity, the **Ca' Foscari**:

King Henry III of France was lodged here during a sumptuous visit in 1474. He was entertained so richly that, in the words of a commentator:

"The King never forgot it nor recovered, His life after was a long, mad dream."

This wonderful building, one of the last examples of late gothic, commands the sharp bend in the canal, the **Volta del Canal**, together with the imposing **Palazzo Balbi** (end of the 16th century). On the first sunday in September, when the Regata Storica is held, rowers and gondoliers head for the Volta del Canal to compete in the festival.

Today the **Ca' Foscari** contains university institutes, while the **Palazzo Grassi**, diagonally across the Canal, is used for exhibitions. This baroque palace, built by Giorgio Massari, was purchased by Fiat in 1984 and has become one of the most important art centers in the city. The Ca' Rezzonico is a museum of Venetian art, including

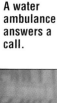

A water ambulance answers a call.

frescoes by Tiepolo, father and son, and pictures by Pietro Longhi. The architect Longhena began this monumental building in 1680.

Before reaching the accademia bridge one passes on the right the late gothic **Palazzo Loredan dell' Ambasciatire**; the figures in the niches have been kept in early renaissance style.

The **Ponte dell' Accademia** is one of the three bridges over the Canal Grande. The wooden structure, with its rather Japanese charm, was built in the 30s to replace a 19th-century iron bridge. This is always a very lively spot. The **Accademia**, right next to the bridge, with its great collection of Venetian paintings, attracts many visitors and from the bridge there is a marvellous view of the Santa Maria della Salute church.

Beyond the bridge one sees on the left the gothic **Palazzo Cavalli-Franchetti**, with striking proportions which

bring to mind the Doge's palace. On the right lies the **Palazzo Contarini-Polignac**, one of the oldest renaissance palaces in Venice.

The next building of interest on the right bank of the canal is the Palazzo Venier dei Leone. Its architecture—it was begun in the middle of the 18th century but never completed—is not so interesting as its owner. In 1951 Peggy Guggenheim, the rich American art collector, purchased the unfinished palace. Until her death in 1979 she managed to scandalise the gossips. She was buried behind the palazzo with her dogs. Her house and her magnificent collection of modern art passed into the possession of the city. (Sculpture and pictures from the 20th century, especially the Surrealists)

Opposite there stands the **Palazzo Corner della Ca' Grande**, a work from Sansovino—some experts say his best—built in the first half of the 16th century. Sansovino did not divide the facade into three parts, he took from Codussi the use of double pillars, regularly spaced, which give an impression of balance.

Right, at the mouth of the Rio Fornace, stands one of the most beautiful palaces in Venice, the **Palazzo Dario**. Its asymetry is striking and so are the colored marble inlays, showing lombard influence. In the year 1487 it was built as one of the first renaissance palaces in Venice; the architect was probably Pietro Lombardo.

Now a quick glance to the left at the **Palazzo Gritti**, today a hotel, famous through Hemingway, and at the small, exquisite **Palazzo Contarini-Fasan**; a gothic building with especially fine ornament on the balustrades. Then one sees to the right the dome of **Santa Maria della Salute** and the **Dogana del Mar**, the famous customs station. Here the Grand Canal is at its widest— 231 ft (70 meters)—and it flows into the St. Mark's Basin.

Left, a Traghetto in the mist. Right, crossing the Grand canal.

GONDOLAS AND GONDOLIERS

The *Gondolieri* are to Venice what the Fiaker cabmen are to Vienna. Since Venice began there have always been gondolieri. For over 1000 years they have not only carried passengers through the natural streets of Venice, the canals, in their little rocking boats they have also transported food and other wares from the markets or the harbor to the palazzi. Since the 11th century most gondoliers were in private service with patrician families. There were about 10,000 gondoliers in Venice in the 16th century, today there are only 400.

Since a regular steamer service began in the 19th century their number has continually decreased. The gondoliers also have to compete with the fast motor-taxis which roused the gondoliers to a spectacular strike in 1978. It proved all over again that, in spite of the steamers, cargo boats and water taxis, Venice without gondolas is unthinkable, for tourists as well as for native Venetians.

For the same price as a meal for two in a good restaurant one can hire a gondola and a gondolier—a song from the gondolier, however, costs extra. There is a fixed price for a one-hour gondola trip, a magical mystery tour through the canals of Venice. On such a romantic journey some of the gondoliers turn out to be experienced guides. Courses in the most important foreign languages, in art history and the history of Venice are offered by the gondoliers' union. They are not given singing lessons—every Italian seems to have a natural talent for singing.

Gondoliers are celebrated for a colorful flow of language—especially when a water-taxi crosses their bows—and for traditionally dry wit and humor, as shown by the following anecdote. When Napoleon conquered Venice in 1797 he issued an edict showing the Lion of St. Mark holding a book with a new motto. Instead of *"Pax tibi, Marce, Evangelista meus."* there stood: "The Rights of Men and Citizens." A gondolier quipped: "At last he's turned the page!"

Steering a gondola through the narrow canals demands great skill. A ten-year apprenticeship with a padrone is required before a gondolier gets a licence and only native-born Venetians can apply. Another barrier to the gondolier's independence is the limited number of licences issued. The young gondolier must wait until a colleague gives up his licence on the grounds of age or sickness and even then he must be content with a quieter place on the canals. The best places, near the Piazza San Marco and the Rialto bridge belong to the oldest gondoliers.

The visitor to Venice in winter will see even fewer gondolas on the canals because this is the time when they are overhauled at one of the three gondola docks, the *squeri*. There they lie at anchor in rows, these slim black trademarks of the city in the lagoon. Until the 16th century they were colorful and expensively decorated, the seats were covered with velvet and brocade. The sumptuary laws affected the gondolas too and ordered them into perpetual mourning.

Every gondola is 36 feet (11 meters long), four feet (1.40 meters) wide and about 1,100 lbs (500

kg) in weight. The elegant swinging motion comes from the fact that the right half of the boat is about nine inches (24 cm) shorter than the left. A gondola is made of eight different sorts of wood: including oak, pine, larch, lime, cherry, walnut, tannen and elm.

The bow of the gondola is decorated with the 44 lbs (20 kg) ferro, a shining silvery piece of iron that makes it stable but also has a symbolic meaning. There are seven horizontal prongs; the one pointing towards the boat stands for the Island of Guidecca, the other six for the sestieri, the six districts of Venice.

In the **Museo Storico Navale** one can see gondolas that are built with the *felze*, the wooden cabin that once protected passengers from prying eyes and also from the rain.

AROUND THE RIALTO

For a long time the name Rialto meant more than a small part of the city. Well into the 13th century it was in fact the official name of Venice and it remained a synonym for the power and wealth of the Republic. On the markets round the Rialto bridge there was a mixture of races and a babble of tongues; merchants of every land under the sun traded busily and the scenes were so lively and colorful that we might expect to find them today only in the bazaars of the orient.

In the warehouses of the Venetians and the great trading houses of foreign nations there lay immeasurable worth of spices, silk, jewels and other luxuries from the fabled kingdoms of the near and far east.

The Rialto functioned as an international exchange between east and west and because of her unique position as intermediary. Venice made fabulous profits that first began to decrease noticeably at the end of the 16th century. The great discoveries of a Christopher Columbus or a Vasco da Gama in 1500 indicated a decline of La Serenissima was inevitable but still a hundred years were to pass before Lisbon could compete with Venice as a commercial city.

The name Rialto is confusing today because it is mainly used for the *Ponte di Rialto*, the Rialto bridge. Traditionally it was used for the whole vaguely defined district near the bridge where the Venetian markets are still to be found. The famous bridge is the starting point for this short trip round the Rialto. The bridge spans the Grand Canal with a strong elegantly curved arch of marble; it is the most important junction between the two halves of the city, divided by the canal.

Until the 19th century it was the only bridge over the Grand Canal. The architect Antonio da Ponte competed against the most famous builders of the epoch, including Michelangelo, Sansovino and Palladio.

The oldest bridges over the Canal Grande were pontoons of boats, such as the one set up today on the festival of Il Redentore (the Redeemer), held on the third Sunday in July. The pontoon bridge is built so that Venetians can make a pilgrimage to the Chiesa del Redentore, Palladio's beautiful church on the island of La Guidecca, to light a candle in thanksgiving for the city's escape from the plaque in 1576.

Towards the end of the 12th century the first wooden drawbridge was built; it finally fell down in 1444 after being renewed several times. This time the drawbridge collapsed under the weight of the crowds during the wedding of the Marchesa of Ferrara. When it was rebuilt the old drawbridge model was used—this can be seen in a painting by

Left, the Rialto Bridge. Right, shops on the bridge.

127

Vittore Carpaccio in the Accademia.

Riding on horseback in Venice became very restricted when the flat wooden bridge was replaced by the stone arch. Venetians in renaissance Italy had the reputation of being bad horsemen; in fact they were known as 'sailors on horseback'.

The necessity of allowing sailing ships free passage through the canal and access to the store rooms of the patrician houses were the reasons which hindered the construction of a stone bridge. It was not until 1588 that a law was passed stating goods must be unloaded on to smaller boats.

Da Ponte's design seemed architecturally a typically Venetian solution: on a light, almost floating structure rose the solid closed arches of the shopping street, broken by the open arch of the middle platform. It was certainly a Venetian touch to have shops on the bridge, putting it to commercial use.

The foundations were erected on 6000 oak piles on either side of the river to carry an arch of istrian marble 92 feet (28 meter) wide. Millions of these treetrunks, the tough resistant wood of oak and larch, form the foundations of the palaces and the churches of the city in the lagoon; for this reason Goethe called Venice 'the beaver Republic'.

City Built on Marsh

The terrain on which the city is built, once consisting of 100 small islands round about the Rivus Altus, the deep riverbed of the Grand Canal, was mainly sandy and marshy land, too unstable for building purposes. The ground was made more stable by the sinking of large numbers of closely packed wooden piles until they were anchored deeply in the *caranto*, a layer of clay.

On the piles there was laid a lattice of

Evening on the Rialto.

larch trunks which was covered with blocks of stone to make foundations. A similar method was used when land was reclaimed from the lagoon but in this case earth and rubble were packed in between the wooden piles. The wood, standing in water, becomes hard and makes a foundation of remarkable stability.

From the Rialto bridge there is a fabulous view of life upon the Grand Canal and the marvelous palaces, swinging away to the **Volta del Canal**, where it makes a great bend leading to the south.

The north side of the bridge is flanked by two large palaces, the **Fondaco dei Tedeschi**, and opposite, the **Palazzo dei Camerlenghi**. Like the Fondaco dei Turchi this trading center for the German merchants, the Tedeschi, was one of the largest warehouses in Venice. Its full extent can only be seen in an aerial photograph.

Like many other words *fondaco* was borrowed by the Venetians from the speech of their trading partners, the Arabs. A *funduk* in Arabic means an inn and a *fondaco* was also used as an inn, because the foreign merchants were not allowed to find lodgings in the city outside their trading center.

Great German firms such as the Fuggers, Welsers or Tuchers, rented chambers permanently in the Fondaco dei Tedeschi. The giant palace with its 160 rooms in four stories grouped around an interior courtyard, offered plenty of room for lodgers. The German merchants dealt in silver and copper ore, furs, wool and canvas. Since it was not allowed to take the price of these wares out of Venice in hard cash they were bartered for Venetian or oriental goods.

Today the Fondaco is the main Post Office. The continual coming and going of customers, the unloading of

The Fondaco dei Tedeschi.

postbags at the water gate, the busy counters, are a reminder of days gone by. The interior courtyard of the finely restored palace is well worth seeing.

The Fondaco is first mentioned in 1228 and in 1505 it was rebuilt at the cost of the city of Venice after a fire. Giorgione decorated the plain, symmetrical renaissance facade with wonderful frescoes but, alas, only a fragment of them remains. His assistant was the young Titian who in later years obtained one of the sought-after broker's licences and made himself extra money as a trader at the Fondaco.

The church adopted by the German merchants, **Chiesa di San Bartolomeo**, is just a few steps south of the Fondaco dei Tedeschi. The present church from the first half of the 18th century catches the eye with its tall baroque tower. Once the right hand choir chapel contained one of Albrecht Dürer's most famous paintings *Das Rosenkrantzfest,* The Feast of the Rosary. The great German artist painted it for the German merchants during his visit to Venice in 1505. Today the work can be seen in Prague; it was brought there at the behest of the Emperor Rudolph II. The old organ in the choir shows a fine *Adoration* by Sebastiano del Piombo (about 1500). The picture at the High Altar, *The Martyrdom of St Bartholomew*, is by Palma the younger.

The square in front of the church, the **Campo San Bartolomeo**, is a popular meeting place for young Venetians. Every visitor who has the time should try to get there one evening. In the little square ringed with shops and cafés boys and girls have a real 'rendezvous' under the statue of Carlo Goldoni, the writer of comedies. The atmosphere is typically Italian—the young people meet and talk and flirt a little then in a couple of hours they drift happily away.

Now our way leads over the Rialto

Laden barges on the Grand Canal.

bridge to the other side of the Grand Canal for a look at the markets. All over the world marketplaces have a great fascination for travelers. Perhaps we are fascinated by the colorful and picturesque profusion of fruits and vegetables, so artistically displayed, perhaps we are curious about the strange and exotic wares. Another reason travelers like markets may be the opportunity they give for slipping undisturbed—and without disturbing anybody—into the everyday life of the local people.

Market Atmosphere

The markets of Venice are no exception. There is a lot of bargaining, full of Italian temperament, the goods are examined, there is time for a friendly chat. The delivery men at the Rialto are something special. The market halls are on dry land but the boats laden up with fruit, fish, greens and other vegetables anchoring at the quays conjure up a picture of a 'floating market'. The built up promenades along the bank of the Grand Canal are unusually long in the Rialto district. Their names: Riva del *Vin*, Riva del *Carbon*, Riva del *Olio*, indicate the goods that used to be handled here...wine, coal and oil.

The sale of more precious wares was concentrated around the little church of **San Giacomo di Rialto**, as we can tell from the **Ruga degli Orefici**, the Street of the Goldsmiths, which begins at the foot of the Rialto bridge. Passing the renaissance palace that housed the city treasury, the **Palazzo dei Camerlenghi**, one comes upon San Giacomo which is supposed to be the oldest church in Venice. It is supposed to have been founded in the 5th century by the first refugees in the lagoon but in fact the oldest parts of the building are from the 11th and 12th centuries.

San Giacomo di Rialto (painting by Canaletto).

The church was rebuilt in renaissance style during the 16th century after a fire and the pictures and statues in the interior come mainly from this period. The High Altar bears a statue of one of the Apostle, James (Giacomo) who is honored here as the patron saint of travelers and pilgrims.

It is hard to get a good look at the church especially in the morning because the square in front of it is packed with market stands. Behind the fruit and vegetable crates we find a little crouching marble figure beside a short granite pillar: the **Gobbo di Rialto** (the Hunchback of the Rialto).

He supports on his back a flight of stairs leading to a stone platform where heralds gave out proclamations. In the middle ages the Gobbo was a welcome sight for 'artful dodgers' and petty criminals—they were forced to run the gauntlet from the Piazza San Marco to the Rialto. Their beating at the hands of

the citizens did not stop until they had kissed the stone hunchback.

Around this square in the olden days there were mainly finance and trading institutions including banking offices under the arcades. These were mainly private banks; the first city bank was opened on the Rialto in 1507. Venice, inventor of the transfer banking system, generally preferred transactions without the use of cash. The merchants deposited their money in the banks who transferred it on paper from one account to another. In the same way one could exchange various currencies; the Ventian ducat was extremely stable.

The **Calle dell Sicurtá** or Security Lane branches off from the church square. Here valuable cargoes for the overseas trade were insured.

There are two ways to reach the Fish Market. Either one goes straight ahead from the Goldsmiths' Street to the **Ruga degli Speziale**, the Street of the Spice Traders, or one turns right to the **Erberia**, in the direction of the Grand Canal. Here there are pretty fruit stands covered with awnings and little delicatessan shops, plus the 'trademan's entrance' to the markets, the water gate.

The market extends right along the bank to the new gothic building of the **Pescheria**. The fishmarket hall was rebuilt in 1907 in the traditional way, with 18,000 piles of larchwood as foundation. Its architecture has been criticized as a 'cold imitation of Venetian gothic' but the two storied brick building with its elegant colonnades is by no means devoid of charm.

Everyday the fishermen bring their catch here and to the surrounding stores and market buildings. Whoever has seen this great array of fishy delicacies will understand why Venetians prefer sea food to meat dishes.

As a reviving finish to our walk through the Rialto what could be better for thirsty travelers than a glass of wine at the **Osteria da Pinto** on the Campo delle Boccarie.

Left, goods are transported by the typical Carretto. Right, the street of the goldsmiths.

133

SANTA MARIA DELLA SALUTE

The visitor traveling from the Lido to Venice sees from far off the spreading white dome of the church of **Santa Maria della Salute**.

It stands in an exceptionally fine position, at the point where the Grand Canal flows into the basin of St. Mark. Together with the Doge's Palace and the church of San Giorgio Maggiore the church has a most evocative silhouette. Some spectators are irritated, however, by the church's grand baroque style which makes it stand out from the other buildings on the Grand Canal.

Santa Maria della Salute was built between 1631 and 1687 from the designs of Baldassare Longhena. It is said that the building rests upon 1,100,000 tree trunks. The church was built as a result of an outbreak of plague which seized Venice in the year 1630. When the plague abated the citizens believed this was due to the intervention of Mary the Mother of God, to whom they had prayed in their hour of need. In thanksgiving Venice built the Salute church in her honor. The church is also symptomatic of the decrease in Venetian power in the 17th century; the self-indulgent and extravagant architectural style is a form of compensation.

The Exterior

The baroque church is an octagonal central building graced with an imposing antique portal on to the Grand Canal. Every facade is richly decorated and this makes it clear that the church was meant to be viewed from every aspect. The total impression of Santa Maria della Salute is opulently baroque but on closer inspection we see that the church is linked to the classical ideals of the renaissance. This can be seen in the central structure and the workmanship of the facades. The lines are straight rather than curved, as in the baroque. An exception are the 14 spiral volutes which give the church its popular name of the 'church with the ears'. The work of decorating the church with over a hundred statues continued well into the 17th century and is also a mark of the baroque. The statue of the point of the dome shows the Virgin Mary in the role of the Mistress of the Seas, (Capitana del Mar), carrying the baton of a Venetian admiral.

The Interior

After the opulent impression of the exterior the interior is surprisingly plain and sober. This plainness is emphasized by the clear and beautiful ornamentation of the mosaic floor.

The dome is supported by eight pillars said to have been stolen from an antique temple in Istria. The High Altar

Previous pages: Santa Maria della Salute. Left, the church in the November mist. Right, Fortune on the Globe (Punta della Dogana).

recalls the story of the church's founding. Above a precious 12th-13th century byzantine icon of the Virgin Mary from Crete there stands a group of sculptured figures. Venice, as a beautiful young woman kneels at the feet of the Virgin while the Plague, in the guise of an ugly old hag, is banished.

There are many beautiful paintings in Santa Maria della Salute. Both the great painters who were sons of Venice, Titian and Tintoretto, are represented. The altarpiece in the great sacristy shows *St. Mark Enthroned With Four Saints*—an early work of Titian's from 1511. In this picture we can see the influence of his teacher, Giovanni Bellini in the arrangement of the figures and in the color tones.

The paintings on the ceiling of *Cain killing Abel*, *Abraham's Sacrifice*, and *David and Goliath* are also by Titian (1543). On the wall hangs, among other paintings, a large Tintoretto, *The Marriage at Cana* from 1561.

Every year on November 21, the city holds a traditional procession of thanksgiving for her deliverance from the plague. The procession crosses a pontoon bridge from the mooring place at Santa Maria del Giglio to Santa Maria della Salute. Those who love the special charm of Venice in winter, when there are few tourists in the city, should not miss this spectacle.

After visiting the church the visitor can catch a particularly fine view of the Doge's Palace and the Riva degli Schiavoni from the **Punta della Dogana**, only a few steps away.

Next to the church is the *Seminario Patriarcale*, with a collection of sculpture and painting that is worth a visit.

Like all the historic buildings of Venice Santa Maria della Salute was seriously threatened by decay. Its restoration has been made possible by a French initiative.

Below, inside the Salute church. Right, young tourist in winter sunshine.

VENICE IN WINTER

Lovers of Venice have always had a secret pleasure: visiting the city in the lagoon in winter. This was supposed to be the time in which the romantic city regained her legendary excitement; she found her personal rhythm and belonged to herself again, not to the hectic hordes of visitors. Then there were loud protests which said the Serenissima had sold her soul to the tourist trade even in winter—the high season in Venice lasted all the year round.

For those who knew the crowded alleyways and the pushing and shoving between the Rialto bridge and the Piazza San Marco during the summer this was sad news indeed. But is it really true? Was this just a way of scaring off visitors so that the secret of Venice in winter would not be made too public? The Queen of the Adriatic can be unfriendly in the months from November to April. She does not always show her sunny side, those pleasant days that her Mediterranean climate definitely has in its repertoire, with a mild, soft light that delights artists and others. Many visitors find the city cold and unwelcoming, a rainy, damp and clammy place with permanently gray skies. But for really incorrigible Venice fans this time of year has its own charm.

A parade of brightly colored umbrellas goes bobbing up and down the bridges; here and there the serenade of the gondoliers still rings out on the canals at night. Venetians are left to themselves, the city is sleepy and has a refreshingly everyday air. One can enjoy all the sights without the summer crowds; the Piazza San Marco is spookily empty.The Christmas season, with lights and gifts, is especially charming in the city on the lagoon; the Basilica radiates a festive dignity that is lost at other times in the babble of countless tourist groups. Those few travelers who are in the city keep meeting each other—with just a nod of recognition to acknowledge another member of the magic circle.

La Serenissima is never more captivating than when she is wreathed in veils of mist. The city, with her fairytale background of palaces, canals and mysterious alleyways threaded with white mist becomes quite unreal. Fantasy knows no bounds. How easy it is to believe that one has gone back in time; who would be surprised if Venetians in medieval dress came strolling out of the fog. No other city makes it so easy to daydream as Venice, especially in winter when everyone can go off on quiet voyages of discovery.

The winter is also the time of the dreaded high water. When the sirens sound visitors should be sure to have gumboots handy because the flood makes the water level rise very quickly. Duckboards are put down on the streets and squares but these end so abruptly that there is not much chance of getting into shelter with dry feet. It is fascinating to see how the Venetians take this disastrous flooding in their stride. House and shops have their entrances barricaded with boards, lower shelves are cleared of goods, but even when the water is knee deep business goes on as usual. With admirable nonchalance one still stands at the counter in a bar to drink espresso and enjoy a brioche.

The wintry stillness is briefly disturbed by the Carnival, revived in recent years, which brings thousands of spectators into the city for ten days to see this fantastic masquerade. In Catholic countries the carnival season comes to an end on Ash-Wednesday, just before Easter. The classic Venetian masks are from the 18th century, and the characters of the Commedia dell'Arte also belong to Venice at carnival time. Arlecchino, Colombina Pantalone and Il Dottore tumble out of every alley dressed in their traditional costumes and masks. Carnival is still a time for gallant adventures, for a moment's warmth and revelry in a glided palazzo or a cheerful tavern before the maskers fade away into the chilly mists that shroud the canals.

EXPEDITIONS THROUGH THE CITY

A charming way of discovering Venice is, of course, just to wander without a planned route and branch off now and then into a narrow dark alleyway. These are just the places where one finds little shops, an antiquarian bookshop, a little gallery or a romantic square hidden away. Venice is like a maze but one in which the pleasure is found in wandering about inside the labyrinth, not in trying to find a way out.

The three expeditions that follow are to show how one can combine strolling with sightseeing. All three begin at the Piazza San Marco and people without much time to spare can combine all three trips. During Carnival and the high season one needs a bit of patience and love of one's neighbor for the alleys

round San Marco are very crowded. One more thing before we begin: Venetians are flexible in their way of writing the names of streets and squares. We mustn't be confused if the Campo Sant' Angelo is written in dialect Sant' Anzolo.

In the Sestiere San Marco

From the Piazza San Marco we wend our way to the west, to Ala Napoleonica and the Salizzada San Moisé which leads to the church of the same name. The **Chiesa di San Moisé**, named for Moses, was built in the 17th century. Over the main portal among the figures decorating the opulent baroque facade are two reclining camels, signs of Venice's connection to eastern lands. Here Egypt is the country denoted for each camel has an obelisk on its back.

Over the Rio di San Moisé the Salizzada continues on as Via XXII Marzo. Halfway along the broad street with its elegant shops is the Calle delle Veste, leading to the **Teatro La Fenice**; as a shield tells us.

After some fine antique shops the Campo di San Fantin opens up before the famous opera house. 1792, the year of its inauguration, is written in roman numerals over the classical portico. The Calle della Fenice which turns off left of the theater, leads to the Camiello Marmori, where the **Taverna La Fenice**, an elegant restaurant, invites us to while away the time.

The lane at the back of the theater is not interesting because of the backs of the buildings but because the orchestra rehearsals and opera performances can be heard from it. A free concert in the open air, so to speak. After crossing over two little bridges and the Calle Caotorta it is only few steps to the **Campo Sant' Angelo** a spacious square with interesting architecture.

It is worthwhile to branch off from the Campo Sant' Angelo in the direc-

Previous pages: everyone has time to chat. Left, artists on the Mole.

tion of the Ponte dell' Accademia before we continue on our round trip in the other direction towards Campo Manin. The **Chiesa San Stefano** forms the boundary between the Campo Sant' Angelo and the **Campo San Stefano**.

The leaning bell tower can be seen a long way off, leaning almost as much as its more famous colleague in Pisa. Already in the year 1445 a masterbuilder from Bologna was given the job of straightening the Campanile of San Stefano. On the day after the scaffolding had been removed, the tower came crashing down and damaged the nearby convent. The foundations of the rebuilt campanile which, by the way, is the highest in the city, were strengthened again at the beginning of this century.

The church, a brick building from the 15th century contains the tombs of the Doge Francesco Morosini and the composer Giovanni Gabrieli. In the sacristy are works by Paolo Veneziano,

The Campo Sant'Angelo with the church of San Stefano.

Bartolomeo Vivarini and Tintoretto.

One can wander across the big busy Campo San Stefano in the direction of the Grand Canal as far as the **Palazzo Cavalli Franchetti**. This wonderfully restored palace from the 15th century, with a park-like garden behind an iron lattice, now houses a savings bank. Opposite, on the same side of the canal, in a small overgrown garden lies the **Casa Barozzi**, which houses the Consulate of the Federal Republic of Germany. From the **Ponte dell' Accademia** there is a picture book view of the Grand Canal. Whoever prefers to walk in quieter streets can turn off now into the Sestiere Dorsoduro.

To carry on with our round trip we retrace our steps to the Campo Sant' Angelo. Anyone who is already tired of walking can turn sharp right at the Campo San Stefano into the **Calle del Spezier**. Here on the right is a music shop with a pretty courtyard where

there are places to sit down and be entertained by classical music while taking a rest.

Following the signs for the Rialto we come from the Campo Sant' Angelo to Campo Manin. These streets are getting busier all the time. More and more shop windows tempt us with legs of Parma ham, pastries or *Pan del Pescatore*. This 'bread of the fisherman' is not a fishburger but a delicious cake which goes well with capuccino.

In the midst of the Campo Manin is the statue of the advocate Daniele Manin, who once lived here. After the rising against Austrian rule in 1848 he was president of the provisionary government of Venice until a year later when Venice was forced to capitulate. At the north end of the Campo stands the sober modern building of the Cassa di Risparmio, the State Savings Bank. In front of the Cassa a little shield tells us the way to the **Scala Contarini del**

Bovolo, a diversion that must on no account be missed.

What could be more surprising after the dark alleys than the courtyard of the Palazzo Contarini del Bovolo. The Scala del Bovolo is a spiral staircase built as a tower against the outer wall of the palace. This typical Lombardy construction is especially charming because of the delicate rows of arches that enclose the staircase. The 'snail staircase' as the Italians call it, was built in 1500. In the courtyard dozens of cats are fed in an enclosure that looks like a miniature lion's cage.

From the Campo Manin we come over the Calle dei Fuseri to Campo Santa Luca. In the the Calle Goldoni that runs off here is the **Teatro Carlo Goldoni**, named after the 18th-century writer of comedies.

Renaissance Architecture

Let us go past the cool, functional front of the theater and turn into the Calle de Lovo that leads to the **Chiesa di San Salvadore**. This church from the 16th century contains some remarkable art treasures and interested visitors should take time to see them. The architects were Tullio Lombardo and Sansovino. The lightness and clarity of the renaissance architecture can only be appreciated in the interior because of the massive facade added to the church in the 17th century. Especially worth seeing are the tomb of the Doge Francesco Venier by Jacopo Sansovino (aged 80 years when he made the design) and two late works by Titian, including the *Annunciation*, painted when he was 76 years old.

Also to be found in San Salvadore are the graves of the Conaro family, at the front of the transept and on the left wall of the nave. This noble family obtained great wealth from their sugar plantations on the island of Cyprus. In 1472 the young Caterina Cornaro was given

Everyday life in the squares with washing hung to dry.

in marriage to King Jacob II of Cyprus; after his death Caterina ruled alone until 1489 when the Venetian Republic took open control of her small kingdom. The poor puppet queen was retired to a castle on the mainland with the title 'Lady of Asolo' and her small court, which inluded dwarfs, apes, parrots and peacocks.

From San Salvadore onwards the crowded streets show that the Rialto bridge is only a few steps away. Early in the morning Venetians take a cappucino in one of the bars on the way to work then shortly afterwards the tourists take their places. They wander along more slowly and aimlessly. At the Campo San Bartolomeo we turn right in the direction of the Rio della Fava and come to the **Chiesa di San Lio** where a fine ceiling by Giandomenico Tiepolo should not be missed.

Next to the church begins the Salizzada San Lio which we follow to the Calle di Mondo Nuovo and then take this street as far as the **Campo Santa Maria Formosa**. Although it is close to the Rialto the Campo has the atmosphere of everyday life in Venice. Stands full of fruit and vegetables, little shops and cafés are refreshingly natural. The **Chiesa Santa Maria Formosa** was built in 1492 by Mauro Codussi; the facade on the square and the bell tower were added in the 17th century. In the interior of the church a Madonna by Bartolomeo Vivarini is worth a visit.

At the back of the church lies the Campiello Querini Stampalia. A narrow bridge over the Rio di Santa Maria Formosa opens right into the entrance of the **Galleria Querini Stampalia**, run by the trust of the same name. Paintings are shown next to a library of old Venetian books and writings. The pictures by Gabriele Bellas are of special interest for their scenes of everyday life in 18th-century Venice. There are

Left, the statue of Carlo Goldoni on the Campo San Bartolomeo; right, the 'Snail Staircase', Scala Contarini del Bovolo.

also works displayed in the gallery by Giovanni Bellini, Palma the Elder and Pietro Longhi. The way back to the Piazza San Marco leads back again to the doorway of the church of Santa Maria Formosa then we turn left into the Calle delle Bande. After a short distance we come to a modern supermarket with no special atmosphere or local color but with very reasonable prices.

This is a good place to buy souvenirs in the form of local products: Italian ham, coffee or pasta. The cozy little old shops we find elsewhere are in fact extremely expensive.

When we pass the Chiesa San Zulian in the Merceria and go through the archway of the Torre dell' Orologio we are on familiar ground: the Piazza San Marco opens out before the weary explorers. This is the time for a rest in one of the cafés; what could be nicer than sitting comfortably and watching other tourists trudging over the square?

In Sestiere Castello

Since it really does get very crowded near the Piazzo San Marco and the alleys nearby we will run away to the east in the direction of the Giardini Pubblici, looking for broad streets and spacious green parks. The early morning when the sun lights up the buildings along the canal banks is the best time for a walk along the **Riva degli Schiavoni**. For more than half a kilometer the promenade curves around the basin of St. Mark. The promenade is called after the Dalmatians, the Schiavoni, who went to sea in Venetian ships. In the famous views of Venice from the 18th century the Riva is a quay at which many ships are moored and today it has the same function for the regular ferries in the lagoon.

The Riva begins at the **Ponte della Paglia**, the popular look-out for the Bridge of Sighs which lies behind it.

Right, looking from the Straw Bridge towards the Bridge of Sighs (shown on the left).

The 'Straw Bridge'—Ponte della Paglia in English—is so called because of the ships laden with straw which once unloaded here. It is the oldest stone bridge in the city and was rebuilt in 1847 in its original 14th-century style, only a little wider.

Just before the next bridge the **Ponte del Vin** is the **Hotel Danieli Excelsior**. This splendid 15th-century palazzo once owned by the Dandolo family, is today one of the most expensive hotels anywhere, not only in Venice. On the other side of the bridge is the bronze equestrian statue of Victor Emmanuel II, first king of a united Italy. It was erected in 1887. Opposite the statue is a *sottoportico*, an underpass, leading to the **Campo San Zaccaria**.

The church and the convent of the same name were founded in the 9th century. At the end of the 15th century the church was erected in its present form by the masterbuilders Camballo and Codussi. One of the art works in the church is *The Madonna Enthroned with Saints* by Giovanni Bellini.

The Convent's Gift

The well-endowed convent was for a long time an exclusive retreat for the daughters of wealthy Venetian families. Here patrician ladies retired from the world more or less volunatrily. There was always a connection to the Doge's Palace. Every year at Easter the head of state came to vespers at the church of San Zaccaria. This tradition began in the 12th century when the convent gave a part of its large vegetable garden to extend the Piazza San Marco. Since then the nuns of the convent also have the privilege of embroidering the Doge's hat.

Back on the Riva degli Schiavoni we cross the Rio dei Greci, a name that reminds us that there was a Greek quar-

A school class on the way to the Riva.

ter here in the middle ages. As a trading metropolis Venice was open to foreign nations and cultures whose influence can still be seen today. Not far from here on the Salizzada dei Greci in the **Instituto Ellenico**, is a collection of icons with works that date from the 14th to 18th centuries.

We stay on the Riva and turn towards the Chiesa della Pietá better known as the **Chiesa di Vivaldi**. The great composer was choirmaster at the church's music school. Regular concerts are held at the church. The ceiling frescoes from Tiepolo are well worth a visit.

The third bridge after the Vivaldi church is the **Ponte dell 'Arsenale**, from which one turns left for the Arsenal. When ships sailed through this canal to the arsenal, the bridge could be swung aside. It was first built in stone in 1936. The former dockyard, closed down since the first world war was founded in 1104 and in the course of the

centuries it developed into the largest ship-building center in the world. At times up to 16,000 men were employed at the Arsenal in an area of more than 75 acres (30 hectares). Work in the Arsenal was top secret because weapons were also produced here. The name Arsenal comes from the arabic *dar assina 'a* which means literally 'house of handicrafts', a factory or workshop. This word now in modern arabic dictionaries is translated with the western word 'arsenal'.

Guarding the Entrance

The entrance on land, built in the 15th century, has the form of a triumphal arch with the winged lion of St. Mark watching over it. This war-like lion does not show the usual open book with its peaceful message *Pax tibi, Marce, Evangelista meus*. Instead his book is closed. The two lions at the gate were

Left, the entrance to the Arsenal; right, a lion at the Arsenal.

brought to Venice from Athens in 1687 as spoils of war after the conquest of the Peloponnese. The watch towers which flank the water gate were erected in 1574. The Arsenal is not open for visitors but one can still enjoy it by sailing through the **Arsenale Vecchio** with the Vaporetto No. 5.

At the Campo San Biagio, back again on the Riva degli Schiavoni, one can see in the **Museo Storico Navale** models of the ships and weapons produced at the Arsenal as well as documents about sea-faring. The entrance is marked by two fine anchors.

After the next bridge, the **Ponte della Veneta Marina**, we turn inland into the Via Garibaldi. What Italian city does not have a street named after the freedom fighter? This Via Garibaldi is wide, spacious and full of small everyday shops and bars. At about the level of the Chiesa di San Francesco di Paola the **Viale Garibaldi** turns off to the right near the Garibaldi monument. The broad avenue leads back to the water, edged by rows of old dilapidated houses. We can just imagine that the Viale Garibaldi had once been a good address. The plentiful greenery of the Viale does not compare with the luxuriance of the **Giardini Pubblici** which begin past the Rio di San Guiseppe.

Originally laid out by order of Napoleon, the gardens are not only a place for refreshment and recreation but wellknown for the exhibition rooms of the Biennale, the famous art show that takes place in Venice every two years. The vaporetto numbers 1 and 4 stop at the western end of the park. Line 1 brings us along the Riva degli Schiavoni back to the Piazza San Marco, a chance to see the route that we have traveled from the water.

In Sestiere Dorsoduro

The expedition through this part of the city begins at the church **Santa Maria della Salute** which is reached from the Piazza San Marco with Vaporetto No 1. *Dorsoduro* means, incidentally, 'hard back', a reference to the long shape and the hard clay soil of the quarter. In contrast to San Marco, Dorsoduro is much quieter and more peaceful. There are few shops and bars but charming streets and squares. Now and again we come upon a little gallery or a bookshop. Instead of eating we can feast our eyes upon the scenery. Next to the mighty church of the Salute stands the small and modest Chiesa San Gregorio with a yellow shield on the wall telling the way to the Peggy Guggenheim collection.

Our route now leads us along a 'parallel street' to the Grand Canal, past the back entrances to the palazzi as far as the Accademia. So we come next to the Campo San Gregorio. On the right it is worth a look through an old iron gate at the wild, picturesque garden in the

A canal.

inner courtyard of the Palazzo Genoese. This palace which naturally faces the Grand Canal, was built in 1892 in gothic style.

The next small square, the **Campiello Barbara**, is not at all barbaric but a pretty spot with picturesque houses. As well as the back of the Barbara Palace we can also see the back of the **Palazzo Dario**: its beautifully ornamented renaissance facade is best seen from the other side of the Grand Canal. After a few steps down a dark lane we come to the gardens of the **Palazzo Venier dei Leoni**. In 1949 the American Peggy Guggenheim, who was married to the painter Max Ernst, purchased this palace and installed her famous collection of modern art.

We go straight on past the Galerie Feruzzi as far as the **Campiello San Vio** which is open to the Grand Canal and has a fine view. On the right stands the Palazzo Barbarigo with modern

mosaics on the facade which are not to everyone's taste. Opposite on the other side of the Rio San Vio, is the **Palazzo Cini** with the gallery of the Cini Foundation which has its headquarters on the island of San Giorgio Maggiore.

We keep on going in the same direction over a little bridge and soon come to the **Accademia**, the 'Louvre' of Venice. The museum is so attractive that crowds of art-loving tourists gather around the Accademia and the pretty wooden bridge.

We turn into the quieter part of the Dorsoduro and go in the direction of San Trovaso. Near the main entrance to the Accademia there begins the Rio Terrà della Carità which we follow as far as the Calle Larga Nani, then bear right as far as the Ponte di San Trovaso. A Rio Terrà, a canal that has been filled can often be recognized by the remains of its plastered side streets.

The pretty **Rio di San Trovaso** is the busy waterway between the Canal Grande and the Canale della Giudecca. Before us on a wide square planted with trees we can see the **Chiesa San Trovaso**, a name that comes from the two patron saints of the church St. Gervasio and St. Brotasio. The church was founded in the 11th century and work on the present building was begun in 1584. In the interior of the—by Venetian standards—plainly built church are paintings by Tintoretto and his son Domenico as well as reliefs of angels from the 15th century on the side altar. Another special feature of San Trovaso is the mighty pipe organ from the year 1765.

Near the church there is one of the last **gondola docks** in Venice. Whoever looks for it on the square will not see any sign of it. If one goes back over the Rio di San Trovaso and then a few yards right along the Fondamenta one sees beyond the Canal a yard with old barn-like wooden buildings. A few gondolas lie on their sides, jacked up, in the open

One of the last gondola docks in San Trovaso.

air and others are being repaired in the workshop. These *squeri*, as the docks are called in Venetian, have become very rare.

The Fondamenta ends in a few steps at the Zattere, the wide street along the bank of the Canale della Giudecca. The nearness to the water, the fresh sea breeze and the view over the canal make a pleasant change after the narrow alleys of the Dorsoduro and accompany us all the way to the Dogana.

The **Fondamenta della Zattere** gained its name from the rafts (Italian *zattere* means raft) which arrived here from the alpine rivers. Left there is the **Dominican Church of the Gesuati**, often confused with the Jesuit church 'I Jesuiti' in Cannaregio. Formerly the church belonged to the Brothers of the Poveri Gesuati and when the Dominican order had it rebuilt in the 18th century it was still called 'I Gesuati'. Its official name is **Santa Maria del Ro-**

sario. In the interior is a ceiling fresco from Tiepolo and a Crucifixion by Tintoretto, both worth a visit.

At the **Ponte dell' Unità** there is yet another place for worldly pleasures where one can even take espresso on a terrace built out into the water.

But now it is not far to the **Punta della Dogana**. We pass the former salt magazine next to the Ponte di Salone and come to the western point of Dorsoduro with the **Palazzo Dogana da Mar**, the former customs house. The two bronze figures of Atlas on the corner tower of the building, who hold up the globe of the world bearing the Goddess Fortuna, are visible far out on the lagoon. From the Punta there is an unusual vista: almost 360 degrees from La Giudecca and San Giorgio Maggiore over San Marco to the Grand Canal. A grand finale...it is only a few steps to the Salute church where we set out and the vaporetto station.

On the Zattere.

THE TEATRO LA FENICE

The Teatro La Fenice is among the most beautiful and most famous opera houses in the world. Whoever has the good fortune to obtain tickets for a premiere can enjoy a most rare pleasure. The richly decorated interior in beige, red and gold, an audience in festive dress in the half circle of the balcony and the five tiers of boxes—all this brings the spectator into another world. It is considered a feast for all the senses. The magic of Italian opera music, the setting and the costumes, vie with the glitter of the opera house itself; on these gala occasions the balcony rails are decorated with fresh roses and in the warmth of the room they give out a bewitching perfume.

Great voices were always to be heard at the Teatro La Fenice. Giuditta Pasta, the muse of the composer Bellini, was often a guest in the 19th century as well as the fiery spanish singers Maria Malibran and Isabella Colbran. Maria Callas, Beniamino Gigli, Mirella Freni—these are only some of the names bound up with La Fenice. Today as well as yesterday the repertoire consists of the best-known works of Italian opera. The work of Richard Wagner was also performed. The great composer made several visits to Venice, which he found inspiring. It is claimed that he incorporated some Venetian melodies into his own music dramas. Wagner passed the last months of his life in Venice and died in the Palazzo Vendramin-Calergi. In 1983 on the 100th anniversary of the death of the Maestro from Bayreuth he was honored by a splendid production of Parsital.

Dramma per Musica

The city in the lagoon has a very long opera tradition but it was not Venice but Florence where opera was born. At the end of the 16th century a small group of scholars called the *Camerata* gathered together to revive antique tragedy. In the belief that the Greeks had sung their dramas they produced works from Greek and Roman mythology in a musical and dramatic form.

These works were not yet called 'opera' but bore the name '*dramma per musica*' because the dramatic element was in the foreground. The name 'opera' was introduced later, about 1639, as the center of production had moved to Venice.

After opera had been consolidated as a special genre in the first decade of the 17th century and had moved away from court patronage Venice became the most important center of early operatic work in Italy. With the opening of the first public opera house, San Cassiano, in 1637, the sociological character of the young art form changed. Its place was no longer the palaces of the nobles; it belonged to every stratum of society. Venice's status as a city-state with a republican constitution played an important role in making opera a popular art form.

The music dramas of the Venetian period hardly differ from the great scandals and the everyday comedy of the time. This was also one of the reason for opera's enormous success. Classical mythology gives only the framework of the heroes and their deeds. The heroes are actually modeled on Italian politicians of the Borgia stripe or power-hungry renaissance *Condottieri*. Disputed inheritance, civil war, betrayal, assassination, conspiracy, rebellion, adultery, abduction and intrigue...these make for colorful and interchangeable plot material.

Very important for the Venetian style was the way in which comic figures entered the action. The way was prepared for the later development of *operbuffa* originating Venice. The

155

improvisations of the Commedia dell' Arte, with its folk characters, played a part in this development. Dramatist Carlo Goldoni (1707-1793) also brought greater depth to simple rustic comedy. His works were the basis for several operas including *I Quatri Rusteghi* , The Four Boors, by the Venetian born composer Ermanno Wolf-Ferrari (1876-1948), who was also Director of the Conservatorium.

The public were also held spellbound by the fantastic portrayal of dreams, mystic oaths and ghastly visitants produced by the surprisingly advanced stage machinery of the time. Whole buildings could be made to collapse with the help of hinged walls; the clouds on which the gods were enthroned grew larger or smaller or divided into three cloudlets as they sank, then joined into one large cloud as they rose. With the aid of blue wave-shaped wooden boards which moved one after the other the sea rose and fell. Natural forces such as thunder and lightning could be produced without difficulty.

In the Florentine opera the dramatic recitative of the chorus was to the fore but in Venice the musical element became more and more important. This is a renaissance development: it is the setting forth of the individual as against the group feeling of the middle ages.

Primadonnas and Castrati

The enrichment of the musical forms, the arias and the coloratura or virtuoso voice passages, paved the way for the soloists of the Venetian opera, the Primadonna and the Primo Uomo, the castrated male singer. The dreadful custom of castrating young boys before puberty to preserve their clear soprano or alto voices may have had to do with an earlier prohibition against women singing in public productions of opera.

A walk behind the theater to hear the rehearsal.

Gradually this became the fashion throughout Europe, lasting in places until the 19th century. Castrati and Primadonnas were so worshipped by their public that they became extraordinarily spoilt and capricious. They decided which arias would be sung and which would be left out and they laid down the coloratura passages which best suited their own vocal virtuosity.

Bravos and Rotten Eggs

In the 17th century the opera was already so popular that the people streamed into the theater every evening. There one amused oneself with the latest gossip and met to play cards or dine in the boxes so that the production often played a secondary role. On the other hand outstanding vocal performances could call forth storms of delighted applause from the public. The spectators vied with each other in their cries of Bravo! and Vivat! or threw roses and lace handkerchiefs at the feet of the primadonnas. After the premiere of the Rossini opera *Semiramis* in Venice an enthusiastic crowd brought the Maestro home with a convoy of gondolas while an orchestra kept on playing the most beautiful melodies from the opera. Singers who were indisposed, however, came to feel the public's disgust in no uncertain manner. The throwing of rotten eggs and tomatoes, radishes or leeks—the traditional symbol of ridicule—was as common as lampoons for the primadonna or gales of boos and whistles.

Phoenix from the Ashes

After the first opera house, the Teatro San Cassiano, was opened in Venice in 1637 there quickly followed four other theaters: the Teatro San Salvador, the Teatro Novissimo, the Teatro San Moisé and the Teatro SS Giovanni e Paolo where in 1640 and 1642

Monteverdi's *Ulisses* and *Poppaea* were first presented. In the 18th century the number of opera houses in Venice had risen to 19. The only theater from this time that exists today is the Teatro La Fenice. It was built in 1792 by the architect Giovanni Antonio Selva and inaugurated on the March 16 of that year with an opera by Paisiello. It was the scene of such brilliant premieres as Rossini's *Tankred*, *The Italian Girl in Algiers* and *Semiramis*. Bellini received a great ovation for a version of the Romeo and Juliet story *I Capuleti ed i Montecchi* and Donnizetti also brought out several of his works here.

In December 1836 the theater was burnt to the ground and a year later rebuilt exactly as before. The name "Fenice" was meant to give the impression that the building had risen from the ashes bright and new like that fabulous bird, the phoenix (Italian *fenice* = phoenix). In the early 17th century there was

Goldoni relief at the theater entrance.

157

a very short opera season, the *stagione*, lasting from December 26 to March 30, as long as the Carnival time. Later two further seasons were added, the *Ascensione* from Easter Saturday until June 15 and the Autumn Season from September 1st to November 30. During a stagione the same opera was played every night. Then the work was laid aside and only revived in the next season if it had been unusually successful.

Verdi and La Fenice

The Teatro La Fenice had to thank Guiseppe Verdi, one of the most important opera composers of the 19th century, for five great works. After his opera *I Lombardi* he signed a contract with La Fenice which was already one of the leading Italian opera houses. He declared to his friends that the Scala in Milan needed a rest after four Verdi operas in four years.

The truth was that the composer was becoming more and more annoyed by the incompetent productions at La Scala. So in 1844 *Ernani* came out at the Fenice. The public were overwhelmed by the enchantment of Verdi's music and a critic wrote that the crowds coming away from a performance were still humming the melodies they had just heard. Seven years later the popular hit of the season was "*Donna émobile*" from *Rigoletto*.

Verdi's next great success in Venice was *Attila* in 1846; this opera, combined with *Ernani*, *I Lombardi* and *Nabucco*, made him a national hero in Italy. The composer was a great patriot and he had the skill to give his operatic scenes patriotic undertones in the year 1848 as Italy was fighting for national unity. Verdi's name itself became a slogan for his countrymen in the fight for freedom: V (ittorio) E (manuele) R (e) D'I (talia)—a reference to the first king of a united Italy, 1861.

After *Simon Boccanegra* and *Rigo-*letto there followed in 1853 *La Traviata* at the Fenice and at first it was not a success. This may have been because Fanny Salvini-Donatello was too fat to play a person dying of consumption convincingly. Every time she coughed to indicate her approaching end the public doubled up with laughter. A year later the Venetians heard a revised *Traviata* and from then on it was successful. The story of Violetta who has 'wandered from the paths of virtue', has had a place in the repertoire of the Fenice ever since.

The Present Day

The name Verdi was a milestone in the history of La Fenice—the last representative of the Italian belcanto opera who composed for this theater. In the 19th and 20th century however the Fenice kept up its reputation. In 1873 it produced the Italian premiere of Wagner's *Rienzi* and in 1883, after the composer's death the whole *Ring des Nibelungen* in German. While most of the opera houses of Europe could only offer makeshift programs during the Second World War the Fenice presented 68 premieres. In 1854 and in 1938 the house was renovated so that it always retained its old brilliance.

In 1930 the directors of the Teatro La Fenice began the festival of contemporary music. Every two years until 1936, then every year with many important productions. In 1951 there was the world premiere of *The Rake's Progress* by Stravinsky, in 1951 *The Turn of the Screw* by Benjamin Britten and George Gershwin's *Porgy and Bess*, and in 1961 *Intolleranza* by Luigi Nono. This Venetian born composer, who is married to the daughter of Arnold Schönberg and lives in Venice, wrote the work specially for the Teatro La Fenice. So we see that La Fenice feels itself pledged not only to uphold tradition but also to support modern music.

VIVALDI AND THE VENETIAN MUSICAL TRADITION

One of the most famous sons of Venice in the musical field is **Antonio Vivaldi** (1678-1741). He entered the priesthood as a young man and was called 'il prete rosso', the red priest, because of his red hair. Since he had been drawn to music from childhood Vivaldi devoted himself more and more to composition and he obtained a post as composer and teacher of the violin at the exclusive girls' conservatorium, the **Ospedale della Pieté**.

Vivaldi's great musical talent, encouraged by his father who was a famous violin virtuoso of his

time, and his gift for melody, made him successful in almost every area of music but his favorite instrument remained the violin. He created the three movement concerto in which the violin as a virtuoso solo instrument is balanced against the rest of the orchestra. His best known work of this kind is *The Four Seasons*.

Vivaldi's relationship to the Ospedale conservatorium was good at first but over the years it deteriorated. He was accused of being closer to his pupil, Anna Giraud, than he should be as a teacher and as a priest. Vivaldi, in his disappointment, turned his back on his native city and went on extended concert tours which took him to Dresden, Paris, Prague, Amsterdam and Vienna, where he died in poverty in 1741.

It is impossible to understand today how the works of such a celebrated composer, who had so much success, could be forgotten for nearly 200 years, until he was rediscovered in 1926. He composed over 770 works, including 46 operas (*Orlando Furioso, Tamburlaine*) most of them written for performance in Venice. The place where Vivaldi worked for many years, the **Chiesa della Pieté**, which belongs to the Ospedale, is now called the **Chiesa di Vivaldi** and his works are regularly performed there by a chamber orchestra.

Another important Venetian musician is Claudio Monteverdi (1567-1643). As the choirmaster of San Marco he was the traditional successor of Andrea Gabrieli (1510-1586) and his nephew Giovanni Gabrieli (1557-1612), the early masters of massed choirs and baroque polyphonic music. Monteverdi himself is regarded as the founder of Venetian opera and was summoned to Venice after he had spent the first years of his musical career at the court in Mantua. In Venice he wrote seven of his twelve operas, Monteverdi showed himself a master of musical characterization, especially in his later works *Poppaea* and *Ullisse*.

Composers such as **Francesco Cavalli** (1602-1672) and **Antonio Cesti** (1623-1669) brought the early Venetian opera to a high point of distinction. Cavalli, who was a pupil of Monteverdi, composed 49 operas including *Ercole Amante*, 'Hercules in Love', to celebrate the marriage of Louis XIV of France, which was produced with great success at Paris in 1602.

Still following in the footsteps of his great teacher, Monteverdi, Cavalli wrote heroic-dramatic operas while Cesti tended towards the more popular regional genre. Characteristic for his rhythmic, lyrical style is the swinging 6/8 beat that recalls the songs of the Venetian gondoliers. This *barcarolle* sound (from *barca* a boat) has been characteristic of Venetian opera from this time and in the 19th century it was used by Jacques Offenbach in the Venetian scenes of his opera *The Tales of Hoffman*.

Another local composer is Ermanno Wolf-Ferrari, born in Venice as the son of a German father and an Italian mother. He was for a time director of the Conservatorium of Music and is remembered for operas such as *The Jewels of the Madonna* (I Giojelli della Madonna), (1911) *Inquisitive Women* (Le Donne Curiose) (1903), from a Goldoni play, and *The Secret of Susanne* (Il Segreto di Susanna) first performed in 1909.

Above, Antonio Vivaldi.

AROUND
SAN ZANIPOLO

San Zanipolo is the name in Venetian dialect of the Basilica of **SS Giovanni e Paolo** (St. John and St. Paul). A comfortable walk from the Piazza San Marco, following the shields marked Ospedale Civile, leads to the spacious square before the church. There is a book shop here with the same name as the square which has a good choice of books on Venice in English and French as well as Italian art books (Santi Giovanni e Paolo, Campo SS Giovanni e Paolo, 6358, Castello). There are many inviting cafés in which the visitor can take a coffee break.

On the broad **Rio dei Mendicanti**, the Canal of the Mendicant Friars, one can see cargo boats chugging by or an ambulance boat rushing to the **Ospedale Civile** with its siren blaring. This is the largest hospital in Venice and it has been housed in the **Scuola Grande di San Marco** eversince the Napoleonic occupation.

The Scuola, like so many other honorable institutions in the Serenissima, was dissolved by the French conqueror. The marvelous facade of the Scuola has been preserved and amazes the beholder with the richness of its fantasy. After a fire destroyed the medieval building of the Brotherhood of San Marco (founded in 1260) it was probably Pietro Lombardo and his sons who erected this masterpiece of renaissance architecture between 1485 and 1495.

The left wing, crowned with rounded gables over the hall of the brotherhood and the chapel, is especially inventive. On either side of the main door the lions of St. Mark, heraldic beasts of the Brotherhood, step out of the '*trompe l'oeil*' entrance to a lobby. The artists of the Lombardi family had grasped the

Previous pages: San Zanipolo and the Scuola San Marco. Below, the equestrian statue of Colleoni.

use of central perspective, rediscovered in Florence, and used it for illusions and '*trompe l'oeil*' effects on buildings.

The mighty **equestrian statue of Colleoni** is a counterpoint to the Scuola and sets the imposing scene for this square full of wonders, as the Campo has been called. As we dreamily sip a *cappuccino* it is easy to move back in time 500 years to the very day on which the monument of the famous general was unveiled.

Thousands crowded the square and admired the powerful elegance of horse and rider, all in gold. Verocchio, the man with the *true eye*, the celebrated artist from Florence, teacher of Leonardo da Vinci, was prepared—after his honorarium had been doubled by the city fathers—to design a suitable monument for the most famous Condottiere in Italy.

Bartolomeo Colleoni was the son of a family of provincial aristocrats. As a leader of mercenaries he served many masters. The seductive Queen Joanna II of Naples granted him a coat of arms with two roaring lions. After this he called himself *Col-leoni*, literally 'with the lions'. On the other hand the unpredictable Duke of Mantua, last of the Viscontis, threw him into the notorious 'oven of Monza', a dungeon from which he made an adventurous escape after a year.

Already as a young man Colleoni had fought for Venice and everyone spoke of his brilliant tactics. He was first named as *Capitano Generale* by the Signoria March 10, 1455 when he was 55 years old. Under his leadership the terra firma was conquered and Venetian power on land was consolidated. Colleoni spent his old age in his country castle of Malpaga as a patron of the arts and let others win battles for him. When he died in 1475 he was immeasurably rich.

He wanted to pay off the 'Moneybags of Venice' who had often treated him shabbily and he tried to beat them at their own game. The city was to receive 10 percent of his estate, about 200,000 ducats, (he purchased Castle Malpaga for only 100 ducats) if they granted him an equestrian statue before 'St. Mark's'. This was against all Venetian policy and tradition, to have a statue outside St. Mark's church on the Piazza San Marco...but how were the city fathers to get their hands on Colleoni's money? After five years a solution was finally found: the *Scuola* not the *Basilica* of St. Mark would answer to the terms of the will. So all was formally and correctly arranged and Venice collected the tidy sum.

Now let us turn to **San Zanipolo** itself. It is over 330 feet (100 meters) long, the largest sacred building in Venice and in its stylistic perfection an imposing example of Venetian gothic. The west front, following the rule of the Dominican order, has been kept very

Plan of San Zanipolo.

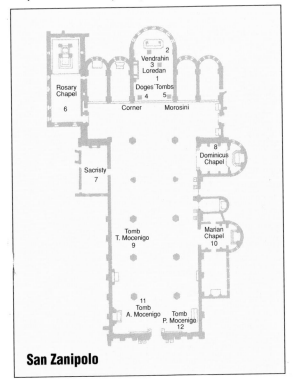

San Zanipolo

plain. Even if it had been clad in marble, as originally planned, it would never approach the monumental look of the French gothic cathedrals.

The interior is surprising because of its height (including 115 feet of vaulting) and there is a typically gothic feeling of space, in the clear structure of the three naves and the dominance of the vertical line. The windows of the nave and the choir have been preserved in their pure gothic style and elegant lancet shape. In the right transept we can admire—a rare sight in Italian churches—a piece of fine stained glass from the end of the 15th century, out of the workshops of Murano. Flanked by the Saints George and Theodore we see the two patrons of the church, John and Paul, not the ones familiar to us from the New Testament, but two roman martyrs from the time of the persecution of the Christians. Their costumes and classical attitudes showed renais-sance influence, however, since they were created in this era.

The **Chapel of the Rosary**, left, joining on to the transept, was donated nearly a hundred years later in 1585, as a memorial for the victory at Lepanto. The paintings by Tintoretto and Palma the younger were destroyed by fire in 1867 and replaced by a beautiful cycle of pictures by Veronese. The altar statue of the Virgin Mary enthroned is the replica of an original by Alessandro Vittoria who made his name in the 16th-century Venice as a pupil of Sansovino.

The **Chapel of St. Dominic** in the right aisle contains a fantastic painted ceiling by Piazzetta. It shows the founder of the Dominican order glorified, in glowing light and color; it was completed in 1725.

A much simpler example of Venetian paintings takes us back a hundred years into the history of the Dominicans: the **altarpiece** in the right aisle is attributed to Giovanni Bellini, one of the most famous masters of the early renaissance. A golden ornamental frame surrounds a number of pictures which show St. Christophorus, the Spanish Dominican Vincent Ferrer and, right, St. Sebastian. In the upper frieze there are scenes from the life of Jesus and in the lower scenes from the life of St. Vincent.

After the Dominicans had received a building place and permission to build from the Doge Jacopo Tiepolo in 1234 they had to wait many years before enough money had been donated by the faithful for building to begin. The nave was almost complete in 1368, the choir and the dome were not finished until the middle of the 15th century.

Municipal contributions and the prestigious acts of patronage of the Venetian patricians had to be organized before the church could at last be consecrated in 1430. The Franciscans, who were putting up their church, the *Frari*, were the greatest competitors for dona-

Tomb of the Doge Pietro Mocenigo.

tions to cover the enormous building costs and both orders of mendicant friars cultivated this rivalry. The Dominicans scored one important point over their heartily detested brothers in Christ and won great prestige. Since more and more Doges were laid to rest in San Zanipolo the Signoria ruled at the end of the 15th century that the Requiem for all the Doges would be celebrated in this church even if the body of a departed Doge was buried elsewhere. So San Zanipolo became the state church and the **Mausoleum for 25 Doges**.

This custom was begun by the first patron of the order, Doge Jacopo Tiepolo (died 1249). His sarcophagus is the second from the left under the gothic arches of the facade. Although the stone may seem very plain, it tells many tales. An inscription recalls the generous and at the same time politically wise gift to the Dominicans. The doves are a reminder of the pretty—and very useful—legend that Jacopo saw in his dream of doves with golden crowns flying over a beautiful garden of flowers and he heard a voice that said: "*Here is the place that I have chosen for my preachers.*"

The Doge Pietro Mocenigo allowed himself a much more opulent tomb. This monument can be admired at the front of the right aisle; it is the work of Pietro Lombardo, architect of the Scuola San Marco. The Doge was himself celebrated as a great military commander and this illustrated with a costly array of pictures with Christian and classical motives. While the Doges had usually been shown lying on their tombs Pietro Mocenigo is shown in a heroic pose, standing over his tomb. Only three mourning figures of Youth, Maturity and Old Age personified are reminders of natural death. The whole concept of this tomb is new: it no longer

The Chapel of the Rosary.

'hangs' on the wall but stands on a pedestal on firm ground. It flows organically into the architectural structure of the church and shares in the monumental character of the whole building.

About the middle of the left aisle there is the grave of another member of this family, the Doge Tommaso Mocenigo. His burial place, still in the tradition of the raised wall graves, shows the deceased resting on his sarcophagus framed by a draped baldachin worked in stone.

In the **Main Choir Chapel** we find the graves of four Doges, the two in front from the 14th century. On the left lies the Doge Marco Corner (died 1368) and on the right Michele Morosini (died 1382), who held office for only one year. The two graves at the High Altar are much more opulent. The tomb on the left is one of the most beautiful of all the Doge's monuments in Venice: it is

the tomb of Andrea Vendramin (died 1478) and was designed by Tullio Lombardo, son of Pietro Lombardo.

In the splendidly sculptured architecture of a Roman triumphal arch the Doge, resting on a stretcher over his sarcophagus, is watched by his servant. The renaissance love of the antique is shown in the figures decorating this monument. The two statues of warriors in the side niches are regarded as the masterworks of Tullio Lombardo.

The grave of Doge Leonardo Loredan (1501-1521) was completed 50 years after his death. Loredan's political role as mediator between Venice and the League of Cambrai is shown here in beautiful sculptured form. Framed by magnificient pillars the Doge sits between two female figures personifying the League and Venetia, his native city.

In the right aisle one comes upon the monumental baroque tomb of the Valier. In the year 1700, when the optimistic mood of the foundation years, as shown by Jacopo Tiepolo, and the proud display of power by Pietro Mocenigo were no more than dreams of other days, Silvestroq Valier, who followed his father Bertucci Valier as Doge, was laid to rest. Their giant mausoleum stands in inverse relationship to the power they actually retained as representatives of a small, third class state. The architect, Andrea Tirali, apparently took the papal graves of the 17th century as his model.

The figure of death no longer appears, indicating his own presence. Grave architecture is far more the stage for a grandiose presentation of a brilliant career. The two princes and the Dogaressa, Elizabeth Querini, the wife of Silvestro Valier, look more as if they are going to an Opera Ball rather than to meet their Maker. The allegorical scenes between the pillars and the beautifully shaped canopy increase the theatrical effect of this last monumental tomb of the Doges of Venice.

Left, the Bellini Altar. Right, the lobby at the Scuola San Marco with 'trompe l'oeil' effect. The sculptured lion actually stands before a flat background.

I FRARI: THE FRIARS' CHURCH

"The poor brothers of St. Francis (Grey Friars) wandered through Italy, preaching in Italian as simple folk to simple folk, and going everywhere, as well into remote hamlets as into the poor quarters of large towns, with their call to poverty and repentance. The movement was the more effective because the early disciples were neither churchmen nor schoolmen. The illiterate multitude could understand a message, pure of all subtlety or artifice, and delivered in the vulgar tongue by men and women who practised the doctrines of poverty and contentment, love and humility, which they preached to others."

A History of Europe— H.A.L Fisher

Santa Maria Goriosa dei Frari is called simply *I Frari* by the Venetians.

Left, *Christ before Pilate* **(Painting by Tintoretto). Below, plan of the** *I Frari* **church.**

I Frari

[plan labels: Tizian Assunta 1; Doges Tombs 2; 3 Monteverdi Tomb; Pesaro Altar Bellini 4; Pesaro Madonna Tizian 5; Canova Tomb 6; Tizian Tomb 7]

After the visitor has threaded the labyrinth of alleyways from the Rialto to the **Campo dei Frari** the imposing church building appears before his astonished eyes like a beautiful mirage. It took over a hundred years (1340-1450) before the whole complex of church, bell tower, monastery and cloisters were completed. Today the monastery contains the state archives and is only open to the public for special exhibitions. Once a small church stood here, built by the Franciscan friars in the 13th century. The building site in Santa Croce, sparsely settled in those days, was a gift from the Doge Croce Jacopo Tiepolo. The church was soon too small for the crowds of worshippers and it was replaced by the present building.

In this district full of such splendid palaces and churches the exterior of the Frari is unusually plain and simple. Even the clearly structured gothic facade with its bare brickwork is almost devoid of ornament. Only the three gothic turrets crowned with pointed gables, also to be found on St. Mark's church, are a reminder of the richness of Venetian architecture.

This atypical simplicity can be explained by the building rules of the Franciscans, the order of brothers who built I Frari. Poverty was the first principle of the three great orders of medicant friars, the Franciscans, the Dominicans and the Augustines, founded in the 13th century. Their main calling was to do missionary work among the people. The rules of the order are also reflected in the structure of their churches, built throughout Italy in the 14th century. The rule of poverty was apparent in the sparse decoration of these churches.

In order to fulfill their missionary calling the mendicant orders made their churches large and roomy. The junction of the nave and the transept gave the ground plan the form of a large T. In the center of the transept was a main choir chapel, resembling an apse, symmetrically framed by side chapels. All these building ordinances have been put into practice in the church of I Frari. It is not known for certain who the master builders of the Friars' Church were, but the architecture of the nave is attributed to a priest, Pater Scipione Bon.

Today one enters the church through a side entrance but one has the best impression of the interior from a standpoint before the main doors. A giant, lofty hall with bare brickwork rises up over the T-shaped ground plan. The space is dominated by the choir screen from the 15th century which divides the nave. These screens were included in almost all the churches of this period; their function was to divide the area for laymen from that of the clergy. They were mainly removed in the course of the 18th and 19th centuries so the screen in I Frari is the only one of its kind in Venice today. The screen, al-most 23 feet (seven meters) high, fills the whole breadth of the central nave and acts as a dividing wall. The pulpits on the upper corners, to left and right, were used by the monks for their sermons. The reliefs showing the Prophets are by Bartolomeo Bon, who also played a major part in the decoration of the Ca'd'Oro and the main entrance of the Doge's Palace.

A rounded archway in the center of the screen gives a view of the high point of the Frari church, the altarpiece in the choir, Titian's **Assunta The Master** aligned this painting of the *Assumption of the Virgin Mary* (Italian *Assunta*) exactly with the opening of the screen so that the congregation, beyond the choir, could see it. Even at this distance details are visible. The picture is divided into three, both in composition and content. On the lower, worldly level there is a group of Apostles whose excited gestures draw attention to the

Reflections: the facade of the Frari church.

center of the picture: the Virgin Mary floats towards God the Father on a wreath of clouds carried by 'putti' or cherubs. The whole conception of the work, which has as its theme the striving to reach God, is completed by the use of color. The two red-robed apostles form, together with the flaming red of the Virgin's gown, a triangle pointing upward to the heavenly sphere and God the Father.

It is not surprising that such an exciting, strongly colored altarpiece, of monumental size attracted attention. It is 23 feet by 12 feet (6.90 meters by 3.60 meters) and was the largest in Venice when it was painted in 1518. The monks of I Frari considered taking back the contract for the picture but artistic genius triumphed over ancient tradition.

Titian's Grave

The tomb of the great painter is in the right hand aisle close to the main portal. Here one seems to meet Titian's *Assunta* a second time: The Assumption of the Virgin, a relief plaque, a copy of the picture on the altar, is set into the back wall of the tomb. The marble figure sitting on a high pedestal before the relief bears Titian's own features. This monument was erected 300 years after the death of the artist by the pupils of the classical sculptor Canova; the commission came from the Austrian Emperor Ferdinand I. Titian himself had thought of having a painting over his grave: the *Pietá* which is to be seen today in the Accademia.

The Grave of Canova

Directly opposite in the left-hand aisle is the mausoleum of the sculptor Canova himself, who died in Venice in 1822. Only his heart is buried here, while the rest of his mortal remains were taken to his birthplace, Passagno, near Treviso. Canova, who planned the

tomb himself, strove for pathos with the pyramidal construction, reminiscent of the graves of the Egyptian pharaohs. This pathetic effect is repeated in the group of mourners on the left at the entry to the tomb. Even the winged lion of St. Mark is crouching upon the steps in a sorrowful attitude.

Not only Titian and Canova have their tombs in the Frari church, it is a veritable mausoleum for the Doges and the patrician families of Venice.

The Pesaro Altar by Bellini

One of the most famous tombs is the chapel of the Pesaro family located on the short side of the transept, on the right. It has always served as the Sacristy of the church. The radiant focus of attention in this small room is the tryptic by Giovanni Bellini. Venice's great renaissance painter has repeated the ornamental motives of the gold frame in

The High Altar with Titian's *Assunta*.

perspective within the picture in such a way that all the separate scenes seem to be enacted upon the same stage. In the center is the Madonna enthroned with the Child Jesus; St. Peter and St. Benedict are in the left hand field; St. Nicholas and St. Mark on the right. These are the patron saints of the donor Petro Pesaro and his sons.

In 1488 he commissioned the painting in memory of his deceased wife. The plasticity of the composition, the dignified poses of the saints impressed Albrecht Dürer so much when he visited Venice that he used them as a model for his picture *Four Apostles* (Alte Pinakothek Munich).

The Choir Chapels

Two of the six chapels in the choir deserve special attention. The first chapel right of the High Altar houses a wood carving, about three feet (one meter) in height by the Florentine sculptor Donatello. This statue is of **John the Baptist**, the patron saint of the city of Florence, set up in their oratory by the Florentine community living in Venice. In spite of poor lighting the lively characterization and gestures of the figure are easily recognizable. The shadows emphasize the life-like pose of the 'Harbinger of Christ' who is shown with raised hand and parted lips, speaking to the people. It was characteristic of the renaissance sculptor Donatello to catch his subjects in action. John the Baptist was also carved by Sansovino for the Conaro chapel in 1550.

In the adjoining choir chapel one can admire Titian's Assunta close up. The colors are even richer and the movements of the figures even more dramatic. The tombs of Doges have been let into the side walls of the chapel: on the left the sarcophagus of **Niccoló Tron** (died 1473) the work of Venice's

The interior of the Frari church.

only important sculptor, Antonio Rizzi; on the right the tomb of the Doge Francesco Foscari, under whose rule (1423-1457) the conquest of the terra firma, the hinterland of the island state of Venice, took place.

In the third side chapel to the left of the main choir a plain marble tablet set into the floor marks the tomb of the great composer **Claudio Monteverdi**. The composer of *Orfeo* and *Ulisses* who died in 1643 is counted as the 'Father of Opera'.

The Pesaro Madonna by Titian

On the way out, down the left aisle we come to the second great painting by Titian in the Frari church. This Madonna was painted by Titian between 1519 and 1526 for the same Pesaro family whose great tomb is in the sacristy. The picture is a typical *Majestá* but the Madonna and Child are not in the center as usual but far to the left. In the middle is St. Peter, symbol of the Papacy, standing as mediator between the kneeling figure of Jacopo Pesaro himself and the Virgin Mary with the Holy Infant. The prominence of St. Peter as well as the presence of figures with banners and turbans are explained by the fact that Jacopo Pesaro fought against the turks in the service of the Pope. With this picture Titian broke all the rules of composition for religious subjects. For the first time the portrait of a patron and his family were made part of devotional picture, thus breaking the strict division between the sacred and secular worlds.

A last highpoint of the art treasures in the Frari is the wall grave which lies directly over the side entrance. This tomb was designed by Venice's most important baroque builder Baldassare Longhena for Doge Giovanni Pesaro (died 1659).

John the Baptist by Donatello (wood carving).

The Scuola San Rocco

Behind the choir of the Frari lies the Campo San Rocco, tucked away in the sharp angle between the church of San Rocco and the Scuola San Rocco, like a corner backstage at a theater. The facades of both buildings—with pillars, gables, double-arched windows in high renaissance style—seem ready to crush the tiny square. This strange architectural arrangement came about in the 16th century. First the church was built in the year 1508—the present building, however, stems from the 18th century—for the bones of St. Roche, which were brought to Venice in 1458. It was hoped that the bones of this saint who worked among the plague-stricken and was himself miraculously healed, would protect the Serenissima, always threatened by pestilence.

The Scuola San Rocco was put up later between 1535 and 1560. The building was never used as a temple of education as its name implies but was the meeting house for the Brotherhood of San Rocco, founded in 1578. The Brotherhoods were societies of men who came together as members of a craft guild, as regional groups or as laymen with the same religious interests. They met under the protection of a chosen name saint and saw charity work and patronage of the arts as their main tasks.

These Brotherhoods existed throughout Italy but in Venice, where, in contrast to other city-states, the guilds and the churches were excluded from government, their members saw in the Brotherhoods the possibility of taking part in the community life of the Serenissima. There were, as a result, 40 such institutions in the city in the 16th century, each one with a splendidly furnished meeting house or *Scuola*.

The Brothers of San Rocco held a **Canova's Tomb.**

174

competition to determine who should decorate their building. The entrants were asked to produce a design for a painted ceiling showing the glorification of St. Roche. The best Venetian painters took part, including Veronese, but Tintoretto won by sprinting a surprise on the jury. While his rival painters only displayed the plans for their compositions on the appointed day Tintoretto not only showed a completed painting but had it already in place on the ceiling of the Conference Room.

For twenty-four years from 1564 to 1588 the painter worked on more than 60 paintings for the Scuola San Rocco. The first pictures were made for the Sala dell'Albergo, that same Conference Room for the directors of the Brotherhood. In order to appreciate the artistic development of Tintoretto let us begin our circuit right here in this small room that joins on to the long wall opposite the windows in the large up-

stairs meeting room. The visitor is overwhelmed at once by the moving and at the same time tensely dramatic painting that dominates the room: *The Crucifixion.*

Among the many figures we recognise first the crucified Christ with the disciples and Mary lamenting at his feet, then the figures of the two crucified thieves. The lighting of this central group is strikingly effective and even more life is brought into the picture by the many different events associated with the crucifixion which the painter captures in 'action shots' full of realistic detail. Although one would need hours to examine every little scene the painting works upon the spectator's imagination—the whole story is taken in at once. With first this effect and with the deliberate use of light and shade Tintoretto more than any other artist is able to make us feel and appreciate the mood and the action of a certain event.

This applies to almost all his pictures including the painting over the doorway which shows **The Suffering Christ**. Here Christ is not shown, as was traditional in this genre, as rising above all his sufferings; instead he is exhausted by the Scourging. Once again Tintoretto appeals to the imagination of the spectator: the intensity of the torture is made palpable by something that has already happened. On the right side of the entrance is the painting *Christ before Pilate*. Christ, in a white robe, rising above all the other figures is the central point of the composition. Yet even here many small scenes stand out, for instance the scribe, kneeling on the steps in the foreground, who is taking down the proceedings.

The painting left of the doors shows **The Stations of The Cross**: the serpentine path winding upwards seems long and difficult to the spectator. Christ, pressed down by the weight of the cross is almost at the point of collapse. The dramatic pleasure in story-telling seen

Plan of the Scuola San Rocco.

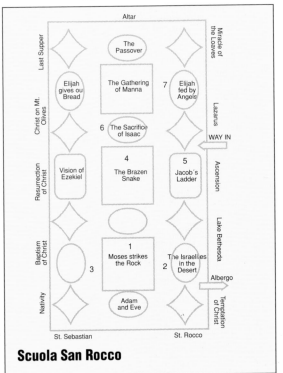

Scuola San Rocco

in the Tintoretto paintings is made clear by comparison with a canvas in the same room on the same theme. The picture, ascribed to Giorgione, shows only parts of the event: the face of Christ carrying the cross, wholly peaceful, not the suffering of the long way to Calvary.

Before leaving the Conference Room one can see overhead the **Glorification of St. Roche** with which Tintoretto won the competition of the Scuola San Rocco.

In the adjoining **Great Hall of the Brotherhood** the splendor of the richly ornamented and gilded frames on the ceiling first catch the eye. The 21 pictures set into the ceiling—painted 10 years after the pictures in the Sala dell'Albergo—have a monochrome red-brown tint. They show scenes from the Old and New Testaments.

The three central square pictures, for example, show *The Gathering of the Manna, The Setting up of the Brazen Serpent, Moses Strikes Water from the Rock*, all metaphors for the charitable work of the Brotherhood. At the center point of the ceiling is fixed a tondo or round picture which shows *The Sacrifice of Isaac*; to be understood as a reference to the sacrifice of Christ.

The paintings on the window wall show from left: *The Birth of Christ, The Baptism of Christ, The Resurrection* and *Christ on the Mount of Olives*.

The Last Supper, right of this scene, is treated in an original way by Tintoretto. The table at which Christ and his Disciples are eating is not front on to the viewer, per usual, but runs diagonally into the room. Once again Tintoretto shows his rich imagination and his willingness to break with traditional rules of composition. This is also seen in *The Temptation of Christ*, to be seen on the entry wall, right of the doors to the Sala dell'Albergo. The devil appears as a graceful youth stretching out his arms to Christ for help, rather than the demonic tempter in the desert.

The other picture on this wall include, from right to left: *Healing the Sick at the Pool of Bethesda, The Ascension, The Raising of Lazarus,* and *The Miracle of the Loaves and Fishes*. The altar piece, *The Vision of St. Roche* on the narrow side of the room and *The Meeting of Elizabeth and Mary*, on its right, are also both by Tintoretto. The two easel paintings with the scene *The Angel visits Abraham* and *Hagar and Ishmael* are by Giambattista Tiepolo.

The **Annunciation** left of the Altar is by Titian. Mary, kneeling, meekly receives the news of her pregnancy from the Angel that hovers before her. It is interesting to compare the picture with Tintoretto's work on the same subject which is to be found in the lower storey.

In Tintoretto's **Annunciation**, set in a crumbling architectural landscape, the Angel storms into Mary's room accompanied by crowds of cherubs and she draws back shocked and afraid. There is none of the peaceful and pious submission to be found in Titian, only dramatic action.

The painting belongs to the eight part **Marian Cycle**, Tintoretto's last works for the lower floor of the Brotherhood. The other pictures after the Annunciation, are as follows: *The Adoration of the Kings, The Flight into Egypt, The Massacre of the Innocents, Mary Magdalene, The Sisters of Lazurus, The Circumcision of Christ,* and *The Ascension of the Virgin*.

As we leave the Scuola San Rocco and the great legacy of Tintoretto we are left with the impression of his genius, generosity and also his own devotion to this body of work. This was so great that for the more than 60 paintings he waived a fee and charged only for the cost of materials. The Brotherhood granted him, a few years after the commission began, a lifetime pension for which he promised to deliver three paintings a year.

The Last Supper by Tintoretto.

THE ACCADEMIA

"We never think of having breakfast before we have first of all set our consciences at rest by seeing four paintings by Titian and two ceilings by Veronese. One can never come to the end of the Tintorettos..."

The Frenchman, de Bosse, was writing to his friend in Dijon, during his visit to Venice in the 18th century. The Serenissima possesses an enormous treasury of paintings in her churches, palaces and galleries. The most comprehensive and famous collection is undoubtedly that of the Accademia, which developed around the Art Academy for painters and sculptors, founded in 1750.

In 1805 Napoleon moved the school from the Palazzo San Marco into the meeting rooms and the church of the disbanded Scuola Santa Maria della Caritá. Paintings and sculpture by famous artists and others less well known were collected as object lessons for the pupils. The collection was enriched by the contents of the secularized churches and donations from patrician families. Soon there were so many works that new rooms had to be built on and in 1882 the gallery was divided from the school. In clearly arranged chronological order in bright rooms flooded with light the Accademia offers an incomparable gathering of Venetian painting. Our tour is orientated to the most important works which show the development of Venetian paintings over a period of 500 years.

Room I: In the former meeting room of the Brotherhood are altar pictures from the 14th to the 15th century. The first of the two main works in this room is the **Polyptich of Paolo Veneziano**, opposite the staircase, free-standing in the room. The great altarpiece delights us through its beautiful golden frame alone, which is given an architectural structure by means of exquisitely fine carving. The gold background and the flat, graphic arrangement shows how the painter was influenced by the Byzantine tradition. In the center of the picture is the Virgin, crowned, framed on both sides with four pictures showing scenes from the life of Christ. Each of the side areas shows a unified group of paintings: on the left we see the *Birth, Baptism*, the *Last Supper* and the *Arrest of Jesus* and on the right the *Way to Calvary*, the *Crucifixion*, the *Resurrection* and the *Ascension*. In the much smaller paintings of the upper frieze the four inner pictures show scenes from the life of St. Francis of Assisi, while the outer ones show the Miracle of Pentecost and the Last Judgment.

The St. Francis scenes make it clear that this work was meant for a church dedicated to this saint. The pleasure taken by the artist in telling a story, which we see in individual scenes, had a didactic purpose in early times. Pictures like these in the churches were the catchechism of simple folk who could neither read nor write.

At the end of the room we find another free-standing work, the **Altarpiece** by **Lozenzo Veneziano**. The middle picture of this polyptych of group of pictures, is the Annunciation, framed by 16 saints. In their golden frames they look like figures in the niches of a gothic cathedral, especially since the massive wooden frames are architecturally carved in gothic style.

It is plain that Venetian art was becoming more open to western influence. The figures are still presented against a gold background but the plastic treatment of the folds of their robes shows a gradual breaking of ties to the *Maniera bizantine*.

Room II: Originally this room was meant for Titian's *Assunta* (Assumption of the Virgin Mary). After the secularization of the churches by Napoleon the picture was taken from the Frari church but it was eventually returned to its place over the High Altar in 1919. Today the room contains one of the most important single canvases of the early Venetian renaissance. **The Madonna Enthroned with Saints** by *Giovanni Bellini*, painted in 1489. This giant altarpiece 16ft.5in. by 7ft.11in. (4.71 meters by 2.58 meters) from the Church of San Giobbe, is regarded as one of the masterpieces of this famous painter. Saints and angels playing music are grouped about the throne of the Mother and the Child Jesus.

In groups of three, left to right, we see St. Francis in a brown monk's habit, who seems to be calling the viewer to worship, then, next to him Job, the patron of the church, (Italian *Giobbe* = Job) and, almost hidden, John the Baptist. On the steps of the throne are the angels and next to them St. Sebastian, pierced by arrows, behind him St. Dominic with the book and St. Louis, dressed as a bishop.

Bellini no longer presents the figures in small separate pictures, as in earlier times, but brings them together in form and content, making a finished composition. The interplay of the figures is not suggested by simply standing them next to each other but is apparent from the life-like composition of the group. Venetian painting had welcomed the revolutionary new ideas of the renaissance, with its fundamental principles of realistic portrayal of the human body and its use of the rediscovered plane linear perspective. This altered conception of composition is to be seen in Bellini's portrayal of the background. He sets the enthroned Madonna in monumental sacred architecture: an apse decorated with mosaics.

Room V: Two cabinets, IV and V branch off from the adjoining room III

with further paintings by Giovanni Bellini. The high point of Room V however, is undoubtedly Giorgione's Tempestá, painted in 1507. In this picture what was formerly the background has now become the main theme. The scene is a city on a riverbank covered with threatening clouds from which lightning bursts; the two persons in the foreground seem almost incidental. A seated naked woman is bent protectively over her child; a man some distance away leans on his staff, apparently uninvolved.

The meaning of this work still arouses controversy. It could, in the religious tradition, show the holy Family. But the painting seems to suggest possibilities of a psychological interpretation, as if the moment of dramatic tension caused by the storm was also reflected in conflicting principles: female and male, nature and humanity, the protection of the mother's lap against the threat of the storm's power.

Room X: From Room III one comes directly across the large Room VI to this room, dedicated to the great Venetian masters Titian, Tintoretto and Veronese.

The entry wall left belongs to **Titian's Pietá**, painted shortly before his death in the year 1576. This monumental legacy of the great painter was originally intended for his grave in the Frari church. The figure of Mary with the body of Christ lying in her lap is set before the heavy architecture of a building which resembles a mausoleum; under a domed arch hovers an angel with a torch. At the sides stand the statues of Moses and of Faith, personified as a female figure holding a cross. Before the body of Jesus stands the lamenting Mary Magdalene, who raises her hand in a gesture of aversion. The whole scene is bathed in a mystic light. With almost impressionistic brushwork and the magic effect of his color tones Titian created a picture of incomparable visionary power. It is clear how the complete work of the master refects a human life; this can be followed in the changing intensity of his colors and powerful representation of human beings right through to the mellow metaphysical beauty of the work of his old age.

Opposite the Pietá hang works of **Jacopo Tintoretto**. This painter's unique use of strong colors and the dynamic rhythm of his composition can be seen especially in two pictures: **The Creation of the Animals** with its magnificent flights of birds and leaping fishes, is a reminder that Venetian painters were unusually fond of animals. In Carpaccio's famous picture "The Courtesans" the two women on their altana have pet dogs and caged birds. Popular saints were associated with certain animals: St. Roche was painted with his dog, St. Jerome with a lion and often with a pet dog as well. Several dogs and a falcon appear in the St. Ursula cycle, while exotic animals-giraffes, camels, lions—appealed to Bellini. A famous rhinoceros was painted in 1751 by the artist Pietro Longhi.

The Miracle of St. Mark began a cycle dealing with the miracles of the city's patron saint, shows the tense and dramatic climax of a legend. The slave of a provincial knight who left his master without permission to pray at the saint's grave in Venice, was to be punished for his deed. He was to be publicly blinded and suffer the cruel torture of having his bones broken. At the last minute St. Mark appeared to save his true follower who already lay tortured upon the ground. The drama of these events is emphasized by Tintoretto through extreme contrasts of light and shade and through the impossibly complex twisting and turning of

The Creation of the Animals (Tintoretto).

the overlapping human figures.

The exaggerated gestures of the figures increase the dramatic tension; this is seen in the figure of the torturer who shows the judge, who is springing to his feet, the broken instruments of torture. The startling perspective of St. Mark hurtling down from heaven showed the way for later baroque painting.

The third great Venetian painter of the 16th century was **Paolo Veronese**. His painting **Supper in the Pharisee's House** measures 42 feet by 18 feet (12.80 meters by 5.55)and takes up the whole short side of the room on the right. He completed it in 1573 for the reflectory of the Dominicans of SS Giovanni e Paolo. The theme is The Last Supper, which is treated as a contemporary Venetian feast. This profane conception resulted in a charge of blasphemy for the painter who was brought before the Inquisition on July 18, 1573. There were objections to many of the

figures near the outside staircase: the dwarfish court fool, the two soldiers in German armor drinking at the right, and a servant who is leaning over the left balustrade holding a handkerchief to his bloody nose. Veronese was not prepared to 'correct' the picture but he was willing to call it something else. He painted the new title clearly on the balustrade in latin, saying that the picture was called "Supper in the House of Levi, the Pharisee", referred to in St. Luke's Gospel, Chapter V.

Room XI: On the short side of the room just opposite the way into Room X is found the work of the most famous Venetian painter of the 18th century **Giambattista Tiepolo: The Finding of the True Cross** (1745) was conceived as a *tondo* or round picture for the ceiling of the Capuccine Church in Castello. The legend it illustrates tells how St. Helena was able to discover the

Procession on the Piazza San Marco (Gentile Bellini).

true cross of Christ.

In her search for this relic she came upon three crosses which she brought from Golgotha to Jerusalem. On the way she met a funeral procession and touched the corpse with each of the crosses. The picture shows the moment in which the dead man wakes to life at the touch of the true relic and sits up on his bier. Meanwhile Helena in a triumphant pose points to heaven before the towering Cross of Christ. The foreshortened lines, so typical for the illusionist ceiling painting of the baroque and rococo, show the influence of Tintoretto in the Serenissima.

Room XVII: From Room IX, on the left at the end of a long corridor is a small room containing *Veduti*. These small detailed views of Venice are the last crowning achievement of Venetian painting in this 18th century. No wonder that this art form developed in Venice where every corner, every alley and every canal provides a picturesque motive. The keenest buyers of these views were the English tourists who came to Italy in the 18th and 19th centuries. Most of the Venetian veduti are not in the museums of the Serenissima but in English galleries. The most important representatives of this genre were Antonio Canal, known as Canaletto (1697-1768), his nephew Bernario Belotto (1720-1780) and his pupil Francesco Guardi (1712-1793).

A charming fantasy *veduti* by **Canaletto** is shown here, titled simply **Perspective**. His best known works nearly always show the famous squares, canals and buildings of Venice.

His nephew Belotto left his home town early and from the age of 26 worked at the court of the Polish King in Dresden. A view of the **Scuola San Marco** by Belotto is here in the Accademia for us to see. After the detailed

Healing of The Possessed (Vittorio Carpaccio).

perspectives of Canaletto *Guardi* produced new effects in the painting of *veduti* with his romantic eye and almost impressionistic technique. An example of this is a view of San Giorgio Maggiore. **Guardi** also went beyond the usual themes of veduti painting by presenting dramatic or topical events such as the **Burning of the Scuola San Marcuola**.

Room XX: The historical paintings of Gentile Bellini or Vittorio Carpaccio 300 years earlier, could be seen as the forerunners of the vedute painting. In order to see them one passes the former chapel of the Scuola and turns left in the corridor after the small inner courtyard. From here we turn left again.

Room XX contains the eight part cycle of the **Miracles of the Holy Cross**: Originally these pictures, on which Bellini and Carpaccio together with other painters whose names are no longer known all worked, were intended for the Scuola Grande di Giovanni Evangelista. The Brotherhood of this Scuola kept as a relic a splinter believed to have come from the Holy Cross, the gift of the Grand Chancellor of Cyprus. The theme of the cycle of pictures is the miracles associated with this relic.

The picture of contemporary Venice in these historical paintings is always interesting for the visitor. Bellini's **Procession on the Piazza San Marco**, shows the only remaining view of the square in the 15th century. We can see that on St. Mark's Church only one of the veneto-byzantine mosaics has been preserved, over the left portal. The clock tower with the moors does not yet exist and neither does the Procuratie Nuove. In its place is still the gothic building it replaced, level with the Campanile.

Carpaccio's Healing of the Possessed shows the old Rialto bridge of wood which fell down in 1444.

Room XXI: In the room opposite is the cycle of **The Life and Death of St. Ursula.**. Vittorio Carpaccio completed this eight part series of pictures for the oratium of the Brotherhood of Santa Orsola between 1490 and 1500, without the help of any other painter. They show how the son of the King of England asked for the hand of Princess Ursula of Britanny, how she made a pilgrimage to Rome with 10,000 virgins, how she and all the maidens were murdered by the Huns. The painter paid no attention to the real places where these events were supposed to have taken place nor to the historical period.

He set the scene in Venice his home city and produced lively contemporary scenes.

Room XXIV: This last room in the gallery is the travelers' room of the Scuola Santa Maria della Caritá, preserved in its original state. Directly over the portal is a monumental canvas: Titian's **The Presentation of the Virgin Mary**. Mary as a child, surrounded by an aureole, climbs the steps to the Temple where the High Priest is waiting for her. The picture, painted in 1538, is full of the glowing colors on which Titian's fame rests. The composition is a fine combination of balanced elements. The group of noble Israelites, before a hilly landscape, makes a counter point of form and content to the single figures of the priest, Mary, and the old woman with a basket of eggs standing before the monumental architecture of the Temple. One can see that Titian conceived his work specially for the place in which it is hung. The natural light in the room corresponds with the way he has the light fall in his picture. The window on the left side of this room acts as a light source for the picture as well as for the room itself.

This picture makes a grand finale to our round trip through 'the Louvre of Venice.'

Pietá (Titian).

184

LA GUIDECCA AND SAN GIORGIO MAGGIORE

The islands of La Guidecca and San Giorgio Maggiore are only a few minutes away by vaporetto from the center of the city. They are both very different not only in shape but in character: the long drawn out and rather homely La Guidecca in contrast to the splendid buildings of the much smaller island of San Giorgio Maggiore. Both are reached with the vaporetti No 5 and No 8. It is best to take the vaporetti when the island is crossed from west to east, thus showing the visitor a contrast between two extremes.

La Guidecca takes her name from the Jewish settlers on the island who lived here before they moved to Mestre or into the Ghetto at Cannaregio. Today the island is the home of ordinary citizens, workmen and fishermen. It is hard to imagine that this was formerly a wealthy suburb with feudal mansions and fine gardens. Now it is the busy fun of the working class children, playing among the simple houses that give the island a life of its own.

On the western tip of the island there looms a striking industrial ruin, the **Mulino Stucky**, a large mill which was still operating in the 50s. The neo-gothic facade of this brick building, unusual round Venice, shows that the architect's family came from North Germany.

From the stop at **San Eufemia**, the furthest west of the three mooring places, one can stroll along the harbor promenade or take a walk through the residential quarter. One wanders through the streets accompanied by the cooing of doves and the twitter of parakeets in cages, which hang in many

Preceding pages: San Giorgio Maggiore. Below left, view of the Redentore Church; right, a watcher at the church door.

windows and doorways. Washing flutters in the wind and window displays for the Communist Party or the office of the Milan Soccer Fan Club show that there is not a *Conte* nor a *Marchesa* living here any more.

Little Islands

The **Rio del Ponte Lungo**, a broad straight canal, divides the island through the middle and is crossed by only one bridge. Here one can see that La Guidecca is really not a single island but that it is put together out of many tiny islets. Instead of stylish gondolas, squat cargo boats are tied up to thick wooden posts.

It is not easy to reach the south side of the island which faces the open lagoon. Many of the streets that seem to cross the island turn out to be dead ends. Near the **Ospedale Inglese** lies the **Parco Quatiere** which one reaches over the

Calle San Giacomo and the Calle degli Orti. When this small park is open it gives a view of the Lido.

Back on the harbor promenade we find on the right the *Chiesa del Redentore*, the Church of the Redeemer, built between 1577 and 1592 by Andrea Palladio, in gratitude for the end of the outbreak of plague in the year 1576. It was a severe epidemic in which at least a third of the population died; a famous victim was the painter Titian, almost one hundred years old.

The stark classical facade reminds us of an antique temple. The architect achieves an overall effect of harmony through his splendid gradation of the single architectural elements, from the rounded arch of the portal to the central dome, the triangular gables, set one above the other and the recurved roof.

The interior is impressive because of its clear architectural quality, the decorations and paintings are less important.

Christmas at the Redentore Church: a Nativity scene.

The best paintings are the *Baptism of Christ*, from the workshop of Veronese and *Christ laid in the Tomb*, by Palma the younger.

Every year on the third Sunday in July the Feast of the Redeemer is held, in memory of the island's relief from the plague. Then La Guidecca comes alive: a bridge of boats over the Canal della Guidecca makes a path for the procession and splendid fireworks light up the night.

There is another church on the island that is also associated with Palladio, **Santa Maria della Presentazione**, only a minute away. Its popular name, *Le Zitelle*, which means something like 'the unmarried girls', seems to indicate that there was once a girls' home here. On the way we pass on the Fondamenta the **Youth Hostel**, **Ostello di Venezia**, with one of the few pizzerias on La Guidecca right next door.

Le Zitelle, as the church of the Pres-

entation is called, comes from the 16th century. The facade resembles the Redentore Church but is not quite so impressive. Andrea Palladio is supposed to have made the design, and the work was carried out by Jacopo Bonzetto. The main building of the present day church is clearly from the 18th century.

On the southeastern shore of the island, in the midst of a magnificent park, lies the famous **Hotel Cipriani**. This luxury hotel, the only one in Venice that will not take tour groups, offers its guests the highest comfort with international flair. The name of its founder, Cipriano, is a guarantee of high quality and the family runs a more moderately priced establishment on La Guidecca: **Harry's Dolci**, not far from the Mulino Stucky. This restaurant, a branch of the famous Harry's Bar, has beautiful lawns which invite us to eat out of doors in summer.

Everyday is wash-day on La Guidecca.

San Giorgio Maggiore

Pomp and popularity are the key words for the changeover to the island of San Giorgio Maggiore. It is only a stone's throw from La Guidecca but the two islands are worlds apart.

The abbey church of the Benedictines, also designed by Andrea Palladio, is one of the classic motives in the panorama of Venice and was undoubtedly a deliberate addition to the city's splendid setting in the lagoon.

Andrea Palladio did not live to see the completion of this church or the dedication of the Church of the Redeemer. This architectural genius was born in Vicenza in 1508 and, according to the political boundaries of the time, he was a Venetian.

His patron, Giangiorgio Trissino, took the 37-year-old Palladio with him to Rome in 1545 where he studied antique Roman architecture for two years. This visit and his continuing study of the 20 volume treatise on architecture of Vitruvius, a master builder from the time of the Emperor Augustus, determined his future development.

His clear classical style was put into practice in the building of villas as well as churches, his churches are found only in Venice; the villas that he built for the Venetian aristocracy can be admired near Vicenza and along the Brenta Canal. A famous example is the **Villa Foscari**, erected between 1550 and 1560. It bears the romantic name of "La Malcontenta" after an unhappy lady banished to her Palladian retreat.

Both the writings—the Four Books on Architecture—and the buildings of this master architect of the 16th century spread far beyond the borders of Italy. His influence on the architecture of the 20th century is indisputable.

A church is said to have existed on the island of San Giorgio Maggiore at the end of the 8th century. An actual church was built in 1566 after a design by Andrea Palladio and finished after his death in the year 1580 by Vincenzo Scamozzi.

The interior of the basilica, with three naves and a central dome, is brightly lit and clearly arranged, in an antique Roman style. The *Last Supper* and the *Rain of Manna* by Tintoretto, on either side of the High Altar are particularly worth seeing.

On the left, behind the High Altar a shield shows the way to the lift for the **Campanile**, from which one has marvelous view of Venice and the lagoons. The lift for the 231 foot (70 meter) tower is worked by a monk, for a modest donation.

A small paved path leads to the eastern side of the island and the buildings of the **Fondazione Giorgio Cini**. Vittorio Cini, the industrialist, created this foundation in memory of his son Giorgio, who was killed in a plane crash in the year 1949. The dilapidated church buildings, which had been used for other things since the secularization by Napoleon, as well as all the monastery buildings, were restored with money from the Cini Foundation. The newly laid out parks filled the island with beauty and dignity.

The main work of the Foundation is focussed on the international center for culture and history, in the former monastery, which holds courses and congresses. An **Art and Trade School**, together with a *Naval School*, whose pupils live partly on the island, also belong to the Foundation. Behind the monastery buildings an avenue leads past the sports fields to the park, where there is an indoor swimming pool and an open air theater.

In the year 1987 the heads of government of the western industrial powers met on San Giorgio Maggiore. During this meeting the security regulations were so strict that the Benedictine monks were not allowed on to their own island.

CAFÉS, BARS AND RESTAURANTS

Venetian trade with the Orient brought many new things to Europe including coffee. As the Venetians began to import coffee beans from Arabia in the 17th century the stimulating black drink was first regarded as a medicine. Soon afterwards it was found to be delicious and refreshing; in 1638 the first *bottego del caffé* was opened on the Piazza San Marco. Under the arcades of the Piazza we still find the most famous coffee houses in Venice: **Florian**, **Quadri** and **Lavena**. As soon as the first rays of sunshine promise warmer weather tables and chairs are set out. In spite of high prices, visitors to Venice should treat themselves to a cappucino or an aperitiff here. The fairytale setting and the colorful comings and goings on the Piazza make up for everything.

The **Caffè Florian**, (accented on the last syllable: Floriàn) was founded in 1720 and is not only the oldest café in Venice but in the whole of Italy. The small, tastefully decorated rooms are both distinguished and cozy, especially in winter. Venetians and foreign guests spend quiet, pleasant leisure hours here. The new owners, Signora Daniela Vevaldi and her husband, Paolo, both professors at the University of Padua, have brought new life into the famous old coffee house while keeping the decor and style intact. Journalists and artists meet in the Caffè Florian; cello and violin virtuosi give performances. It is a place for art shows and musicans among its guests: Goethe as well as Thomas Mann, Marcel Proust, or Ernest Hemingway. Richard Wagner, however, kept away from the Caffè Florian so as not to run into Guiseppe Verdi; Wagner preferred the Lavena on the other side of the Piazza. It was rumored that both Verdi and Wagner were inspired to write arias by the coffee house musicians.

A custom that can be seen in oriental cities today is the Coffee Seller who walks the streets. He was a familiar figure in old Venice and Venetians could take a cup of mocca in passing on every street corner. This led to the habit seen in all Latin countries, not only in Venice, of pausing to drink a cup of espresso at a bar. A **Bar** has nothing to do with night life in Italy and should not suggest a counter in a pub or a place where only alcohol is sold. Italian bars are more like stand-up cafés where one can have a continental breakfast. Show cases with crisp pastry, savories, and appetizing *panini* (bread rolls with fillings) invite the visitor to have a snack.

Bars like this are to be found every 50 yards in Venice but *the* Bar is of course, *Harry's Bar*, in the Calle Vallareso 1323. The proprietor of this small, exclusive establishment—which is a

restaurant as well as a bar—is Arrigo Cipriani, son of the founder, Guiseppe. Arrigo is a marvelous host; he receives his guests personally, chatting wittily with them in many languages. Venetians who want to know which prominent personalities from the jet set or the cultural scene have arrived in town, go to Harry's Bar and drink a *Bellini* at the counter.

The real *Bellini*, peach juice with champagne, not to mention the colorful Tiziano (of grapefruit juice, and champagne, colored pink with grenadine or bitters) as well as the Giorgione are among the original creations only to be found at Cipriani's—whether in Harry's Bar, in the **Locanda Cipriano**, a country hotel on the island of Torcello, or in **Harry's Dolci**; on the island of Guidecca, Fondamenta San Biagio.

At every one of these addresses we find exquisite cuisine as well as a spe-cial atmosphere. The same quality awaits the guest in 'Harry's', the newest gourmet creation of Arrigo Cipriani on 5th Avenue, in New York.

Recently Arrigo published a book in honor of his father. It gives amusing sketches of his most prominent guests from Churchill to Mastroianni and Fellini. One of the best-known was Ernest Hemingway who could always find new inspiration over a glass of the best in his favorite bar.

The name Cipriani is also connected with one of the most exclusive hotels in the world. The **Hotel Cipriani**, on the island of Guidecca, was founded in 1958 by Arrigo's father and today is in American hands. The hotel owns motor boats which whisk guests from the Molo, near St. Theodore's pillar, to an oasis of peace, with azaleas, rhododendrons and oleanders framing the wide expanse of the swimming pool. A dinner by candlelight in the **Restaurant** Harry's Bar.

Orient Express is a very special experience.

A good place for a celebration is also the **Danieli Terrace** or the **Mansarda** of the **Hotel Londra Palace**, both on the Riva degli Schiavoni. From high up one has a lovely view over the Bacino di San Marco. How romantic it is in the evening, when the lights are reflected in the dark waters of the lagoon. At the **Terrace Restaurant of the Gritti Palace** we have a grandstand view of the most beautiful street in the world: the Grand Canal. This exclusive hotel, now owned by Karim Aga Khan, lies diagonally opposite the church of Santa Maria della Salute.

Venetian specialties are also well cooked in simpler restaurants. The difference between a *Trattoria* and a *Ristorante* is small but very important. In the trattoria, a family business, 'Mamma' is usually the cook and the recipes have been handed down for

generations. A harmonious blend of local garden produce and seafood makes up the menu. *Spezie*, herbs and spices are the secret of good Venetian cookery: pimento, tumeric, ginger, nutmeg, vanilla, show the oriental influences; pine-nuts, raisins, almonds and pistachios are also used. These exotic ingredients are also enriched with a dash of French or Austrian cuisine. Here is a short guided tour through the Venetian menu.

The **Antipasto**, the appetizer, must be of fresh seafood, raw, fried or boiled, for example: *Tartuffi di mare*, sea truffles, *Granseola*, sea spider, *Peoci Salati*, mussels cooked in the pan with parsley and garlic. Those who don't care for seafood should try the delicious vegetable dishes. A speciality are *Castraura*, artichoke hearts that only grow so well on the island of San Erasmo, Venice's market garden.

A typical **Primo** or first course is

Terrace café on the Zattere.

Pasta e Pasioi, pasta with beans. The ingredients are white beans, celery, carrots, onions, rosemary, basil and sage. Lots of vegetable and just a little pasta with a dash of olive oil make this really delicious. Also *Risi e Bisi*, rice and peas, is a speciality, the star of the many rice dishes, for rice and pasta are popular in Venice as in the whole of Italy. Pasta is made by hand in a good trattoria and is called *Pasta fatta in casa*. Two dishes that taste especially good are *Bigoli in Salsa* and *Pappardelle alla granseola*.

As **Secondo**, second course, fish of every kind is to be recommended. Whoever is not afraid to get black teeth should try *Sepe in tecia*, squid cooked in its own ink. With this dish one eats *polenta*, maize porridge, white or yellow according to the trattoria.

As **contorno**, side dishes or accompaniments, there is a whole palette of different vegetables to choose from. A special delicacy is *Radicchio ai ferri* which is radicchio fried with oil and pepper.

It is more fashionable than ever to eat *sorbetto*—a lemon ice—between meals. It helps the digestion.

Good wine is part of a good menu and there are many varieties to choose from: dry white wines from the Veneto and Friaul, such as *Soave, Verduzzo or Pinot Grigot*, all go well with fish dishes. An alternative to bottled wine is the *vino della casa*, the house wine, which the host usually picks out at the vintners himself.

This sort of meal can be ordered from Signora Ada. She is the proprietress and the cook at the **Trattoria da Ignazio**, Calle dei Saoneri, near the Campo San Polo. In summer one can sit outside in the little garden.

The **Trattoria Montin** on the Fondamento Eremite, Dorsoduro, also has a pretty garden. The walls of this artists' restaurant are decorated with many paintings and one can enjoy good food in a friendly atmosphere.

The trattoria **Citta di Vittorio**, San Marco 1591, in a side street of the **Frezzeria**, is a favorite eating house for gondoliers. And they know where the food is good.

For the end of the meal one should not forget the Dolci, the sweet things. Those with a sweet tooth will enjoy *Tiramisu*, which the Venetians brought from Byzantium and which is rather like English trifle. Krapfen, strudel, kranz, waffle, brioche and bigne all came to the city from other lands and were adopted by the Venetians.

The best ices can be found on the **Zattere**, behind the Salute church. This is a secret...please don't pass it on! Here are all the Venetians with their wives and families—including Grandma and the baby in the pram—visiting **Nico, Cucciolo, Franco or Aldo** and enjoying *La Coppa giganta con amarena*, the giant ice with a shot of sour cherry syrup.

Left, Bar do Leoni.
Right, gondolier.

THE OTHER VENICE

Whoever has a little more time should take a longer walk into those quiet, idyllic districts on the edge of the city, the winding alleyways of **Santa Croce**, **San Polo** and **Cannaregio**. They not only show the visitor more of everyday life in Venice but lead to hidden historical treasures or cast interesting sidelights on Venetian history. The Rialto bridge is the junction for the two following walks which can be taken separately or—as described—joined together to make a round trip. So as not to get lost in the tangle of alleys and lanes, bridges and canals, it is advisable to take along a map of the city.

Sestieri of San Polo and Santa Croce

We begin at the **Piazzale Roma**, the

hectic terminus of all motor traffic to and from the mainland, and go first of all to the **Giardini Papadopoli**. The pretty park, once privately owned, was a botanical garden and zoo in the 19th century, famous for its exotic plants and animals...and for its riotous summer festivals.

A short way behind the park, following the signs *Per Rialto* we come to the **Chiesa San Nicoló dá Tolentino**. The classical open portico built in front of the facade in the 18th century gives the church the look of a Greek temple. The main body of the Theatine church was built to the plans of Vincenzo Scamozzi and—it is believed—Andrea Palladio. Two paintings in the interior by Bernado Strozzi and Johann Liss are worth seeing. One sees architecture students sitting on the steps of the church—their faculty adjoins the church at the left.

Still following the signs in the direction of the Rialto we come to the **Calle delle Chiovere**, where tastefully and carefully restored residences with little palm gardens reminds one of villas on the Riviera.

Shortly afterwards we reach the **Campo San Rocco**. The little square is framed by the end walls of the mighty Franciscan church of **I Frari**, of the **Chiesa San Rocco** and of the renaissance **Scuola San Rocco**, all decked out with cypresses. The Church of San Rocco, built in the 18th century, does have some works by Tintoretto but it is overshadowed in this respect by the Scuola. The Scuola San Rocco, with its great treasury of works by this master, counts as one of the most beautiful museums in Italy.

Our way leads over the Campo dei Frari to Campo San Stin from which it is only a few steps to the **Scuola Grande di San Giovanni Evangelista**. The Brotherhood of St. John the Evangelist was founded in the 13th century. For their meeting house Giovanni Bellini and Vittorio Carpaccio

Portico of the Chiesa San Nicolo da Tolentino.

painted the famous cycle of **The Miracles of the Holy Cross**, now shown in the Accademia. The atrium of the building is very pretty: its walls, decorated with marble incrustations, give it a charm of its own. Today the rooms of the Scuola are used for exhibitions and lectures.

Some Peace and Quiet

A little further north the **Chiesa di San dell'Oro**, stands calm and peaceful, out of the way of the crowds of tourists. It is supposed to be one of the oldest churches in the city and was indeed founded in the 9th century. The present building, however, stems from the 15th-16th centuries. The picture at the High Altar by Lorenzo Lotto is worth a visit.

Not many visitors come to this district. A good indication of the degree of 'tourist influence are always the goods displayed for sale. The shopkeepers here live from everyday commodities not from the glittering luxuries sold by their colleagues in San Marco. This quarter of the city is more natural and genuine. There are also nice little eating houses such as the **Osteria La Zucca**, near the Ponte del Megio. Although it is named after something big, for example the pumpkin, (Italian *zucca*) the Osteria is a tiny restaurant, but cosy with reasonable prices.

On the way to the Campo San Polo we wander through a number of narrow alleyways and through the dusty panes we glimpse craftsmen at work, especially shoemakers. If there were statistics available on the numbers of worn-out shoe soles Venice would be at the top of the survey.

The **Campo San Polo** is the largest square in the city after the Piazza San Marco. In former times there were even bull-fights held here. The **Chiesa San**

Left, delivering wine by boat. Right, reflections: A view of the island of San Michele.

Polo stems from the 15th century but was extensively rebuilt in the 19th. It contains among other things a very fine *Last Supper* by Tintoretto, that is too easily missed in the semi-darkness of the interior. Two further paintings of the same subject by Tintoretto can be seen in the Chiesa San Marcuola and San Giorgio Maggiore.

San Polo also contains paintings such as the *Assumption of the Virgin* by Tintoretto and, in the second side altar to the left *The Virgin Mary with St John Nepomuk* by Tiepolo. The altar painting shows *The Betrothal of the Virgin* by Veronese.

The size of the Campo makes it a popular meeting place; mothers bring their children here to play during the day and everyone meets here for a chat in the evening. The rest of the way to the Rialto is packed with shops.

At last we come to the vegetable stands at the Rialto market and plunge into the crowds round the bridge.

In Sestiere Cannaregio

Our way leads us out of the bustle of the Rialto quarter into the district of Cannaregio. On the other side of the bridge, from the Campo San Bartolomeo, we pass the Fondaco dei Tedeschi, today the main Post Office, and follow the Salizzada San Crisostomo as far as the Campo dei Santi Apostoli. Here the *Strada Nuova* begins and we are already in Cannaregio. The Strada Nuova has a lot of shops, large and small, but not many cultural sights. The things on exhibition here are juicy hams, appetizing vegetables and rich fruits, pasta, vino and gelato. The sightseer in search of culture should branch off the **Ca'd'Oro**. A side entrance shows the way to the **Galleria Franchetti**, an extensive art collection that show specially chosen examples of

Romantic gondola ride.

Venetian painting of the 15th and 16th centuries as well as fine furniture.

Further along the Strada Nuova we come to the *Campo di Santa Fosca*. Here there is a statue of the Venetian monk, Paolo Sarpi, who defended his home town so passionately in the quarrel between Venice and the Vatican in the 17th century. His famous last words over Venice were: "*Esto perpetua!*" May it last forever.

To the right a bridge over the Rio Santa Fosca leads to the Campo San Marziale. Beyond the Rio della Sensa we go along the Corte Vecchia to the *Ponte di Sacca*. From this bridge there is a wonderful view of the cemetery island, San Michele, and the northern lagoon. At twilight, especially when the boundary lights of the waterways are lit, this is a unique picture, its magic tinged with sadness.

From the Ponte di Sacca we go further along the canal to the **Chiesa Madonna dell'Orto**: This lovely church from the 15th century is a masterpiece of Venetian gothic. A point of interest is the unusual Campanile with a roofed top. The church is named after a miracle-working picture of the Madonna found in a garden, (Italian *orto* = garden). In 1937 a memorial bust of the painter Tintoretto was placed on his grave in a side chapel. He was buried here in his own parish church. Many of his works and those of his son Domenico decorate the interior of the church, together with works by Cima da Conegliano, Palma the younger and Giovanni Bellini, making this a treasury of Venetian painting.

Before crossing the bridge over the Rio Madonna dell'Orto to get to the **Campo dei Mori**, one should look from the Fondamento at the **Palazzo Mastelli**, opposite. There one sees a charming relief of a man leading a camel which has given the palace its popular name of the **Palazzo del Cammello**. It once belonged to the brothers

Rioba, Sandi and Alfani, merchants who came to Venice in the 12th century from the Peloponnese. These brothers are identified with the romanesque statue of a turbaned oriental on the front of their property on the Campo dei Mori. It is also suggested that the Campo dei Mori, the square of the Moors, has its name from the **Fondaco degli Arabi**, the trading house of the Arabs, which once stood here.

Only a few yards along the nearby Fondamenta to the left is the **Casa Tintoretto**. A plaque tells us of the house's claim to fame: the painter lived here for many years with his large family. The house was restored in 1881 and its next restoration is long overdue. Today Tintoretto's neighbor is Giovanni Tadora, with his trim vegetable shop. Giovanni is getting on in years but he still enjoys a chat and likes to point out the advantages of peaceful Cannaregio as compared with the hectic life in San Marco.

Sior Rioba on the Campo dei Mori.

Now we cross the Rio della Sensa as far as the next Fondamenta, on which we turn right. Our way lies south along the Rio di Girolamo to the **Campo di Ghetto Nuovo**, the oldest Jewish quarter in Venice. Here in Cannaregio the wide streets along the straight canals, flanked by pleasant, relatively flat house, have a Dutch air. What a contrast to the high tenements of the Ghetto. Beyond the spacious square of the Ghetto Nuovo, which is surrounded by water, like a moat, we cross a bridge into the Ghetto Vecchio. At the **Campiello della Scuole** one can take a guided tour through the **Museum of Jewish History** and also see the **German Synagogue**, built in the 16th century. The **Scuola Levanti** and the **Scuola Espagnol**, two more of the five synagogues in the Ghetto, are also open to the public.

A shield marked *Ferrovia* shows the way to the railway station over the

Canale di Cannaregio. On the south side of the Ponte Guglie, on the **Campo San Geremia** there is an interesting contrast: a huge modern antenna rises up from a splendid restored palazzo. Since 1969 a station of the RAI, the Italian radio and television service, has been installed in the **Palazzo Labia**. The former owners, the noble Labia family, were renowned for their extravagance, as shown in the following anecdote. After a sumptuous banquet, the left-overs, including the golden dishes and cutlery, were flung into the canal, and the host cried out: *"L'abbia o non l'abbia saro sempre un Labia!"* "Whether I have it or whether I don't I'll always be a Labia!" It was rumored that there were nets in the water to catch the precious dishes, but the wealth of the family is obvious from the luxurious interior of the 17th-18th century palazzo. Giovanni Battista Tiepolo, the greatest Venetian painter of the day, painted the frescoes in the salon. Today this room is also used for exhibitions.

After the Campo San Geremio comes the **Lista di Spagna**, the extension of the Strada Nuora. It is very lively and busy with more and more jewelry stores and boutiques. Many little streets branch off the wide shopping boulevard and end sometimes in pretty courtyards with a restaurant.

Here we find the **Trattoria Roma di Povoledo**, a restaurant which is very handy for travelers because it opens early, and also the **Piper Discotheque** a popular meeting place for Venetian teenagers and young travelers.

The bustle in the street reaches a high point at the Railway Station which is crowded with young 'rucksack' tourists, without much money, so often cursed by Venetian tourist managers. The stream of visitors crosses over the square on the way to the gondolas and the vaporetto. This is a good place to end our expedition or set out in a different direction on foot or on the water.

Left, a funeral gondola. Right, Madonna dell' Orto.

THE GHETTO: JEWS IN VENICE

The former Jewish quarter is quiet and unobtrusive, far from the main tourist attractions. There is nothing about the neglected facades of the houses to suggest that until the 17th century this was one of the largest and most important Jewish communities in Europe. The persecution of the Jews in neighboring lands drove waves of refugees into the Italian states, seeking a safe and lasting home. They often sought in vain. Even Venice's policy over the centuries wavered between toleration, expulsion and protection.

Jews were first officially mentioned in the 10th century when they were forbidden to travel on Venetian ships. Venice, the ambitious trading city feared competition from the world-wise Jewish merchants. Already, from 1090, Jews settled one by one on the island *Spinalunga* because the city was closed to them. In the course of the 13th century other Jewish immigrants increased the small unofficial community on the island which was now called **Guidecca**, after the inhabitants.

The unfriendly attitude of Venice first began to change in the year 1298, as a result of internal social problems. The church forbade the Christians to take part in banking and financial transactions and this prohibitions encouraged loan-sharks who charged enormous rates of interest. Other cities had found a way out: rich Jews, who were not bound by the Christian prohibitions against banking and money-lending, could provide credit. The Serenissima also followed this example.

First on the mainland in Mestre then in Venice itself three 'banks for the poor' were opened in 1366. The rights and duties of the Jewish bankers were laid down by contract. Although they were now tolerated as money-lenders and traders they were still second class citizens. The Jews not engaged in bank-

ing were allowed to remain in Venice but they had to wear a sign showing their race. First of all this was a sign on their clothing then a distinctive headgear, first yellow then red.

When Mestre was destroyed by enemy troops in 1509 the Jews sought refuge in Venice and were allowed to stay there for a time. In 1516 the Jewish community, which had greatly increased in numbers, was given its own closed living quarters—the ghetto. Other ethnic groups had formed communities in certain parts of the city but they were able to choose them freely. Only the Jews were forced to move into an out of the way unhealthy area, the sight of the former 'new foundry' *il gheto nouvo*. Since then 'ghetto' means a closed Jewish quarter.

The Ghetto in Venice was ringed with canals, like a moated prison. The gates were locked at night. It was damp and dark and the living space was always too small because the Jewish community multiplied in spite of persecution. With the years the houses grew higher and higher, as far as the foundations permitted. The density of population was three times as high as in the most heavily settled Christian suburbs. Two new ghettos nearby, the *gheto Vecchio* and the *gheto nouvissimo* improved the situation only for a while.

Many Jews left the ghetto during the day and many Christians came in. They visited the three banks, called the red, the yellow and the green banks after the color of their promissary notes. Other Christians visited the Jewish doctors in the ghetto, whose healing arts were highly valued. The Jewish festivals, music and theater were also popular. Jews in the ghetto wore splendid clothing and rich jewelry—the only way of showing their wealth for those who were not allowed to own houses and land.

The Jewish community was held together by close religious, social and economic ties. There were many charitable organizations caring for every emergency and free education for children was already taken for granted in an age in which only a few of the Jews' Christian contemporaries could read and write. The ghetto also contained one of the most important centers in Europe for printing of Jewish books.

The elected representatives of the ghetto had limited powers of self government; they kept carefully to their contract with the Venetian state, collected taxes, settled legal problems and examined new immigrants. The Jews of three nations were recognized by Venice: the **Tedeschi** from Germany, the **Levantini** from the Orient, and the **Ponentini** from Spain and Portugal. These groups lived quite separately and used their own rituals in their own synagogues.

While Venice's greatness declined during the 16th and 17th centuries the Jewish community enjoyed its highest development. The main source of their wealth was the lively trade with the

Jews of the Levant, but they also dealt in second hand goods and clothing. Just in this phase of their economic decline Venice found the Jews very useful, consumers and employers, thus benefitting the people.

The fall of Venice affected the Jews; in 1655 there were still almost 5000 people in the ghetto, a century later only 1500. They were poor in numbers and in capital; their tax burden led to bankruptcy. Their long agony was ended in 1797 with the Napoleonic invasion. At last the ghetto gates were flung open: it seemed that even Jews could share Liberty, Equality and Fraternity. This was a brief dream quickly interrupted by the restoration of the Austrian government. But times had indeed changed and Jews were among the most passionate upholders of the revolutionary aims of 1848—Daniele Manin was their hero. They became full citizens in 1866, when Venice became part of the Kingdom of Italy.

They found no peace, however, in the 20th century: a bronze relief in the Campo di Ghetto Nuovo recalls the fascist holocaust in which 200 Venetian Jews lost their lives. Today there are about 650 persons in the Jewish community in Venice but only a few live in the former ghetto.

The synagogues are as unobtrusive as the ghetto itself, usually hidden away behind the facades of the house, mostly on the second floor as a protection against flood. Outwardly so modest their interiors are extravagantly rich, reflecting the enormous wealth once possessed by the Jews of Venice. The five synagogues in the ghetto—the Italian, the Spanish, the Levantine, the Great German Synagogue and that of the Family Canton—were admired by Christian visitors.

For their last journey the dead of the ghetto were rowed down the Canale degli Ebrei to the Lido. Here is the small outcast cemetery where, among important scholars, there lies the poet Sarah, Coppio Sullam, famed beyond Venice.

ISLANDS IN THE LAGOON

Would you like to search for traces of a once rich and powerful city which disappeared mysteriously over 500 years ago? Would you like to have lunch at a picturesque country inn? Or would you like to enjoy 'Italian life' on a real fisherman's island? Perhaps you're thrilled by a romantic boat trip at night through the softly lit waterways, back to Venice.

When, after all the beautiful but hectic exploration of Venice, you think you would like some of these experiences too, then take an excursion to the islands in the lagoon: **Murano**, **Torcello** and **Burano**. If you have time take two days for this trip. If you have only one day to explore the lagoon…well, a great deal can be done in a day!

From the **Fondamenta Nouve**, the ferries of Line 12 follow the course Murano-Torcello-Burano all day long until late at night. On these larger ships, which can take 45 minutes to reach Burano, the journey, in fine weather, is already a treat.

A word about the lagoon: it is the size of Lake Constance, or one could say, one hundredth of the size of Lake Michigan. Venice is situated on almost 200 islands, some of them uninhabited, to be reached only by private motorboat. Lord Bryon, who spent quite a lot of time in Venice, swam non-stop across the lagoon in 1812, to the Lido. Visitors are advised not to repeat this venture because of the polluted state of the water.

Murano

From the Fondamenta Nuova it is ten minutes by ship to Murano. On the way you pass the cemetery island, San **The lagoon.**

THE ART OF THE GLASS BLOWERS

Visitors who have the time to make a side trip to Murano find a world all to itself. From the 13th to the 18th century this island was the center of European glass work. A glance at the graceful shimmering objects in the glass museum of the Murano shows the high artistry of the glass blowers of other days and their mastery of the craft. Some of the vessels are like the finest lace; others are covered with a network of white threads in beautiful patterns. There we see a chalice, covered with sparks of shining gold, which gleams mysteriously like dark brocade.

This Aventurine glass was an invention of the Venetian glass maker Briani and in the 17th and 18th century the secrets of its manufacture were closely protected. The glittering effect came from tiny particles of copper set into the molten glass. The most beautiful and subtle creation of the Murano glass makers' art is the netted or *reticelli* glassware. White glass rods are melted and formed into fantastic ornaments by constant twisting and cooling. The antique art of the mille-fiori glass was rediscovered in Murano. It took 18 years before the complicated technique was mastered again.

Venetian Mirrors

For a long time the making of mirrors was a monopoly of the Venetians. Already in the 14th century a man named Muzio de Murano made the discovery that a reflecting surface could be obtained when a glass sheet is coated with a solution of tin and mercury. Venetian mirrors with their magnificent glass frames were admired throughout Europe and the glass makers attempted to guard the secrets of their craft. It was forbidden on pain of death for the glass makers to leave Murano. On the other hand glass makers were allowed to marry into patrician families. But neither threats nor rewards could prevent a few from escaping. It is known that in the 17th century several glass makers went to the court of Louis XIV where, after giving up their secrets, they were poisoned.

Glass making first began in Venice in the 13th century. At that time the Republic of St. Mark stormed Constantinople and won as part of its booty precious Islamic and Byzantine glassware and also craftsmen who built up a local glass industry. In 1291 the Venetian government used a fire in the city as an excuse to move several glass workshops to safety on the island of Murano. This was really an attempt to keep closer control of the flourishing industry which was one of the pillars of the Venetian economy. From this period come

the first craft guild regulations which were set down in special books. An especially beautiful example of one of these books is the *Mariegola*, a folio from 1447, encased in silver and velvet, which is today in the **Museo Correr**.

Glass was not only fascinating to the people of the renaissance. Since the middle of the 3rd century B.C. there was glass making in Babylon and later in Egypt and Rome. The main ingredients of glass, quartz sand, lime and soda, were heated to 900 degrees and then formed into small vessels around a kernel of clay.

At the beginning of the Christian era the use of the glass blower's pipe, which was a metal tube about a yard long, was discovered and made it possible to create larger vessels. The ingredients were heated to a glowing red mass at 1400 degrees centigrade and blown to the desired shape as it cooled. Various colors were obtained by the addition of metal oxides. At first glassware was regarded as jewelry and was made to resemble precious stones.

The special character of Murano glass was that, thanks to the best raw materials from the Orient, a very light-weight, thin-walled and unspotted glass could be blown. The purity and clarity of the glass recalled rock crystal, so that colorless glass since the 16th century has been called *cristallo*. The variety and refinement of the Murano technique were unique in Europe at this time: the chalices and the violins and organs of glass made Murano famous.

The glass makers of Murano were also skilled in the art of designing and making beautiful stained glass windows for churches. Although many examples of the stained glass of the middle ages and the renaissance have survived in England and in France not many examples have survived in Italy over the centuries. One genuine window from the 15th century can still be seen in the church of San Zanipolo (SS Giovanni e Paolo) in the right hand transept. The two patrons of the church, St. John and St. Paul—not the better known saints from the New Testament but their namesakes, two Roman matyrs—are shown flanked by St. George and St. Theodor.

The decline of the Venetian art of glass making began with the industrial revolution in the 19th century. The old craft was almost lost but thanks to the initiative of the Brothers Teso it was revived. Today there are about 100 glass hearths employing 6000 workers on Murano. Sixty percent of the objets d'art produced are for export and bear witness to the fact that the quality of Venetian glass is as high today as it has been for hundreds of years.

Michele settled in the 13th century by Camalduline monks. Whoever wishes to visit this island must take line 5 which makes regular journeys to it: it is not on the route of the larger ferries. The cemetery, where Ezra Pound, Igor Stravinsky and Serge Diaghilev are buried, is worth seeing: the chapel is one of the earliest renaissance buildings in Venice.

Whoever hears of the name Murano thinks at once of the famous glass. There was already a flourishing community of glass blowers here at the end of the 13th century, with more than 30,000 inhabitants. This traditional craft is still practised but most of the things produced are not very original and too much influenced by the tourist trade. The many glass workshops on Murano are (free of charge) open to visitors and it is very interesting to see the glass-blowers at work. These displays of glass-blowing are supposed to encourage tourists to buy souvenirs of the glass work. It is better to be patient and look for some more tasteful pieces in the shops of Venice…lamps for example.

Those who wish to see what was made in the good old days should visit the **Museo Vetrario** (the Glass Museum) on the Canale di Donato. On the way lies the Church of **San Pietro Martire**, from the 14th century, which is worth a side trip. It has a beautiful Madonna from 1488, an Assumption from the Bellini workshop and two paintings by Veronese.

The Museo Vetrario contains the most important collection of glass-blowing work from antique times to the present day. Examples of Roman work are on the lower floor and Venetian work on the upper floor. Most of the exhibits are from the 16th and 17th centuries, the greatest epoch in Murano: the beautiful renaissance glass is

Carnival in Murano.

especially worth seeing.

After the glass museum we continue on to the nearby **Campo SS Maria e Donato** to visit the church of the same name. It is in Venetian-Byzantine style and was probably built in the 7th century. It is one of the oldest buildings in the lagoon, once the cathedral of the Bishops of Torcello, and one of the most beautiful buildings in the whole of Venice. The church contains relics of St. Donatus which were brought to Venice from Sicily. A feature of the interior is the fine mosaic floor from the 12th century, which was restored with the help of a private American initiative, at the beginning of the seventies. There is also a gilded icon of St. Donatus in relief and frescoes from the school of Vivarini.

Murano, with its broad canals, looks like a smaller edition of Venice and it is difficult to imagine that the island was once full of flourishing gardens. It was a retreat for the great humanists of the renaissance Pietro Bembo, Tasso and Aretino, exiled at various times from Florence. The first botanical garden in Italy was laid out on the island of Murano and many noble Venetians had their villas here.

On the way to the wharf visitors can go to the old taverns on the Fondamenta dei Vetrai for a relaxing glass of wine or a coffee before traveling on to Torcello.

Torcello

The journey from Murano to Torcello takes 25 minutes. The Campanile of the medieval cathedral of Torcello can be seen for a long way as if it floats above the calm water. Torcello is a swampy green island, not very prepossessing. At the same time it gives visitors a strong impression of the original landscape of the lagoon.

The sight of this wild uninhibited

A canal in Murano.

looking island makes it difficult to imagine that it was for hundreds of years a rich and powerful trading city, with a large population and many palaces, churches and monasteries, the place where Venice had her origins as world power.

The history of Torcello began in the 7th century with the destruction of the towns of the Veneti on the mainland by the Lombards. The Veneti, led by their Bishop, fled to this inhospitable island and founded the town of Torcello in the year 639. Little by little the inhabitants built Torcello into the most important port of the Veneti. Its heyday was between the 9th and the 12th centuries and it was also a merchant from this island who 'liberated' the remains of St. Mark from the so-called heathen in 827 and brought them to Venice.

Already in the 15th century Torcello was depopulated, sinking back into its marshes. It is still not clear how this happened—war was not the reason. One of the many legends declared that it was the small river Sile which caused the overthrow of the city. Possibly a string of natural disasters caused the disappearance of Torcello. Perhaps it is this mystery that gave Torcello a unique charm. Only two palaces now remain, as well as the Cathedral, **Santa Maria Assunta** and the little church of **Santa Fosca.**

Although many tourists visit the island Torcello never lost its atmosphere of stillness and loneliness. Here and there among the green thickets there are still a few solitary houses: about 100 people live on Torcello, mostly farmers or innkeepers.

Santa Maria Assunta

The cathedral was begun in 639 but reached its present form in the 11th century. The foundations of the former baptistry can be seen from the cathedral and we go past them into the 14th-15th

century entrance hall. After paying a small fee visitors go into the cathedral on the right hand side of the nave. At once we see the wonderful mosaics decorating the apse and the rear wall. These mosaics are the art treasure of Torcello, without parallel in any other Venetian church.

The condition and the dates of origin of the mosaics vary greatly. The oldest mosaics from the 7th century are found in the vault of the apse and in the side chapel. They show four angels bearing a wreathed medallion showing the Lamb of God. The lower mosaics come from the 12th century and it depicts the saints Ambrosius, Augustine, Martin and Gregory.

The Madonna with child from the 13th century in the upper part of the apse is very beautiful and moving. Opposite the Madonna stands a wonderful Byzantine mosaic—a picture of the *Last Judgment* from the 12th-13th century. In contrast to other works in this style which often have a static look this mosaic is full of life. Other treasures in the church are the choir stalls and a bishop's chair from the 11th century.

Whoever has the chance to visit Torcello more than once should not miss one of the concerts in the cathedral. Right next to the Cathedral stands the small church of Santa Fosca, simple and beautiful, named for a martyr from Ravenna. It is a romanesque building from the 11th-12th centuries and impressive through its harmonious blend of different architectural elements.

The **Museo dell' Estuario** or Museum of the Lagoon contains many interesting archaeological finds from the earliest days of Venetian history. There are antique Roman statues and grave shrines as well as fragments and inscriptions from Altinum and the ancient sites of the lagoons. We can only see homely domestic articles from palace kitchens and from farmhouses together with farm implements and other artifacts illustrating the long history of Torcello. Of particular interest are the hellenistic lamps and sculpture. In the adjoining Palazzo del Podestà there are fine examples of the goldsmith's art, made after byzantine models, some of the most beautiful examples of this art from the 11th-12th centuries. A fragment of the *Pala d' Argento* the silver altarpiece of the Cathedral of Torcello still remains.

Now, since our cultural tour is over, we deserve a pleasant lunch. In good weather one should not miss a visit to the **Villa Seicento** diagonally opposite the cathedral. The villa, a handsome country inn, situated right on a canal, invites the visitor to sit under the awnings in the large garden. The food is good and reasonably priced, the host and his wife are extremely nice people who know how to give their restaurant a pleasant friendly atmosphere.

Before making the short journey to Burano, only five minutes away, it is worth making the short trip to the **Locando Cipriano**. The only hotel on the island of Torcello is famous among other things for its high prices. Famous guests who came to the island seeking a little peace and quiet include Queen Elizabeth II of England and Winston Churchill. Ernest Hemingway—a great lover of Venice—often stayed here and greatly admired the wild and lonely landscape of Torcello.

Burano

After the quiet austerity of Torcello Burano gives the visitor a colorful and lively welcome. The bell tower leans over the island at a dangerous angle but nobody seems to worry.

Burano is one of the most beautiful islands in the lagoon—perhaps the most beautiful of all. The narrow alleys,

The Cathedral of Torcello.

with their houses painted in rainbow colors, are criss-crossed by little canals and their bridges. In spite of tourism Burano is still a genuine idyllic fishing village, not very rich in art history but full of interest for those who like to see 'real Italian life'.

The best time for a visit is the late afternoon with the tourist rush, it begins at 11 o'clock in the morning when the arrival of the ships from Venice begins to slacken off. Before eleven and after seventeen hours the island belongs to the *Buranelli*, as the inhabitants are called. The few tourists still about are simply part of the picture of life on Burano. There is no hotel on Burano and the community had decided to keep things this way. However, there are a few simple rooms to rent over a Trattoria in the main street.

The island is teeming with life. Fishing and cargo boats ply the narrow canals or lie at anchor. In front of the cafés there is a colorful mixture of locals and tourists; on the main shopping street children, women and men all talk cheerfully to each other. Many painters can be seen sitting before their easels along the canal.

About 5000 people live on Burano. Many of them work as fishermen in Venice, from the Lido, or as glass workers in the factories of Murano.

In summer on June 21, there is a festival for the patron saint of Burano whose relics lie in the church of San Martino. First there is a procession to this church followed by the blessing of the fishing boats, a colorful ceremony. All the houses on the island are decorated for the occasion.

Embroidered lace was for Burano what glass was for Murano. Burano lace was once famous and in great demand. In the 15th and 16th centuries this precious lace became one of the most important sources of income for **Burano.**

the island. Under Louis XIV the importation of Burano lace into France was prohibited and its manufacture began in France with immigrant workers from Burano.

These laces were not made with bobbins but stitched with needle and thread. There were once many lace schools in Burano where young girls endanger their sight by stitching these laces for very low wages. A lace school can be seen in the **Palazzo del Podestà** on the Piazza Galuppi. This costly art of lace stitching is still also practised by the old women of the district who can be seen sitting at their work in front of their shops in the peaceful side streets. Today lace is sold in many shops but it is factory made lace of rather doubtful quality. Real Burano lace would be almost priceless.

Burano is mainly a place to wander about comfortably and enjoy the local life and color. Restaurants, cafés and bars invite us to while away the time. The restaurant **Da Romano** on the Piazza Galuppi, is highly recommended. It is an old traditional restaurant with a pretty interior lit by glass lamps and decorated with paintings in every style. The atmosphere is reminiscent of a dance-hall of the twenties.

The food is excellent—try the specialty of the house: *Riso Nero*, a risotto with black squid sauce. In the evenings one can eat in the open air on the terrace and see the natives of Burano taking their nightly stroll.

Two even quieter restaurants are the **Da Forner** and the **Gatto Nero**, both on peaceful side streets directly on the canal; they both serve good food.

A happy evening can be rounded off by a romantic boat trip through the darkness. We sit on the open deck of the ship, take in the fresh air and sail back to Venice through waterways marked with golden lanterns.

Evening on the lagoon.

THE FILM FESTIVAL AT THE LIDO

The Venice Film Festival is world famous and is one of the most important of its kind, together with the Festival at Cannes and the Academy Awards in America. The film industry is an important part of our mass media society. In spite of hard marketing the film medium has never lost its charisma. A world of celluloid dreams. A colorful world of sophistication, adventure, hope, starlets, tough guys and tons of money. Everyone dreams of being in a movie or at least taking part in the making of a motion picture.

The sensitive and imaginative Italians were, not by chance, among the first to discover film as a new art form. The first film festival in the world opened, not by chance, in Venice, on August 6, 1932. One of the most beautiful spots in the city on the lagoon had been chosen for this occasion: the **Lido**. This long strip of land, between the city of Venice and the waters of the Adriatic, is the site of the most elegant hotels (Excelsior, Hotel des Bains) and has a lovely bathing beach as well as a small airfield.

There is a touch of unreality about the Lido, as there is about Venice itself, and it has often been used as a film background. The famous Visconti filming of Thomas Mann's *Death in Venice*, starring Dirk Bogarde, was set in the Hotel des Bains.

The powerful hotel owners of the city founded an association in 1908, the Societá dei Grande Alberghi (C.I.G.A.). The happy combination of many interests, both financial and cultural, resulted in the opening of the first film festival on the terrace of the Excelsior Hotel, in the presence of illustrious guests from all over the world in the summer of 1932. Forty films from nine countries were shown, no prizes were presented.

Stars of the Film Festival

The undisputed darlings of the public were the stars Helen Hayes and Fredric March. Films of high caliber such as Alessandro Blassetti's documentary *Assisi*, Ruben Mamoulian's *Dr. Jekyll and Mr. Hyde* and Leontinė Sagan's *Mädchen in Uniform* contributed to the unexpected success of this new manifestation, the film festival. The gentlemen from the Biennale decided at once that it should be a regular event.

The second festival in 1939 exceeded everyone's hopes. Seventeen nations accepted the invitation to take part: 40 feature films and 40 short films were shown. This time prizes were awarded to directors, script writers, actors and actresses, cameramen and composers of film music. Robert Flaherty won the Mussolini Cup for *Man of Aran*, as did the Italian Guido Brig-

none for *Teresa Confalionieri*. The prize for the best actress went to Katherine Hepburn for her performance in *Little Women* an attractive film version of Louisa M. Alcott's famous girls' story.

In 1937 the Film Festival Hall was built with the financial support of the hotel association C.I.G.A. and it still houses the festival. The generous financial backing of the hoteliers brought its own rewards because the international folk from the film branch became regular hotel guests on the Lido. Filmstars and producers attracted the film fans to Venice—who wouldn't take the chance to see the heroes and heroines of the silver screen in the flesh? The fans believe that it is always worth the trip, yesterday and today.

In the year 1935 Clarence Brown's production of *Anna Karenina*, with Greta Garbo, won the film prize and an Austrian actress, Paula Wessely, won the award as best actress for her role in the film *Episode*. Three years before the outbreak of the Second World War the titles of the winning films seemed to give warning of its approach. These were productions such as the socially critical *Der Weg der Helden*, the documentary *Jugend der Welt* (Youth of the World) and the Italian film *The White Squadron*. A noted director of this era was Leni Riefenstahl, a gifted film-maker whose work was compromised by her association with the Nazi hierarchy. In this year, 1936, there were fewer outstanding films but some light entertainment including *Der Kaisser von Kalifornien* with Luis Trenker, a young mountaineer popular in Europe for his climbing adventures.

The popular film medium has always been used for educational films in the field of science and technology and for political propaganda. In 1937 the German film maker Walter Ruttmann received a prize for *Mannesmann* a documentary about heavy industry. The Venice Film Festival has tried to include documentaries as well as feature films and to provide more than fantasies and dreams.

The Second World War put an end to the festival. The doors of the **Palazzo del Cinema** on the Lido did not open again until 1946 and no prizes were awarded in that year. A year later the Biennale inaugurated a new prize, the *Gran Premio Internazionale di Venezia*. In 1947 it was awarded to the Czech producer Karel Steklys for his film *Sirena*. In 1948 England presented Laurence Olivier's classic *Hamlet*. The film won a prize and so did the actress Jean Simmons for her role as Ophelia.

This post-war period was a time of brilliant artistic development for the Italian film industry.

These were the years of the great neo-realist Italian films *Bicycle Thieves* from Di Sica and *Open City* from Rossellini, followed by the rise of Visconti and Fellini. Film fans all over the world were dazzled by the beauty of Italian stars such as Sophia Loren and Gina Lollobrigida.

Prestigious Awards

Since the beginning of the Biennale art exhibition in 1895 the Biennale has had its own coat of arms showing the golden Lion of St. Mark. In 1949 this noble beast was used as the trophy of the

new directions for film production generally.

At the beginning of the 60s however the famous film forum had altered. Sliek sophistication and commercialism corrupted and controlled the festival. The Italians and others were just discovering film as an art form when it began to be degraded into a piece of merchandise. The protest movement of the wild 60s had its influence on the festival. Cinema lovers from all over the world streamed into Venice and engaged in fiery all-night discussions over the function of film in contemporary culture. The festival went on at the Lido almost as planned but with no awards.

Film Festival. The prize—*Premio Leone di San Marco*—is a symbolic rival of the Oscar and is almost as highly valued in the film world.

In the year 1956 there was an important alteration in the organization of the festival. So far every country had been able to choose which of its films would compete but from now on the international commission of experts decided which films could enter the competition. The new selection procedure led to a marked improvement in the quality of the films shown at the festival. The character of the festival was now truly international and it helped to give new standards and

Above, young travelers waiting on wharf.

Something good remains from those exciting days namely the spread of the film festival to the city itself. For the first time in the 60s a great fan festival was held on the Campo Santa Margherita; today it has become a tradition to hold special events on all the larger squares of Venice during the 10 days of the festival.

As the years passed the mood of the festival was mellowed. In 1980 the Golden Lion of St. Mark was awarded again, this time without protest. The high quality of the prize-winning films—*Atlantic City* from Louis Malle, *Gloria* from John Cassavetes, and Margarethe von Trotta's film *Die Bleierne Zeit*—proves that the Film Festival of Venice is once again of international standard.

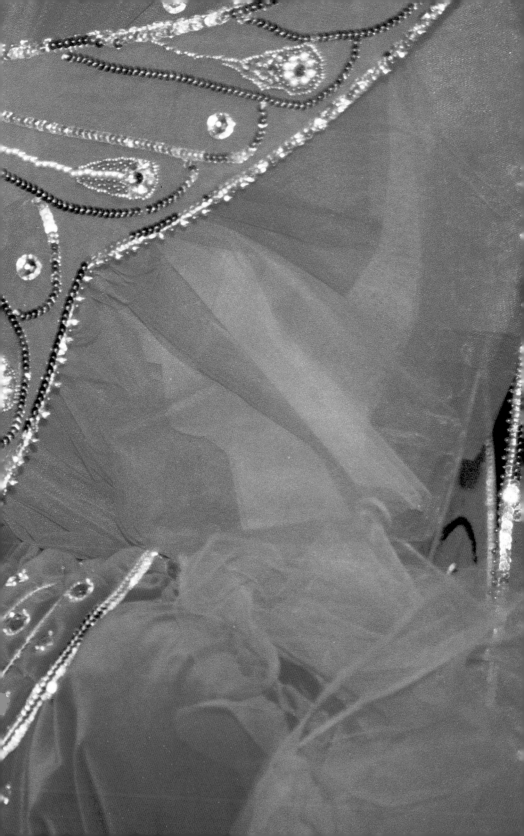

VENETIAN MASQUERADE

"At the Venetian festivals the processions, not on land but on water, were marvelous in their fantastic splendor...In the 16th century the nobility were divided into corporations with a view to these festivals, whose most noteworthy feature was some extraordinary machine placed on a ship. So, for instance, in 1541, at the festival of the 'Sempiterni', a round 'universe' floated along the Grand Canal and a splendid ball was given inside it. The Carnival, too, in this city was famous for its dances, processions and exhibitions of every kind. The Square of St. Mark was found to give space enough not only for tournaments, but for 'Trionfi' similar to those common on the mainland."
—Jacob Burckhardt

One used to visit Venice in February to enjoy the quiet melancholy of the city in its winter sleep, wreathed in mists. For several years now the Carnival has broken in upon this pleasant other-worldly mood. Every year for ten days the quiet and leisurely winter days are changed into a time of over-flowing gaiety and colorful masquerade.

When Napoleon conquered Venice in 1707 the Carnival went the way of the Venetian Republic. Now it has been reawakened. It began with the Theater Festival during the thirties: there were already performances on the Piazza San Marco, in the courtyard of the Doge's Palace and on the Lido.

In 1980 Venice went a step further: the whole city was declared to be a stage, the distance between the audience and the actors vanished and everyone was invited to wear a mask. The Theater Carnival became a festival of the Venetians for Venetians, with playful processions and happenings every-where, an act of homage to 18th-century Venice and its splendid costume festival.

The *Compagnie della Calza* played an important part in this rebirth of the carnival.

Previous pages: masks. Left, bananas à la Venezia. Above, a mysterious beauty.

This group of carnival societies, including the *Antichi* and the *Nuove Cortese*, which had existed since the renaissance, gained their name from the custom of wearing a colored sign on the right stocking (Italian: *calza*). Since the 15th century the organization of the carnival was in their hands until Doge Gritti passed it to the government in the middle of the 16th century. The companies withdrew into *Ridotti*, private clubs where, in the exclusive world of the palaces, their members preserved the old customs of the carnival until the present day.

The special excitement of the 'feast of fools' in Venice lies in the character of the city itself: the marvelous palaces, the Piazza San Marco with the gondola mooring place and the elegant campanile—no theater could provide a finer setting for such a festival. One doesn't find commercialized artificial merry-making, with ready made costumes and papier maché noses.

The Venetian carnival is pure love of dressing up; the costumes are lovingly prepared for weeks, with talent and fantasy.

227

Everyone has the chance to put on a show and everyone has a sympathetic audience. The *Antichi* and the *Nuove Cortese* also give masked balls, theater performances, sketches, literary readings, interspersed with classical music and dance, so that every year the Serenissima wakes to life again in a whirl of colors, masks and costumes. For ten days *Sior Maschera* rules Venice and her citizens and leaves behind a wistful memory of a time filled with possibilities beyond the world of every day.

Carnival in Venice—what an alluring

picture! For a moment one can realize that ancient desire to slip into a different skin, to change, to become another person. The costumes are so perfect that all these masks seem to take on a life of their own—perhaps the person behind the mask does not exist any more. Does this love of disguise express a longing to loosen the ties that bind us to a single personality, a longing for new experiences? We feel the power of ancient pagan festivals which expressed the need for change, the striving for development and perfection—perhaps this is the secret of the Venetian carnival today.

Carne Vale: Farewell to Meat

The Carnival contains a mixture of pagan and Christian elements. Folk festivals celebrated in the middle of winter go back at least 3000 years before the Christian era and are linked with the Winter Solstice and the fertility gods. The winter must be overcome and the sun be persuaded to return—and that can only be done by life in its most vital and concentrated form. So in Rome on December 17, the fertility festival of the Saturnalia was celebrated with a free and easy masquer-

ade in which even the slaves took part.

Christendom gave the carnival new significance: the words *carne vale*, Latin for 'farewell to meat', meant abstinence from the pleasures of the flesh and a redirection towards things spiritual. Carnival was the last chance for gaiety and revelry before Lent, the period of fasting which was a preparation for Easter. In France during the Middle Ages it was the custom to have a parade of decorated floats accompanied by clowns and jesters whose tricks and games lessened the general fear of death and decay.

Throughout Italy, especially in Naples

and Venice, extravagant masked balls were the fashion. Today Carnival is celebrated mainly in countries with a strong Roman Catholic tradition: Italy, Spain, France, parts of Germany and Switzerland, South America, Mexico, Haiti.

From the beginning Carnival encouraged the breaking of social rules. It was and is the expression of 'a world turned upside down', a time when the mask gives everyone the chance to question authority or make 'the Establishment' ridiculous without fear of punishment.

as the Egg Game (*Giuoco dell Uovo*) in which young men dressed as devils stood outside the houses of their ladies and pelted them with egg shells filled with perfume. Rope dancers, acrobats and fire eaters showed their skills on the Piazza and at the carnival in the year 1751 everyone could admire a rhinoceros.

The high points of the carnival are the *Giovedi Grasso* and the *Martedo Grasso*, the Thursday and the Tuesday before Ash Wednesday. On both these days the traditional festival was celebrated with all its old

Festival Traditions

The history of the Serenissima is always present in its carnival. Political and military events, town rivalries and defeats are shown in the festival traditions.

In the 12th century young men covered in fur and decorated with twigs went through the city with musical instruments serenading their sweethearts. Later this became known

Left, monks at the carnival? Right, carnival. Above, children's carnival.

customs. The 'volo del Turco', the flight of the Turk, recalled the conquest of Aquileia in 1162, when the Patriarch of the town was captured with 12 of his priests and ransomed for 12 pigs and a bull. After this, at the carnival 12 pigs were flung down from the campanile while a bull was beheaded. The 'flight of the Turk' is a less cruel survival of this old custom in which an acrobat slides down a rope from the bell-tower and gives the Doge a bunch of flowers. The first acrobat to make this flight was a Turk, hence the name of this festival.

Another event was the Battle of the

Bridges which harked back to an old rivalry between the islanders of Jesolo and Eraclea. At the *Festa dei Tori* bulls were chased in the squares of Venice, as in the old Roman custom of animal baiting. On the last days of the Carnival the *Forze D'Ercole* (strength of Hercules) was a display of huge pyramids of men and boys supported by the local strongmen. The evening ended with fireworks.

Right at the end of the festival on *Martedo Grasso*, the Tuesday before Ash Wednesday, all Venetians gather for an orgiastic masked ball on the Piazza San Marco until

ordinary citizens. The *volto*, the white half-mask covered the face and for a finishing touch there was a black three-cornered hat with white feathers. During the carnival everyone was addressed as "Sior Maschera"; there were no more differences in rank or of sex. The mask made everyone equal.

Besides this costume the *Commedia dell' Arte* characters joined the carnival. Today typical Venetian carnival masks can be bought as souvenirs everywhere in the city.

There are the classic pair of servants *Arlecchino* and *Brighella*. Both these fellows

midnight when the fasting bell would ring out from the campanile which signaled everyone to forgo the joys of carnival.

Sior Maschera

The classic costume of the 17th and 18th centuries was the *maschera nobile*, the fine masks for ladies and gentlemen. The head was covered with *bautá*, a black cloth that covered the back of the head and hung down to the shoulders, while over the masker's clothes a short cloak (*tabarro*) was worn, in black silk for the nobility, in red or grey for

come originally from Bergamo and speak the local dialect. A typical feature of the popular extempore comedy was that every character spoke in a special regional dialect. So *Arlecchino* and *Brighella* spoke Bergamask, *Pantalone*, Venetian, and the *Dottore* Bolognese dialect. The comedy focused on the contrast of many dialects and in the funny situations that arose as a result of misunderstood words.

The costume of the merry *Arlecchino* is made of many scraps of material stitched together, a sign of his poverty. Later this became his red, orange and green suit of lozenge shaped patches. *Arlecchino* is the servant of the miserly old skinflint *Pantalone*, from Venice. The name comes from his long black trousers (Italian: *pantaloni*) with which he wears a black cloak and red stockings. A little brown mask with a bristling moustache and a long crooked nose completes the costume.

The foil to the *Pantalone* is the self-important *Dottore*. He is a great scholar and thinks he knows all there is to know, so his trademark is a constant stream of talk—no-one else can get a word in edgewise. The *Dottore*

ing up some intrigue. The bilious green color of his mask shows his bitter nature and so does his broken nose and ugly face. He wears a kind of white livery, with green diagonal stripes, for he is one of *Pantalone's* servants.

There are many other characters besides, often developed from these main types. For example the maid servant *Columbina*, *Arlecchino's* female partner, and *Pulcinella*, the lovable clown, popular with children. In England he has turned into Mr. Punch of the popular seaside *Punch and Judy* puppet show, while in Germany he has become the

wears the robes of a Bolognese lawyers: black knee breeches, stockings and a wide cloak, with a white shirt and a white ruff, crowned with a scholar's hat. His black half-mask has a bumpy forehead and nose and recalls a learned disputation. One of the *Dottore's* opponents, driven mad by his incessant talking, threw an ink well in his face and the black stain can still be seen. *Brighella*, the wily servant, is always thinking up some intrigue.

Left, The Lagoon: an original costume. Above, the Orient in Venice.

jolly puppet *Kasper*. Other characters are seen in France: *Arlecchino*, *Truffaldino*, *Tantaglia*, *Capitano*—the list is endless.

A Masquerade in 'the finest drawing room in Europe'

This was Napoleon's rather overworked expression for the Piazza San Marco. Every year the carnival is opened here in the presence of thousands of masqueraders. The revived carnival has a new theme or motto every year. One year it might be "New York in Venice", the next "Lights of Venice and the Orient". During the ten days spectacle masqueraders come tumbling out of every alley; the sound of renaissance and baroque music is heard everywhere. Pantomimes and comedy numbers are put on everywhere and operettas, concerts and literary readings are presented in Venice's famous theaters and on the squares of the city. Masked balls, fireworks and historical happenings are produced by the *Compagnie della Calza*, one colorful event follows another and every Masker tries to attract the attention of the merry throng.

The masks of the Carnival are ageless, as we can see. Every year since the great festival was revived there is a certain select group of Venetians and their international guests who appear in Tarocco costume. These famous Tarot cards, used for fortune-telling, are believed to have reached Europe from the East, through Venice. Now we see maskers dressed as Kings and Queens of Cups, Batons, Swords and Coins, masked in gold and silver, their rich robes worked with cabalistic signs in primary colors. The number of this mysterious group of merry-makers, glimpsed on a moonlit terrace,

threading the alleyways or crossing the Piazza, never seem to grow less.

The elegant costumes of the 18th century, the *Maschera nobile* and the *Commedia dell' Arte* masks are not the only ones to be seen: there we see a perfect reconstruction of the death mask of Tuntankahmen: everything is correct from the blue and gold stripes of the Pharoah's headdress to his pectoral and the vulture and cobra on his brow; even his face is pure gold.

Ahead there dances a bunch of laughing Marguerite daisies. The four have made their bodies into stalks, with long green robes while their yellow faces are framed by rows of giant white petals which nod gently as they walk. Venetians love to go in groups to the carnival, all wearing the same masks and costumes.

Masked Feelings

There is another mask from the floral kingdom on the Rialto bridge—his face…or is it her face?…has been changed into a poison green leaf, its upturned ends like tongues of flame, an effect intensified by the glowing red mouth and the dark leaf veins. It is really more than just an original costume—one thinks of Nature Spirits, of a divine power spreading through the whole of the natural world.

Another Mask interrupts my fantasy; I almost collide with a creature in a sunny yellow robe, with the mask of a laughing face, laughing so heartily that no-one can help laughing too. And how funny this other mask is, a creature with his head between his shoulders, shaking with laughter all the time. His hands are clasped helplessly, his red-rimmed eyes so filled with tears of laughter that they hang down at the corners. What a wonderful idea? It reminds us that joy and laughter belong to the carnival; this was how the people of other days conquered their fears of death, darkness and cold. For just a short time they laughed their fears away.

Left, "Sior Maschera". Right, Turandot…a man?

LA TRIBUNA ILLUSTRATA
della Domenica

ABBONAMENTI

Nel Regno . . . . Anno L. 5 —
All' Estero . . . . » » 7.50

Il numero cent. 10
(Tiratura: 125,000 copie).

Zinchi dei Fratelli Danesi.

L' INAUGURAZIONE DELL' ESPOSIZIONE DI VENEZIA.
S. A. R. il Duca di Genova e il ministro Baccelli nella Sala della Cupola.

THE BIENNALE

In this old and melancholy city on the lagoon the visitor—fascinated by the unique calm of Venice—may not guess that it is also an important center for modern art. Perhaps Peggy Guggenheim was fascinated too by this contrast when she decided to settle her collection of modern paintings and sculpture in the Palazzo Venier dei Leoni on the Canal Grande, which she purchased in 1949. High points of the collection are works by Max Ernst and Jackson Pollack.

Venice was already at this time a popular meeting place for contemporary artists. For this we have to thank the broad vision of a small elite group of intellectuals who met regularly in the Caffè Florian on the Piazza San Marco and developed the idea of an exhibition of modern art. Riccardo Selvatico—litterateur, poet and mayor of Venice—belonged to this illustrious circle. On the occasion of the silver wedding anniversary of their majesties Umberto I of Italy and his Queen, Margherita of Savoy, the Biennale was inaugurated.

Everyone quickly agreed on the place where this exhibition would be held, namely in the public gardens on the eastern tip of Venice, before the island of St. Helena. Napoleon had the gardens laid out in 1807 by the architect Gianantonio Selva. Valuable buildings had been destroyed to make way for this project. The monastery of Sant' Antonio Abate and also that of Santo Domenico, both from the 14th century, as well as the Sailors' Hospital, Ospedale dei Marinai, founded in 1476 and the church of San Nicolo di Bari were all torn down.

The gardens had never played an important part in the social life of the Venetians. Some visitors to Venice might regard them as a spacious and idyllic public park, to others the Giardini Pubblici were no more than a little patch of green which could not compete with the dazzling beauty of the Piazza San Marco. At any rate the gardens lay there for decades and saw the Austrians come and go until finally the Biennale honored them with its presence.

Everyone was pleased. The old concert chamber was extended to make an exhibition building by the engineer Trevisanto. The painter Mario di Maria created the neo-classical facade of stucco, plaster and wood, which lasted only twenty years because of its perishable materials. This was not a tragedy for the Biennale—alterations, extensions and new buildings were to be a part of its history. The far-reaching building schemes of some well-known architects such as Louis Kahn, could, alas, never be carried out. But this shady story would lead us too deeply into Italian politics which have put an end to so many Biennale projects.

A Scandalous Start

On April 30, 1895 the opening of the Biennale was celebrated in the presence of the royal pair. Over 180 paintings and 100 sculptures from well-known Italian and foreign artists were displayed in the large hall and its nine adjoining rooms. The spectators, with ladies in their long gowns and elegantly clad gentlemen in top hats, strolled through the flower-decked rooms of the **Palazzo dell' Esposizione**.

One did not have to wait long for the first scandal. His eminence Cardinal Guiseppe Sarto, later Pope Pius X, thought that a 'modern' work of art must not injure public morals. His letters of violent protest could not prevent the showing of a work entitled *Il Supremo Convegno* (The Supreme Congress) by Giacommo Grosso. The Italian painter presented in his florid oil painting a crowd of naked women draped in voluptuous attitudes about the flower laden coffin of Don Giovanni. The picture was the success of the year and the 'excellence' of its artistic content brought the painter and his work the first prize, awarded by the public.

This prize was the most prestigious because it came from a public vote. It put in the shade the other prizes from the city of Venice, the members of the assembly, the community and the municipal Savings Bank, who offered 5000 and 10,000 lire. An honorary jury issued personal invitations to foreign and national artists. The Biennale generously paid the costs of transport for these invited artists. A shimmer of hope still remained for those artists who had not been invited to exhibit—they could send work to Venice at their own expense and hope that the jury would be merciful and include it in

1914) are unjustly ridiculed today. The idea of a Biennale was apparently more far-sighted than the actual works of art displayed: historical subjects and the traditional academy painting of the 19th century tended to dominate the exhibition.

Art for Art's Sake

These opening years of the Biennale, however, cannot be compared to the salon exhibitions of former years. It was a time of confrontation and discussion between the

the exhibition.

The Biennale proved to be a great success. About 224,327 visitors were counted and 186 art works to the value of 360,000 lire were sold. The prestige of the Biennale continued to grow and by 1907 the number of visitors had risen to 357,356. By 1976, almost seventy years later, when transport had been revolutionized and when visitors to Venice itself were counted in millions, it had doubled to 692,000, proving perhaps that the public visiting these art shows is a fairly constant number.

The early years of the Biennale (1895-

traditional and the progressive. Society and the artist must both deal with a new reality. Artists experienced the end of centuries of patronage by the aristocracy and the church; society had to come to terms with the possibilities and the limitations of the new industrial age. It was not by chance that the Biennale was instituted at just this time.

Moreover, in this period following the unification of Italy, the Biennale encouraged the development of a national consciousness; artists from every region of Italy could display and compare their works. The confrontation with foreign art helped to increase the flexibility and tolerance of Venice and to give the city a new identity as a lively cultural metropolis within the young Italian nation.

The presence of renowned artists such as James Ensor, Gustav Klimt, Max Liebermann, James Whistler, Auguste Renoir and Franz von Stuck tell us of the high standards of the first years of the Biennale. It is doing the organizers of the new exhibition—a debutante in the European art world—some injustice to criticize them for turning down a Picasso in the year 1910. But at that time

The story of the founding of the Galleria d'Arte Moderna di Venezia illustrates the new spirit of the age. Prince Alberto Giovanelli purchased at the second Biennale in 1897 those pictures which were to fill the ground floor of the new gallery. In 1899 the Duchess Felicita Bevilacqua La Masa left the community her **Palazzo Pesaro** which was used as the Museum of Modern Art.

International Exhbitions

In the following years there was a com-

everyone was turning down Picasso, today things are different.

By the time of the third Biennale in 1899 prizes were no longer awarded; instead the works were purchased for the **Galleria Internazionale d'Arte Moderna di Venezia**. This was a clever move which brought many works right to the door of the gallery. In the years 1928 this practice was stopped. The popular prize-giving was already reinstated in 1903 and continued until 1968.

Left, painting by Coluso. Above, in the German Pavilion.

petitive feeling between the Biennale and the Galleria d'Arte Moderna which began when the 23 year old Nino Barbantini became director of the gallery. Until 1907 the Biennale was responsible for the new museum. The young Barbantini preferred, contrary to the Biennale, artists who had not had any great public success. There was a lively quarrel between Antonio Fradeletto, director of the Biennale at that time and the young Barbantini. The Venetian press had a piquant topic and there was eager discussion in the cafés.

Another problem arose over the years

with lack of space in the Palazzo dell' Exposizione. A clever idea was ready at hand: sections of the Biennale grounds were sold to the nations taking part, who built exhibition pavilions at their own expense. One after another these temples of art were erected until today 27 exhibition buildings stand in the Giardini. The Belgian pavilion was built first in 1907, then followed Hungary, Germany, England, Sweden, Holland, France, Russia, Spain and many others.

With the years a lively discussion sprang up over the function and relevance of the

Biennale for these displays and these locations alter from year to year. The old Salt Magazine and the old Rope Works proved excellent for this purpose and their old walls make a fascinating contrast to the modern works of art.

Designer Pavilions

Some of the pavilions are works of art themselves, designed by famous architects: the Dutch pavilion, for example is a concept from Gerrit Thomas Rietveld. Another

structure of the exhibition. Since it was oriented towards national exhibits it seemed no longer able to do justice to the international development of art. It became very difficult to give the exhibition a suitable overall theme. Although the national pavilions remain to this day the custom of giving the Biennale a theme was also continued, to give the jury members of the guest countries a criterion for their selection.

In addition to this an international jury of experts make the selection for smaller thematic exhibitions. It soon became necessary to find space outside the grounds of the

architectural treasure is the Austrian pavilion designed by Josef Hoffmann. Other pavilions are fascinating examples of folk art which have become a popular part of the history of the Biennale. The visitors can, with a little fantasy, imagine that they have returned to the days of the Great Exhibitions of London and Paris.

Perhaps some visitors will shake their heads doubtfully at some of the art objects

Above, The Biennale buildings in the gardens seen from the water.

and wonder about their meaning. There are always those who would rather return to the times when art was aesthetically "beautiful" and easy to understand. But art is the herald of the Zeitgeist and a debate over art is always rewarding.

The Biennale has not always been able to get together the most important avant-garde art. After the 'learning years' there followed the time of fascism under Mussolini who used the Biennale as an organ of culture propaganda. The number of cultural events in Venice was increased: in 1930 the first music festival was held, then came the film festival in 1932 and the theater festival followed in 1934.

After the Second World War the Biennale was used to make up all those "sins of omission" caused by war and the men in power. Impressionists, Expressionists, Futurists, Fauves, Metaphysical Art, Surrealists, Cubists—everything was to be seen. Solo exhibitions, group shows and retrospectives of 'classic' modern art were presented. Great artists including Henri Matisse, George Braque, Pablo Picasso, Henry Moore, Max Beckmann, Diego Rivera, Alfred Kubin, Vassily Kandinsky, to name only a few, rehabilitated the Biennale.

The Emergence of Pop Art

American art began to attract attention. In the year 1964 the great art prize of the Biennale was awarded to Robert Rauschenberg and thus Pop Art was made acceptable by European standards. Guiseppe Santomaso, a Venetian artist of the first rank, former member of the jury that awarded the prizes, remembers how the French jury members campaigned against an American victory. It seemed to them that France's leading position in the art world was being challenged.

It was also a fact that the Americans had done some campaigning themselves. The best known New York gallery owners Helena Sonnabend and Leo Castelli were the generous patrons of the arts who represented America at the Biennale in 1964. Besides

this the Americans tried to increase the size of their exhibition by using their former embassy as a temporary gallery: Pop Art everywhere was their motto. This strategy was not allowed by the committee but the Americans were allowed to temporarily extend their pavilion in the gardens…a more acceptable arrangement. In any case Robert Rauschenberg did receive the prize and the year 1964 has a special place in the history of the festival as the year in which Pop Art, a most important new development, took its place at the Biennale.

In the year 1968 the Biennale experienced a crisis caused by the student protest movement which had sprung up in America and moved to Europe. There was a strong protest against the bureaucracy in all institutions from Universities to art shows. Students and artists occupied the exhibition grounds. Pictures were taken down or hung upside down. The awarding of prizes was declared to be absurd and it did not take place in the following years. This decision was not without its reasons. The opponents of the prize asked how a work of art could be judged. As with the film festival the protests of the late 60s and early 70s died away. The prize giving was reinstated in 1986 and without protest: times had changed.

Everything seemed to have returned to normal until a fresh breeze blew through Venice. The age of patronage had never died in Venice and now it was Signor Agnelli of the Fiat Motor Company who purchased the fine **Palazzo Grassi**, on the Canal Grande and had it restored for use as an art display center. Ponthus Hilton, former director of the Centre Pompidou in Paris, was chairman of this new handsome center, with a completely free hand. Venice has a valuable new cultural institute and the Biennale definitely has some competition.

The Biennale has now lasted 90 years. The experience and dedication of many highly qualified people have made the great exhibition what it is today. It is to be hoped that there will still be those who are prepared and willing to carry on the work with dignity and responsibility.

IN SEARCH OF BEAUTY

A legend tells us that St. Mark was once shipwrecked upon an island in the lagoon. An angel declared to him that on this spot the most beautiful of all cities would arise and he, Mark, would be its patron saint. In fact the bones of St. Mark were purchased and brought to Venice by a trick 750 years after his death.

The tales surrounding the foundation of Venice seem to have been invented as a cloak for unpleasant facts. What of the literary myths and legends of Venice?

Over the centuries Venice has been gushed over, swamped with admiration and praise. While the traveler in other cities has trouble finding anything at all extraordinary, here everything is far too unique. Venice is the extreme, it is fascinating but it can be overwhelming. The words of Nietsche keep ringing in one's ears: *'The Olympus of Illusion...'* Where is the questionable nature of art and the artist's life better illustrated than in this city which is itself a work of art and at the same time rests upon such a shaky foundation? Originally Venice was built in the midst of the sea as a protection against invaders. Today the city lives from the invading hordes. Causeways for trains and automobiles have been built to make it easier for the invaders to get here. Once they came to admire a rare beauty, seeking unconsciously adventure that only this place could provide. Today they come to be present at a deathbed.

City of Beauty and Decay

Venice insists on playing out an operatic death scene. The last aria has been going on rather too long. The city simply will not have done with it all and sink. Goethe could see plainly in 1786 that its heyday was over. Charles Dickens declared it 'a wreck' (1844); Mark Twain called Venice 'poor and completely insignificant' (1869). To Maupassant in 1885 the city gave the impression of a ruin. Is this the stuff that legends are made of?

Poets, especially in earlier centuries, perceived in Venice the phenomenon of its double nature: it was a heavenly and an earthly city at one and the same time. The heavenly edition was the incarnation of pure beauty in all its aspects, particularly those of art, and it hung like a mirage, ageless, above the earthly city. This earthly Venice equally exciting, was a restless place, full of delusions, traps and temptations.

The proximity of beauty and decay runs like a red thread through the literature. Whoever surrendered to the maze of canals and alleyways saw himself beset by temptations which were unique in the Europe of the day. No wonder that Venice became the playground of the privileged classes in the 18th century. The goings on are described in the *Secret Letters* of Charles de Brosse, in Rousseau's *Confessions* and in Casanova's *Memoirs*.

As it became clear towards the end of the 19th century that Venice was sinking slowly but surely into the sea the city changes into a symbol of the decline of the European bourgeoisie. The connection between beauty and the approach of death, one of western culture's most popular notions, had found new meaning.

D' Annungio's novel *Il Fuoco* (1900) translated as *The Flame of Life* is infused with the philosophy of Nietsche; the theme of decline is played out on the private, the artistic and the political level. In Henry James' novel *The Wings of the Dove* (1902), a young woman with an incurable illness comes to Venice to die. Venice becomes a place of catharsis for all those taking part, no-one leaves the city unaltered. In an earlier story, *The Aspern Papers* (1888) Henry James also used a Venetian setting for a sad tale of deception. In order to obtain a literary treasure an editor befriends the plain niece of a very old woman, once the mistress of a Romantic poet. This deception is echoed in the betrayal of the innocent heiress, Milly Theale, in *The Wings of the Dove*. For Henry James the Serenissima suggested not only death but of love betrayed.

Inspired by Venice

For Hugo von Hofmannsthal his character Andreas is "the geometrical meeting point of strange lines of destiny" but this definition could be used for Venice itself, the setting of the novel fragment. *Andreas or the Allies* (published posthumously 1930) is the story of a progressive loss of identity. The psychological entanglements which developed in the labyrinth of Venice give the impression

Der Tod in Venedig (Death in Venice). Aschenbach—"the embodiment of the artist, inwardly exhausted, ready to be transformed or to be plunged into ruin"—is the representative of a bourgeoisie doomed to the same fate. In the 'ailing city' of Venice he is seized by the love for a young boy.

Mann's story, apparently simple, presents a picture that teems with double meanings and superimposed images. Aschenbach wanders "in search of beauty", but here,

that the city itself has taken a hand in the plot and is influencing the characters. The mirrored face breaks into a myriad refracted images: it is an almost magical portrayal of the world of the unconscious.

It was Thomas Mann, another writer aware of the theories of psycho-analysis, who brought the new myths of Venice permanently into our consciousness in his story

Previous pages: 19th-century travelers arriving in Venice. Above, from Visconti's film version of *Death in Venice*.

ironically, it is not the well-worn and obvious beauty of the city of Venice that he seeks but a child named Tadzio. The confrontation between the 'picturesque' city and the professionally esteemed but emotionally impoverished Aschenbach gives the story its intense effect. Here indeed is an Olympus, a magic mountain of illusion. The creed of the artist breaks down under an unexpected upsurge of human feeling.

In Proust's novel *Albertine Disparue* (translated as The Sweet Cheat Gone) the narrator resists the sinister power of this beautiful city. He has to persuade himself with sober scientific arguments in order to escape the allure of Venice. Here, he says, water is no more than H_2O and marble is only a variety of stone—in this way he resists the city's fatal charm.

Hemingway's novel *Across the River and Into the Trees* appeared in 1950. It tells the love story of a 50-year-old American Colonel suffering from heart disease and a 19-year-old Venetian Contessa; it is one of those rare books in which the characters are irritating to the reader. Colonel Cantwell, the main character, is particularly troublesome

Romantic Venice

It is surprising to see that the cliché of 'romantic' Venice, for lovers and honeymoon couples still exist side by side with the literary legend. The German author, Bernard Vesper, summons up a picture of Venice full of kitsch and sentimental hit-songs in his novel *Die Reise* (published posthumously 1977). Just before reaching the city the traveler in the book takes flight at the sight of the masses of tourists, to protect the image of "his" Venice. An equally harmless Venice is

with his endless description of Venice. The reader, alas, has to fight through all the outpourings of Cantwell, the slavering soldier. "A dreadful book" wrote Gottfried Benn, the German critic, "but it does have beautiful passages. Although all this sex before open windows, with the icy wind whistling through, is not my idea of fun."

Icy winds are whistling through a wintery Venice in Patricia Highsmith's psychological thriller *Those Who Walk Away* (1967). But in Venice, the archetypal city of death, she avoids presenting a conventional murder, with corpse.

described by Henri Pierre Roche in his well known novel *Jules et Jim*. The city is no more than an ideal setting for the private happiness of Kathe and Jim.

Are these images of 'romantic' Venice a feeble reflection of the heavenly city, which at some stage disappeared into the clouds? In any case it is definitely *not* possible to be overwhelmed by Venice. One can enjoy it without sinking into a welter of myth or psychological depths. Some great writers have refused to join the admiring throng. D.H. Lawrence who knew and loved Italy, found the city 'abhorrent'.'

In 1910 the poet Rilke was a voice crying in the wilderness declaring that Venice should not be regarded as a product of mankind's addiction to pleasure but rather, through its successful struggle against nature, as a strong expression of the human will. The literature of Venice, however, written mainly by visitors, resulted long ago in the complete division of the real city from the city of legend. A literature that opposed this development did not exist. Venice, whatever is said to the contrary, was never a literary city. Gozzi, Goldoni and Casanova

Pasinetti, for instance, who lived in Venice at the time when *Der Tod in Venedig* was written can show that Thomas Mann made topographical errors. What use is this when Mann is not attempting to present a life-like picture of the city? However, had the Venetian writer Pestriniero tried to lead the visitor off the beaten path and closer to the 'true reality' of Venice it seems a purely rhetorical undertaking. Already in the 50s Dino Buzzatti, not a Venetian but one who knows the place, declared at the sight of the hordes of tourists that the 'true reality' of the city,

cannot alter this fact. The city, may, because of its own foreseeable destiny, be symbolic of a world in decline for others but for its inhabitants, descendants of those strong-willed predecessors, this can scarcely be the case. A few modern Venetian writers have deliberately attempted to correct the literary picture. They must accept that this attempt to fight against the mythological notions of Venice is going to be about as successful as tilting against windmills.

Left, Mysterious Venice: a funeral gondola. Above, a stone beauty caught in a net.

(Buzzatti called it "the secret Venice") had been lost beyond recall. Della Corte adds a surprising touch: in his opinion Venice no longer exists…it vanished long ago. What we are visiting bears the name of Venice but it is only an empty package, a marketing concept to encourage the sale of all kinds of goods and services. How difficult it is to imagine that Venice, the wonderful nexus of symbols and associations, can simply be a place where one happens to live.

Hotcher, Hemingway's biographer, says that Hemingway used to ponder over why one actually lived in New York when there were cities like Paris and Venice. Colonel Cantwell, traveling through Venice, thinks "I should live here." It remains a hypothetical statement because on the very next day Cantwell dies. Naturally Hemingway never lived in Venice and neither did D' Annunzio; they loved the city but did not want to have anything to do with its 'true reality'. The reasons can only be guessed. Richard Dehmel made a point in his poem Punta della Salute from 1910: to die in Venice? Yes! But to live here—no, never.

One detail of the true reality strikes everybody. Maupassant notes with surprise the lack of an adequate drainage system so that 'inhabitants are forced to sail through their own sewage'. D.H. Lawrence asked a friend who had just been in Venice if the city 'still stank as badly as ever.' In his hotel room Colonel Cantwell addresses the portrait of his Contessa Renata: "You're so damned beautiful that it stinks!" This is Hemingway's typically brash way of helping his hero to get over embarrassing feelings but this expression would surely not have occurred to him in any other city. The miasma of rot and decay that hangs over Venice is the link between the real city and its legend.

Venetian novels after Hemingway do not follow the mythic trails so closely. We are in the age of the inventory and statistics are sometimes more important than symbols. It is still amazing what different temperaments can make of the same place: *Venetian Red* by P.M. Pasinetti, *The Doge* by A. Palazzeschi, *The Red* by Alfred Andersch. Then there is the brief irreverent novel *Valid for Ten Days* by Silvio Toddi which opens playful new perspectives. A really unusual book is *Invisible Cities* by Italo Calvino. It is a collection of imaginary conversations between Marco Polo and Kublai Khan, in which Marco describes fantastic cities. They are all based upon Venice, his home town, and each one begins where the previous one left off. In this vision of every possible kind of city Venice has by no means sunken from view: on the contrary it rises transformed every time. The legend of the city is enriched in a book as inimitable as Venice itself.

It is a paradox: the mythical Venice is difficult for us to grasp through literature alone. It must be approached through real experiences. When one arrives at the city itself it does not matter what one has read. Visitors must experience Venice with their own senses and keep their own standards, accepting both its beauty and its ugliness for what they are.

Look at the climate for instance. Heavy summer air, the stink, the clouds of insects: the storms of autumn and the endless rain, then the winter floods. Reality, more palpable here than elsewhere, comes to grips with the traveler. In spite of all this (or perhaps because of it) we are haunted by associations and pictures from other contexts, which intrude upon our fantasy and take control of our dreams.

Bewildering Venice, the place where we fall up and not down. In the morning we feel a strange unease: did we spend the night over or under the water? One is astonished to find, on first looking out of the window, that the hotel is still anchored on the same shore.

Is the last wave of Tadzio's hand the gesture of the death god or the invitation into a life that poor Achtenbusch has missed? In this city embraced by the sea we realize for the first time that the answer to this question of life and death is a kind of decision. The sea contains all possible worlds. All myths end in the sea, blend into one another and rise again, transformed, out of the depths.

Myths and legends which arise from reality but do not obey its laws are the only way we can defeat time. Ancient names come to mind: Babylon, Nineveh, Sheba. No doubt that Venice will take her place among them. Not the actual city that has been described a thousand times but that other Venice which held so much more than our senses could grasp. *This* Venice will remain long after the actual city has sunk beneath the waves. Picasso seems to have recognized this state of affairs: "Some copies are a better likeness than the original itself."

Right, peeling walls, mossy steps: are these the symbols of a sinking city?

INSIGHT GUIDES

Travel Tips

So, you're getting away from it all.

Just make sure you can get back.

AT&T Access Numbers
Dial the number of the country you're in to reach AT&T.

*AUSTRIA†††	022-903-011	*GREECE	00-800-1311	NORWAY◆	800-190-11
*BELGIUM	0800-100-10	*HUNGARY	00◇-800-01111	POLAND¹◆³	0◇010-480-0111
BULGARIA	00-1800-0010	*ICELAND	999-001	PORTUGAL¹	05017-1-288
CANADA	1-800-575-2222	IRELAND	1-800-550-000	ROMANIA	01-800-4288
CROATIA¹◆	99-38-0011	ISRAEL	177-100-2727	*RUSSIA¹ (MOSCOW)	155-5042
*CYPRUS	080-90010	*ITALY	172-1011	SLOVAKIA	00-420-00101
CZECH REPUBLIC	00-420-00101	KENYA¹	0800-10	SOUTH AFRICA	0-800-99-0123
*DENMARK	8001-0010	*LIECHTENSTEIN	155-00-11	SPAIN•	900-99-00-11
*EGYPT¹ (CAIRO)	510-0200	LITHUANIA◆	8◇196	*SWEDEN	020-795-611
*FINLAND	9800-100-10	LUXEMBOURG	0-800-0111	*SWITZERLAND	155-00-11
FRANCE	19◇-0011	F.Y.R. MACEDONIA	99-800-4288	*TURKEY	00-800-12277
*GAMBIA	00111	*MALTA	0800-890-110	UK	0500-89-0011
GERMANY	0130-0010	*NETHERLANDS	06-022-9111	UKRAINE¹	8◇100-11

Countries in bold face permit country-to-country calling in addition to calls to the U.S. **World Connect™** prices consist of **USADirect** rates plus an additional charge based on the country you are calling. Collect calling available to the U.S. only. *Public phones require deposit of coin or phone card. ◇ Await second dial tone. ¹May not be available from every phone. ¹¹¹Public phones require local coin payment through the call duration. ◆ Not available from public phones.• Calling available to most European countries. ¹Dial "02" first, outside Cairo. ³Dial 010-480-0111 from major Warsaw hotels. ©1994 AT&T.

Here's a travel tip that will make it easy to call back to the States. Dial the access number for the country you're in to get English-speaking AT&T operators or voice prompts. Minimize hotel telephone surcharges too.

If all the countries you're visiting aren't listed above, call **1 800 241-5555** for a free wallet card with all AT&T access numbers. Easy international calling from AT&T. **TrueWorld Connections.**

AT&T

TRAVEL TIPS

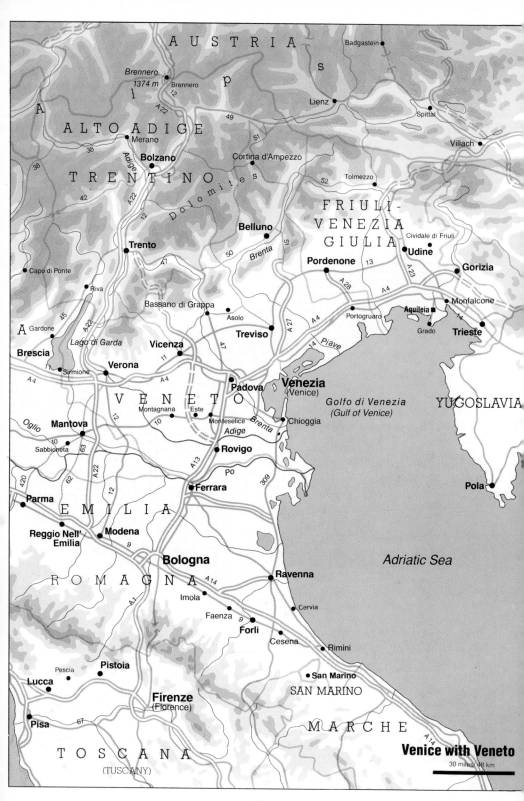

Venice with Veneto

30 miles/48 km

A Wise Man Never Thinks How Far He's Come. He Thinks How Far He Can Still Travel.

REMY **XO BECAUSE LIFE IS WHAT YOU MAKE IT**

Swatch. The others just watch.

seahorse/fall winter 94-95

shockproof
splashproof
priceproof
boreproof
swiss made

swatch■
SCUBA 200

GETTING THERE

BY AIR

The international airport Marco Polo lies on the eastern shore of the lagoon 8 miles (13 km) northeast of the village of Tessera. From here buses (Line 5) run to the Piazzale Roma and motorboats (*motoscafi*) to the Station San Marco. The trip takes about 30 minutes.

There are direct flights to Venice from Frankfurt, Munich, Düsseldorf and Vienna; the flight lasts from 1 to 1½ hours according to the airport.

From the Aeroporto Nicelli, the small airfield at the Lido, one can book for flights over the lagoon. A motorboat runs from the Riva degli Schiavoni to the Station San Nicoló.

AIRLINES

British Airways
Aeroporto Marco Polo
Tel: 5415629.

Alitalia
Aeroporto Marco Polo
Tel: 5415160;
San Moisé 1463, San Marco
Tel: 5200355/5225428

Lufthansa
Aeroporto Marco Polo
Tel: 5415347.

Air France
Aeroporto Marco Polo
Tel: 5415148.

BY SEA

Those holidaying near Venice can also reach the city by ship. From the popular camping place Punta Sabbioni the Line 12 goes to the Fondamente Nuove and Line 14 to the Riva degli Schiavoni.

There are links to all the larger Adriatic ports such as Piraeus or Rhodes. Cruise ships moor at the Stazione Marittima. Information about cruises can be obtained at all travel agents and through the Italian Tourist Department, ENIT.

Visitors can take a very romantic trip from Padua with a small motor boat through the Brenta Canal, passing the summer villas of the Venetians and approaching Venice from the sea. (See also "Things to Do: The villas of Brenta".)

BY RAIL

There are direct rail links with Venice from all the larger cities in West Germany, Austria and Switzerland, with sleeping-couchette and dining-cars. Travel bureaus and Railway stations can provide timetables.

Since 1846 Venice has been linked to the mainland by a railway bridge. The trains run to the Stazione Santa Lucia on the Grand Canal. From here, at the Vaporetto station Ferrovia, Line 1 goes to the city center.

BY ROAD

Buses run to Venice from other Italian cities: Padua, Albano, Montegrotto, Treviso. Tour groups travel by bus to Venice from other European countries. (Get more information from your travel agent.)

BY CAR

One must pay toll on the autobahns in Italy, Austria and Switzerland but not in West Germany. This also applies to the Brenner Pass.

The main traffic routes from West Germany, Austria and Switzerland are:

– from Munich through Innsbruck, the Brenner Pass, Bozen, Trient, Verona, Padua, Venice. 341 miles (550 km), always on the autobahn.
– from Munich through Innsbruck, the Brenner Pass, Bozen, Trient, Bassano, Venice. 319 miles (515 km), autobahn as far as Trient.
– from Zürich over the St. Gotthard Pass, then through Milan, Bergamo. Verono, Padua, Venice. 229 miles (370 km). Partly

on the autobahn in Switzerland, all the way on the autobahn in Italy.

– from Vienna, through Salzburg, the Tauern tunnel, Villach, Tarviso, Udine, Venice. 483.5 miles (780 km), mostly on the autobahn.

The mountain passes in Switzerland and Austria are often closed in winter; motorists should check with the local Automobile Association (e.g. the ADAC in West Germany) or the ACI, Automobile Club Italia.

Travel Essentials

MONEY MATTERS

A passport or other proof of identity is necessary in order to change money or cash travelers' checks or Eurochecks. Some of the larger hotels have a bank or a cambio.

Currency to the value of 1,000,000 lire per person may be taken out of Italy without declaration. Only 400,000 lire in Italian currency per person may be exported. Checks are not subject to control.

BANKS

Opening times: Monday to Friday 0830-1330 and 1500-1600 hrs. Closed Saturdays, Sundays and public holidays.

The **Banca Nationale delle Communi–cazioni** at the Railway Station is open all the time, including weekends and holidays.

From 2100 to 0800 hrs, money can be changed at the ticket offices of the Railway Station. (No cheques).

American Express Bank
San Marco 1471, Salizzada San Moisé
Tel: 5200844
Open in Summer 0800-2000 hrs, Monday to Friday; Winter 0900-1800 hrs; Saturday 0900-1300 hrs.

American Service Bank
San Marco 1336.

Banca Cattolica del Veneto
San Marco 4481.

Banca Commerciale Italiana
Via XXII Marzo 2188.

Banca d'America d'Italia
Via XXII Marzo 2188.

Banca d'Italia
San Marco 4799.

Banca Nazionale del Lavoro
Bac, Orseolo 1118/1121.

CAMBIOS

Information Office
At the Railway Station
Open 0800-2000 hrs.

Thomas Cook (San Marco)
Monday to Friday 0900-1300 hrs, 1500-1800 hrs; Saturday 0900-1300 hrs.

Romeo Tour
Lista di Spagna (at the Railway Station)
Summer daily 0800-2000 hrs. In other seasons 0900-1300 hrs and 1530-1900 hrs.

Cassa di Rsiparmio
(at the Airport)
Daily 1130-1230 and 1330-1630 hrs.

CUSTOMS

Travelers from Common Market countries must follow the usual regulations.

IMPORT

The following goods may be brought into Venice (and into Italy generally) undeclared and duty-free: 1 kg coffee, or 400 g powdered coffee, 200 g tea.

For persons over 17 years: 1.5 liter spirits over 22 percent or 3 liter spirits over 22 percent, 3 liter sparkling wine, and 5 liter wine, 300 cigarettes or 75 cigars or 400 g tobacco. Presents and other goods to the value of 490,000 lire may be brought in addition to the above.

When bringing amounts of money it is better for the traveler to declare them as sometimes there are strict currency controls when travelers leave the country at the border. A declaration form (Modulo V2) can be obtained at Customs. No more than 400,000 lire in Italian currency per person can be imported.

Video equipment must be declared: it is forbidden to bring in large knives, weapons and replicas of weapons.

Detailed information is available from ENIT and travel agents.

GETTING ACQUAINTED

ECONOMY

The most important industrial centers of Venice are the mainland communities of Mestre and Marghera. After the Second World War the area developed into one of the greatest harbors of Italy, with a turnover of 24 million tons of goods per year, 14 miles (24 km) of wharves, an oil storage capacity of 1.5 million tons and a large container wharf, all of which makes Venice the third largest harbor in Italy, after Genoa and Triest. Besides the docks the petrochemical industry, the refineries, the metal-working trades, and the processing and manufacturing centers for agriculture products and cotton are all of importance. Tourism has developed into one of the most important industries. Today 12 million tourists a year visit Venice. In the city's 200 hotels, and in the catering and service trade generally, Venice employs more than half her work force.

Because of the housing shortage, the high rents and the cost of living, many Venetians must commute daily. Many who live in the city have to move to the mainland for financial reasons.

GEOGRAPHY & POPULATION

Venice (Venezia Città), the capital of the north Italian province Veneto, is built on 118 islands and lies about 2 miles (4 km) away from the mainland. Of the 377,000 inhabitants, 251,000 live in the industrial districts of Marghera and Mestre while only 125,000 still live in the historic center of the city in the lagoon. Since 1864 there is a 2.2 mile (3.6 km) railway bridge which links the city to the mainland, and since 1933 a road link as far as the **Piazzale Roma**. Since there is no motor traffic in the city center, vehicles must be parked here or elsewhere (Trochetta, Fusina etc).

Venice is the administrative capital of the province Veneto, the seat of a Catholic Archbishop and, since 1451, Patriarch of the church. The University, founded in 1868, is now in the Ca' Foscari and has faculties for Architecture, Music, Languages and Urban Studies. There are also an Academy of Science, an Art Academy, and a Nautical Oceanographic Institute in the city.

The lagoon, a flat inland sea, belonging to the Adriatic, has an expanse of 24 miles (40 km) long and 9 miles (15 km) wide. Venice itself has an area of 2.7 sq miles (7.06 sq km), and a circumference of 8 miles (14 km) including the island of Guidecca and San Giorgio Maggiore.

CLIMATE

In the High Season (Summer, Christmas and Carnival) one should not visit Venice if it can be avoided because the hotels and the streets and squares are hopelessly crowded and no one can enjoy sightseeing in peace. At these times too, the prices are at their highest. In July and August especially, lots of people holidaying at the Adriatic coast make trips to Venice, until it is bursting at the seams. The average summer temperature is about 23 degrees Celsius but when the *Scirocco*, the hot dusty wind from the Mediterranean blows, it can be much hotter and very humid.

It is more pleasant in late spring (beginning of May to the end of June) and Autumn (September/October). The temperatures are between 15°C and 20°C and the water temperature is about 17°C. A visit to Venice in winter can be a great experience but one should be prepared for the cold and for high water (bring gumboots!). There is very little rain in February and there is a fantastic glowing light: here is the time to enjoy Venice in peace without crowds of tourists. The 10 days of Carnival, from the middle or end of February until the beginning of March, are an exception.

HIGH WATER (AQUA ALTA)

Travelers will find information about the water level in the city traffic shelters, at vaporetto stops, etc. The plans of the city are displayed with the foot ways marked where visitors can walk dry shod. In winter one should always take gumboots to Venice – sightseeing with wet feet is not comfortable and can bring on a cold. *Stivali di gomma* can of course be bought at department stores such as "Standa" Campo San Luca. Elegant Venetian shoe stores don't really handle such humble footwear but some of the better hotels provide them for the use of guests.

CULTURE & CUSTOMS

Toilets: There are very clean pay toilets in the **Alberghi Diurni** restrooms, (literally "Day Hotels"), located at the Railway Station, open daily 0600-2030 hrs, and on the west side of the Napoleonic Wing on the Piazza San Marco, open daily from 0830 to 2000 hrs. The restrooms also have baths and showers and massage and hairdressing is offered.

There are not always toilets in bars and if there are, they are not always clean. Toilets in restaurants can only be used by customers.

ELECTRICITY

The voltage in Italy, at least in the cities, is usually 220. It is best to buy an adaptor for electrical appliances on the spot, for example at the department store "Standa" Campo San Luca, or "Coin" Salizzada San Giovanni, Crisostomo 5788 Cannaregio.

BUSINESS HOURS

The opening times given here are approximate because, in Venice, these times can be changed without notice. Except on their free days, most museums are sure to be open between 1000 hrs and 1200 hrs in the morning. In winter they are sometimes closed in the afternoon.

Shops are generally open from Monday to Friday from 0900-1300 hrs and 1530-1930 hrs. During the hot summer months, the midday break in shops becomes longer. Then they are closed between 1300 hrs and 1600 hrs or even 1700 hrs, but they stay open until 2000 hrs at night. Grocery stores are mostly closed on Monday mornings, other places on Wednesday afternoon. (See also "Banks" and "Medical Services".)

HOLIDAYS & FESTIVALS

Banks and business premises are closed on public holidays. If the holiday falls on a Tuesday, the preceding Monday or the following Friday will also be a holiday.

JANUARY

January 1: **New Year's Day.**
January 6: *Epiphany* (Feast of the Three Kings). On this day, Italians celebrate the festival of the Witch Refana; in Venice and on the island of Sant' Erasmo, she is called *Berolon*. Children are given sweets and allowed to light fires.

FEBRUARY/MARCH

Carnival: After Napoleon conquered the Republic of Venice in 1797 there was no Carnival for almost 200 years. In 1980 the Compagnia della Calza together with the organizers of the Theater Biennale, decided to revive the splendid masquerade that was the Venetian Carnival in the 18th century and regain some of the glory of the Serenissima. At the same time, of course, these businessmen wanted to provide an attraction for tourists during the quiet winter season. So many tourists were attracted that in 1987, angry citizens formed an Anti-Carnival party to stop the new festival. Statistics show that in the last four days of the Carnival, up to 700,000 people filled the streets and squares of Venice and the citizens believe that the city cannot survive this experience unharmed. Prices are usually lower in Venice during the winter months but not during the Carnival. Whoever plans a visit at this time should make bookings in advance because hotels fill up very quickly.

The high points of the event are the Thursday (*Giovedi Grasso*) and Tuesday (*Martedi Grasso*) before Ash Wednesday, the beginning of Lent, the fast season before Easter. On the evening of the Martedi Grasso, the **Compagnia della Calza I Nuova Cortesi** prepares a big surprise presentation for the whole city. Every Carnival has a different motto or theme for the masks and costumes but it is often difficult to obtain a program because the organizers often disagree among themselves.

Information is available from ENIT, **Ente Nazionale per il Turismo,** which has branches in all major European cities and overseas. (Refer to the section on "Tourists Information".)

Many travel agencies arrange a trip or flight to the Carnival for one or two days or longer, sometimes leaving the travelers to fend for themselves once in Venice. A West German agency, the *abr* (Amtliches Bayerisches Reisebüro, Official Bavarian Travel Agency), together with the EZO Art Company and the Compagnia della Calza I Antichi, offer a one-day flight combined with a visit to a masquerade arranged by the Compagnia della Calza.

abr (Amtliches Bayerisches Reisebüro GmbH)
Landshutter Allee 38, 8000 München 19

EZO Kunstdirektion
Dr E. Zorn and Volker Kinnius, Ainmillerstr. 800 München 40
Tel: West Germany 089/347519.

At the following places in Venice, one can rent masks and costumes:

Fiorella
Campo San Stefano

Il Prato
Frezzeria 1770/1

Il Baule
San Marco 583.

The classic masks of the Commedia dell' Arte have become a favorite souvenir and can be purchased all over the city. Beautiful masks, hand-made according to old tradition can be found at:
Gabi Lechner
Salizzada San Lio.

Laboratorio Artigiano Machere
Barbaria delle Tole, 6657 Castello.

MARCH

Su e zo per i ponti (Up and down the bridges): Many Venetians and people from the mainland take part in a run through the city. This festival takes place on the second Sunday in March and begins at the Ponte della Paglia near the Piazza San Marco. The course extends through all six parts of the city (Sestieri) and back to the Piazza.

APRIL

April 25: *Festa di San Marco*, the official Liberation Day 1945, is jointly celebrated by the Venetians as the Festival of St. Mark, the city's patron saint. A gondolier race between Sant' Elena and Punta della Dogana.is held to honor him. It is still the custom for men to give their wives or sweethearts a rosebud on this day. The festival is crowned by a big procession to St. Mark's Church. Traditionally *risi e bisi* is eaten on St. Mark's day.

Easter Monday is a moveable feast.

MAY

May 1: **Labor Day.**
At the beginning of May there is the *Festa della Sparesea*, the great **Asparagus Festival**, with a regatta of little boats in the lagoon. In the city itself, there is a popular race (similar to the run up and down the bridges) and free asparagus with egg can be eaten all day long on the Piazza. At midnight the festival ends with fireworks.
Festa della Sensa (**Ascension Day**): sixth Thursday after Easter. To celebrate the conquest of Dalmatia in the year 1000 by the Doge Pietro Orseolo, the Venetians took part in the famous Marriage with the Sea. The Doge threw a wedding ring into the waters and spoke the solemn words: "We wed thee, O Sea, in token of a true and lasting dominion." After this ceremony, there was a mass in the Church of St. Niccoló at the northern end of the Lido. The Doge in his splendid robes of state, then proceed to the

church in his ship of state, the *bucintoro*, accompanied by the papal Nuncio, the Patriarch of Venice, foreign Ambassadors and a train of followers. After them came a swarm of boats of every sort, including the glassmakers of Murano and the members of other craft guilds. When he had heard mass, the Doge and all his court visited the famous trade fair on the Piazza San Marco, which had been opened the previous day and lasts for 15 days. Since 1180 Venetians, and visitors from Italy and other lands, could wonder at the great display of local oriental products in specially erected wooden stalls.

Today Venetians still celebrate "La Sensa" with a mass in St. Niccoló. Following the old tradition of the Marriage with the Sea, leading representatives of the Clergy, the Municipal Council and the Armed Services sail past the Lido and throw a ring and a wreath of bay leaves into the sea. In the afternoon there is a rowing regatta and in the evening a concert on the Piazza.

Vogalonga: The rowing regatta takes place every year after the feast of the Ascension. The "Vogalonga" or "long row" is a competition between rowing boats of every class which begins at the Molo before the Piazza San Marco and has a circular course, 19.8 miles (32 km) long, passing the islands of La Guidecca, Burano and Murano before it returns to its starting point.

Corpus Christi, the Feast of the Blessed Sacrament, is celebrated in all Roman Catholic countries on the Thursday after Trinity Sunday.

JUNE

June 2: **The Proclamation of the Republic**. On the first Sunday in the month there is a regatta on the island of Sant' Erasmo with other festivities.

June 21: The **Festival of the patron saint of Burano**, whose relics are kept in the Church of San Martino. The houses on the island are gaily decorated; after a procession to the church, the fishing boats are blessed.

June 29: A **regatta** in honor of St. Peter and St. Paul.

JULY

First Sunday in the month: **Gondola regatta** from Murano.

Second Sunday in the month: **Fish festival** in Malamocco (Lido).

Il Redentore (**Feast of the Redeemer**). Between 1575 and 1577 Venice was struck by one of the most severe outbreaks of plague in its history. A third of the population died from this Black Death, the most prominent victim being Titian, alleged to be 100 years old. The council promised to build a votive church if the city were freed from the pestilence. The prayers of the people were answered and so afterwards there was a procession of thanksgiving to the church of the Redemeer, built on the island of Guidecca by Andrea Palladio. Prior to the festival, a bridge of boats was erected so that the Venetians could make their pilgrimage to "Il Redentore" and light a candle. On the Eve of the Festival, which falls on the third Sunday in July, half of Venice sails out into the lagoon in boats decked with paper lanterns and flowers, to eat with friends and relations. Typical "Redentore" dishes are "sardo in saór" – fish in a dressing of vinegar, onions and oil. Afterwards they make music and enjoy the midnight fireworks. Many go on afterwards to the Lido, where, traditionally, one watches the sun come up. The church procession is on Sunday and is followed by a mass in Palladio's church; in the evening, the Patriarch of Venice blesses the city from shore.

On the fourth Sunday in the month, a big **Mussel festival** is held in Alberoni on the outermost tip of Lido. Fantastic mussel dishes are prepared while a regatta takes place.

July 29: A **festival** in Santa Marta, the traditional home of the fishermen.

AUGUST

In the traditional holiday month of the Italians, there are not many events so that most of the shops and restaurants remain closed for several weeks.

First Sunday in the month: A **rowing regatta** in Treponi and Pellestrina.

August 15: The **Assumption of the Virgin and Ferragosto**. All shops are closed.

SEPTEMBER

First Sunday in the month: The **Regatta Storica**. Rowing contests are among the most characteristic sporting events of the city in the lagoon, home of the gondolas. The Venetians show in this way their love and attachment to the craft and to the Sea. The best known and most splendid of these regattas is *Regatta Storica*, which has taken place since the 13th century in boats with up to 30 rowers. These rowing contests were originally held to keep young men in form for war service, a sort of drill on the water. The regatta as a festival also recalls another aspect of Venetian life: the farmers of the lagoon had a kind of race every morning, for everyone wanted to bring his wares to market first and earn the most money. The "caorlina" as their boats are called, are named after the home district of these fruit and vegetable farmers: Caorle.

The young men also raced from the Arsenal to the Lido to practise with weapons. They started with their boats *in riga* (in line) hence the word *Regatta*.

A counter legend is the one the Venetians tell themselves concerning the origins of their love for regattas. Once pirates seized young maidens on their wedding day; their bridegrooms sprang into their hastily prepared boats, followed the robbers and took back their brides. They rowed in races to express their joy at the successful rescue: the present day regattas are alleged to be an expression of spontaneous feeling and the joy of living. Today's *Regatta Storica* consists of a parade of hundreds of historical boats, including a copy of the *Bucintoro*, the ship of state. The rowers wear 16th-century costume and after this parade along the Canal Grande, there is another regatta.

Programs with the route of the boats, the times of the competitions and also tickets and a list of places where one can watch without tickets can be obtained from:

Assessorato al Turismo
Ca' Giustinian, Salizzada San Moisé 1364 A
(under the Napoleonic wing)
Tel: 5209955.
Open 0830-1830 hrs.

Often a small number of tickets can be purchased from desks or porters at large hotels.

Posters from the *Regatta Storica* with reproductions of old pictures can also be obtained in the Ca' Giustinian.

Public transport on the Canal Grande is, of course, interrupted during the *Regatta Storica*.

Second Sunday in the month: Rowing regatta in Murano.

Third Sunday in the month: Rowing regatta in Burano.

OCTOBER

First Sunday in the month: A **wine festival** on the island of Sant' Erasmo, to celebrate the end of the regatta season with dancing and the traditional trampling of the must or grapes for the new wine, hence its name: *Festa di Mosto*.

NOVEMBER

November 1: **All Saints Day**.
November 4: **Day of National Unity**.
November 11: **St. Martin's Day** or Martinmas. Biscuits or little cakes in the shape of St. Martin are given to children, along with other sweets and small presents. The children go from house to house saying traditional verses. The grown-ups meet in the taverns for wine and hot chestnuts.
November 21: *Festa della Salute*. Like the festival of the Redeemer, this festival has its origin in an outbreak of plague, this time in the year 1630. The church of Santa Maria della Salute was built as an act of thanksgiving to the Virgin Mary for this city's escape from the plague. There is also a pontoon bridge from one bank of the Grand Canal (Station Santa Maria del Giglio) to the Salute Church on the other. The Venetians light candles in memory of the plague and its end.

DECEMBER

December 8: **The Annunciation**.
December 25 and 26: **Christmas**.

OTHER FESTIVALS

Biennale
The Biennale Art Show takes place every two years (in the years ending in even numbers). The exhibition grounds are the *Giadini Pubblici* the public gardens, and almost every

European and several non-European countries have their own exhibition pavilions in the park. In the last few years there were also Biennale exhibitions in the Rope Works, at the Arsenal, and in the old Salt Magazine.

Four other festivals are organized by the E.A.B.V. (Ente Autonoma la Biennale di Venezia).

• *Festival of Contemporary Music* (since 1930) every year in Sept./Oct.

• *Film Festival* (since 1932). First took place in the Hotel Excelsior on the Lido, now it has moved to the specially erected Palazzo del Cinema. Every year August/September.

• *Theater Festival* (since 1934) with exciting productions from famous directors, in theaters and in the open air on the squares. Every October, the organizers of the theater festival also organize the Carnival, a celebration of classical 18th-century Venice, every year in February/March.

• Since 1970 there is also an *Architecture Festival*.

Information of all the Biennale festivals from can be gotten from: *Ente Autonoma la Biennale di Venezia*, Ca' Giustinian, San Marco, Tel: 5200311.

RELIGIOUS SERVICES

Venice is a Roman Catholic city and mass is celebrated continuously in the churches on Sundays and religious holidays, the times are announced outside the churches, also in the brochure *Un ospite di Venezia*.

A Latin mass with Gregorian chants is celebrated at San Giorgio Maggiore, Sundays 1100 hrs and at San Simeon Piccolo (at the Railway Station) on Sundays and holidays 1030 hrs.

OTHER CHURCH SERVICES

Anglican Church
St. George's, Dorsoduro,
Campo San Vio 870
Tel: 5200571
0830 and 1130 hrs.

Methodist Church & Evangelical Waldensian Church
Santa Maria Formosa 5170
Tel: 5227549
Sundays 1100 hrs.

Lutheran Evangelical Church
Campo SS Apostoli, 4443
Tel: 5211176 Cannaregio.

Greek Orthodox Church
Ponte dei Greci 3412
Tel: 5225446
Sundays and holidays at 1100 and 1200 hrs.

RACE & RELIGION

The Venetians are the descendants of illyrian (indo-germanic) tribes who settled north of the river Po up to the 3rd century B.C. These Venetians had their own religion, speech and script, which had some resemblance to those of the neighboring Etruscans. Their main cities were Ateste (Este), Patavium (Padua) and Tarvisium (Treviso). In the Second Punic War (218-201 B.C.) the Veneti were allied with the Romans and afterwards the increasing political influence of Roma was apparent, which brought with it a strong Roman cultural influence.

Today 99 percent of the Venetians are Roman Catholics, under a Cardinal-Archbishop who has since 1451 also borne the title of Patriarch.

COMMUNICATIONS

MEDIA

NEWSPAPER DAILIES

Christian Conservative (*Il Gazzettino*), which is sold throughout the Veneto contains up-to-date information, a calendar of coming events and the names of the Pharmacies on all-night duty.

La Nuova Venezia (Liberal Left Wing) also contains up-to-date information.

WEEKLIES

With political views:
Europeo: Middle of the road.
Espresso: Liberal Left Wing.
Panorama: Left Wing.
Veneziasette: Published since 1982 by a group of young journalists. A hard-hitting critical weekly with articles about the political and social problems of Venice. A good and comprehensive survey of coming events.
Marco Polo: A cultural monthly magazine in an attractive and expensive format of cultural events, a list of coming events and an English summary of the most important articles. Published since 1984.
Il Mondo: Deals with politics and the economy.

Grazia and *Amica* are good women's magazines while *Gente*, *Oggi* and *Nouvelle 2000* are gossipy picture papers.
Pamiglia Cristianna: One of the most widely circulated papers in Italy, this is a Catholic newspaper sold more in churches than in kiosks.

NATIONAL NEWSPAPERS

Corriere della Sera: A liberal newspaper with good topical and literary articles.
La Republica: Left Wing intellectual with an excellent cultural section and well-researched political background material.
Il Giorno: Left Wing Liberal
Il Messagero: Left Wing Liberal
La Stampa: Liberal
Il Tempo: Right Wing Catholic
Il Cironale Nuovo: Right Wing

PARTY PAPERS

Avanti: Socialist
L'Unitá: Communist
Lorra Continua: New Left
Il Popolo: Christian Democrat
Il Manifesto: Far Left

FOREIGN PRESS

These are available about noon on the day of issue at the Railway Station. Piazzale Roma, on the Campo San Bartolomeo near the Rialto, at the Kiosk near the Post Office behind the Napoleonic Wing and at the passage from the Riva degli Schiavoni to the Church of San Zaccaria.

English Newspapers:
The Times
The Wall Street Journal
Financial Times
The Independent
Daily Telegraph
The Guardian
International Herald Tribune
Time Magazine
Newsweek

German Newspapers & Magazines:
Spiegel
Frankfurter Allgemeine
Frankfurter Rundschau
Die Welt

French Newspapers:
Le Figaro
Le Monde
Le Canard

POSTAL SERVICES

The main Post Office is just behind the Rialto Bridge in the Fondaco dei Tedeschi, the former German Trade Center. This fine building is worth a visit in any case; its inner courtyard surrounded by galleries is especially impressive.
Opening times: Monday to Saturday 0900-2000 hrs; Sunday 0900-1200 hrs.

There is another central post office behind the Napoleonic Wing on the Piazza San Marco. This office and all the other city offices are open Monday to Friday 0815-1400 hrs and Saturday 0800-1200 hrs.

Stamps are not only sold at Post Offices but in bars and in tobacconist shops, which are marked with a white "T" on a black shield (for *tabaccheria*). Stamps are called *franchobolli* in Italian.

TELEGRAMS

Telegrams can be sent at the Main Post Office which is always open: Ufficio Principale, Telegrafico Centrale.

Telegrams can also be sent at the Railway Station and at the *Poste e Telegrafi* Calle dell' Ascensione, open Monday to Friday 0815-1400 hrs.

TELEPHONE

In Italy, tokens or *gettoni* are used for tele–phone calls and these are available every-where and also given as change. They are mainly useful for local calls. Overseas calls and calls to European countries should be made from Post Offices (see above) and from the places listed below.

There are also public telephones for long distance calls in all bars, restaurants and tobacconist shops, marked with a yellow dial. There are now modern automatic phones which are operated with a telephone card, available from the SIP, State Telephone Company, San Polo 1976/A; also in Mestre, Via Dante 5. Automatic phones marked *interurbana* or *teleselezione* can be used for direct dialing outside Italy.

Within Italy there are various tariffs: Monday to Friday from 0800-0830 hrs – normal tariff; 0830 to 1300 hrs – a higher tariff for the peak hour, then normal tariff again from 1300-1830 hrs. From 1830-2200 hrs there is a reduced tariff or night rate, and from 2200-0800 hrs a double reduced tariff which also continues on Saturdays and Sundays and on Mondays until 0800 hrs.

When calling outside Italy dial 00, the code for a foreign connection then the dialing code of the required country. Overseas and European calls can be made at reduced rates from Monday to Saturday 2200-0800 hrs and all day Sunday.

EMERGENCIES

SECURITY & CRIME

Metropolitan Police (Vigli Urbani)
Venice and Mestre: 112 (Robbery Squad)
Central Police Exchange: 5204777
General Emergency Number: 113

In case of theft one should go straight to a Carabinieri station and swear out a com-plaint. This may also be important for col-lecting insurance. If the language difficul-ties are too great, go to your consulate, which you should also do in the case of a lost passport.

LOSS

Lost Property Offices
(Uffici oggetti rinvenuti)
1. Metropolitan Police at the City Hall, Palazzo Farsetti-Loredan Riva del Carbon, (right at the Rialto Bridge) San Marco Tel: 5224063/5236010. Open Monday-Friday 0800-1400 hrs.
2. Lost Property Office at the Railway Sta-tion Tel: 5289600. Open daily 0800-1200 hrs and 1500-1800 hrs.
3. When things are lost on public transport: City Traffic Dept. ACTV, Corte dell' Albero 3380 San Marco Tel: 780111. Open Monday to Friday 0830-1230 hrs.

MEDICAL SERVICES

PHARMACIES/CHEMISTS

Opening times in Summer: 0830-1230, 1600-2000 hrs.
Winter: 0830-1230, 1530-1930 hrs.
Saturdays: 0900-1200 hrs.

Information from the Emergency Phar-macy Service, Tel: 192. At the door of every pharmacy hangs a notice showing which shop has night duty. This information can also be found in the newspaper *Il Gazzettino* under the heading *Farmacia di turno* and also in the brochure *Un ospite di Venezia* and in other daily papers.

MEDICAL TERMS

Many words for common ailments and remedies are very similar in English and Italian. For example: tranquillizer (*tranquillante*), Laxative (*lassativo*), diar-rhoea (*diarrea*), fever (*febbre*), influenza/grippe (*influenza*), sedative (*sedative*). Other useful expressions include:

Sore throat
mal di gola

Headache
mal di testa

Stomach ache
mal allo Stomaco

Plaster
cerotto

Sleeping tablets
sedative, sonnifero

Pain-killer
calmante, analgesico

Cotton wool
ovatta

Toothache
mal di denti

DOCTORS

Travelers should enquire about travel and health insurance before leaving home.

Private hospitals and the addresses of doctors and dentists can be obtained from your consulate.

HOSPITALS

Ospedale Civili Riuniti
Campo SS Giovanni e Paola (near the church of the same name)
Tel: 784111 Stop: Fondamnee Nuove.

Ospedale Fatebenefratelli
Fondamenta Madonna dell' Orto
Tel: 709355.

Ospedale al Mare
At the Lido; Lungemare d' Annunzio 1
Tel: 5261750, 765900.

Ospedale Civile
Umberto 1, Via Circonvallazione 50, Mestre
Tel: 5056590.

First Aid (Pronto Soccorso)
Tel: 113.

Red Cross (Croce Rossa)
Piazza San Marco
Open 0800-2000 hrs. Closed Sunday.
Tel: 5224704.
In Mestre 950988
Open 0700-2000 hrs. Closed Sunday.

Blue Cross (Croce Azzura)
24 hr service.
Tel: 5230000. This is also the number for an Ambulance. (Ambulanza).

General Emergency Number
Tel: 113.

GETTING AROUND

ORIENTATION

Venice is divided into six suburban districts (*Sestieri*): San Marco, Castello, Cannaregio, Santa Croce, San Polo and Dorsoduro.

When addresses are given, the name of the suburb and the house number are given but not the street name. This is supposed to stop mix-ups because in Venice there are the same street names used in every suburb. Complete addresses can be found not in the telephone book but in the **Guida topo-nomastica**, a street directory.

Many streets, squares or churches can be written in several ways, sometimes in Italian, sometimes in the Venetian dialect.

Piazza
There is only one in Venice: the Piazza San Marco.

Piazetta
The name given to the two small squares between the Doges Palace and the Molo and between St. Mark's Church and the Clock tower. Further out there is the Piazzale Roma, where cars can park.

Campo
Usually the square in front of a church with the same name.

Campiello
A smaller square than a Campo.

Corte
A small courtyard surrounded by houses, usually closed in.

Ponte
All the bridges in Venice have a name, often that of the canal that they cross or the street of which they are a part. There are only three bridges over the Grand Canal: at the Railway Station, at the Rialto and at the Accademia.

Rio
The name for all other canals beside the Grand Canal.

Rio Terrá
A street along a canal that has been filled in. Sometimes the old footpath can be recognized by the paving.

Sottoportico (Venetian: sottoportego)
A passage or a little alleyway entered through an archway.

Ramo
A side street that can lead to a canal…but doesn't always do so.

Ruga/Rughetta
A business street, with shops.

Sacca
A dead-end canal, a watery *cul de sac*.

Canal
Only the Canal Grande has no final "e" at the end of Canal. Like Lewis Carroll, who created another Wonderland, the Venetians are fond of "portmanteau words". They combine canal and palazzo to make *Canalazzo*, a reference to the many palaces along the Grand Canal.

Calle
A long, narrow alley.

Callessa
An alley that always leads to a canal but not necessarily, as one would think, to one of the *traghetti*, where one can pick up a gondola.

Salizzada
The main street of a quarter. In the Middle Ages the only one that was paved.

Fondamenta
The street along a canal. When very wide, it is called Riva.

MAPS

Plans of the City: Good plans of the city can be purchased at every kiosk and in photographic supply shops. Free plans of the city are available at all information centers. The blue folding plan from Studio F.M.B. Bologna, "Pianta della Cittá VENEZIA and Murano, Burano, Cavalli, Pallestrina, scale 1.5000" is recommended. This gives a good coverage of Venice with directions to the main sights so that the travelers can easily find their way.

WATER TRANSPORT

VAPORETTI

The Vaporetti, small motor boats, provide public transport on the Grand Canal and to the islands of the lagoon. In contrast to the Motoscafi or Water taxis, which are very expensive, the Vaporetti are the main form of transport for tourists, unless they decide to walk for short distances which is often quicker. At the height of the season the boats are often full and cannot take on more passengers. A first impression of Venice, however, should really be experienced from Vaporetto No 1, along the Canal Grande.

Tickets: These can be purchased at all boat stations where there is an official on duty or on the boat itself. On board they are about 500 lire dearer. The tickets must be cancelled in the automatic stamping machine as one goes abroad; extra tickets must be obtained for pieces of baggage. Since the counters at the stations are often closed in the evening and at night, it is best to purchase a book of tickets or a 24-hour ticket. This costs 8,000 lire, including one piece of baggage but cannot be used on the lines 2, 19, 25 and 28. If you are planning a longer stay in Venice, you can also buy a "Carta Veneziana" at a greatly reduced price. The "Carta" is valid for 3 years and can be obtained by presenting a passport, passport photos and 8,000 lire to: A.C.T.V. Corte dell' Albero 3380 San Marco, open from Monday to Friday 0830-1230 hrs. (Vaporetto Station Sant' Angelo, Line 1).

Traveling Times: Usually 0600-2300 hrs, but many Lines also offer a night service. The exact times can be obtained from the brochure *Un Ospite di Venezia* which is available at all hotels and information counters. A plan with all the Vaporetto Lines can also be obtained from the A.C.T.V.

WATER TAXIS (MOTOSCAFI)

They have a taxi meter and must display a list of charges and a plan of the city. A trip with a water taxi is very expensive: a journey for four persons from the Railway Station to the Rialto costs about 25,000 lire and prices are always going up. Information about prices are found in *Un Ospite di Venezia*.

Water Taxi Stands
Piazzale Roma Tronchetto (the parking island)
Rialto
San Marco/Giardinetti
San Marco/Molo
Fondamente Nouve

Lido/Viale Santa Maria Elisabetta
Marco Polo Airport

GONDOLAS

A gondola ride costs 50,000 lire for 50 minutes (up to five passengers); every 25 minutes after that costs 25,000 lire. From 2000-0800 hrs, the same time costs 60,000 lire. If visitors have any special requirements they can be arranged with the individual gondolier but the price must never sink below 50,000 lire an hour.

Gondola Stations
1. Bacino Orseolo (behind the Procuratie Vecchio)
2. Calle Vellereso (near the Vaporetto Station San Marco)
3. Riva del Carbon (near the Rialto bridge)
4. Riva degli e Schiavoni (near the Hotel Danieli) Castello
5. San Marco, Molo (right in front of the Doge's Palace)
6. Campo San Moisé, San Marco (near the

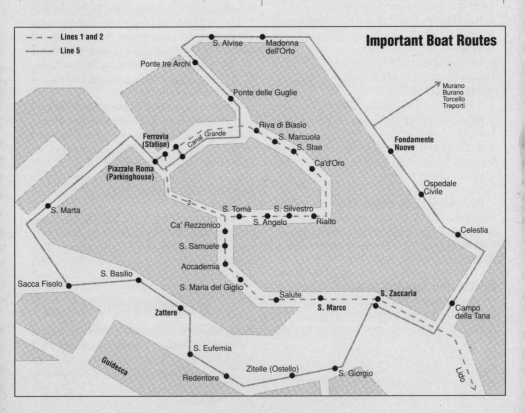

Important Boat Routes

263

Hotel Bauer-Grünwald)
7. Vaporetto Station San Tomá, San Polo
8. Vaporetto Station Santa Maria del Giglio, San Marco (near the Hotel Gritti)
9. Ferrovia (at the Railway Station)
10. Tronchetto, Santa Croce
11. Near the Piazzale Roma.

Prices can be obtained from the hotel reception desk or the brochure *Un ospite di Venezia*. Price lists should also be displayed in every gondola.

Visitors who would like to get the feel of a gondola ride without going to great expense can cross the Grand Canal with the Traghetti, boats very similar to gondolas, which leave from many stopping places on both sides of the canal.

1. Calle Vallaresso-Punta Dogana 0800-1800 hrs.
2. San Marcuola-Fondaco dei Turchi, daily except Sundays and holidays 0700-1400 hrs.
3. San Samuele-San Barnabas 0730-1400 hrs, except Sundays and holidays.
4. Santa Maria del Giglio-San Gregorio 0700-1800 hrs, in summer until 1900 hrs.
5. Ca' Garzoni-San Tomi 0700-2100 hrs on weekdays, 0800-2000 hrs Sundays and holidays.
6. Riva del Carbon-Riva del Vin 0745-1430 hrs on weekdays, 0845-1330 hrs Sundays and holidays.
7. Santa Sofia-Pescheria 0700-2100 hrs on weekdays, 0700-1900 hrs Sundays and holidays.
8. Railway Station-Fondamenta San Simeon Piccolo, 0745-1430 weekdays, 0845-1330 Sundays and holidays.

Between May and September, gondoliers sing serenades with musical accompaniment in the evenings. They set sail from the Gondola Station at the church of San Moisé at 2100 hrs.

Information and Bookings:
CIT (Compagnia Italian Turismo)
Piazza San Marco 4850
Tel: 5 28 54 80

PUBLIC TRANSPORT

District Buses: Buses run to the mainland and surrounding district including Brenta. There are also buses to Padua.

Line 5 – Airport
Line 6 – between Venice and Triest
Line 11 – runs at the Lido between Santa Maria Elisabetta and Pellestrina
Lines A, B, and C also run at the Lido
Line 17 – runs between the Piazzale Roma and Tronchetto

PRIVATE TRANSPORT

PARKING

Since there is no motor traffic in the city of Venice vehicles must be parked out of town. The two nearest parking areas, **Piazzale Roma** and **Tronchetto** (a parking island on reclaimed land across the 2.2 mile or 3.6 km Ponte della Libertá) are usually full, especially during the summer and at Carnival but parking space is available in **Fusina**, outside the industrial zone at the mouth of the Brenta Canal. Visitors can travel by ship through the lagoon to Venice and there is also the possibility of finding quiet and reasonable accommodation in the area, in Malcontenta, Dolo or Oriago. Parking charges at Fusina are 3,000 lire up to 6 hours.

The parking areas at **Fusina, San Giuliano** (on the mainland near Mestre) and **Punta Sabbioni** (near Jesolo) are run by the ACI which provides various services for tourists including hotel reservations, money changing, bookings for excursions and gondola trips (with serenade) and a car wash (at San Giuliano).

Warning: Never leave baggage or valuables in an automobile, certainly not where they can be seen through the windows. This applies to all parking areas, even those with a security patrol.

BREAKDOWN SERVICES

Auto Repairs: Repair workshops are called *Officina* in Italian. Workshops that repair tires are called *Riparazione Gomme*. Only the ACI can tow automobiles off the autobahn.

ACI in Venice

Automobile Club Venezia, Fondamenta S, Chiara, Piazzale Roma 518a
Tel: 708828; in Mestre: Corso Popolo 147.

ACCIDENTS

Emergency help (Italian: *Pronto soccorso*) can be reached under the Police Emergency Number 113, throughout Italy.

GAS STATIONS

Many petrol stations are shut on Sundays and holidays. On working days they are open from 0700 hrs (0730 hrs in winter) until 1230 hrs and from 1500 to 2000 hrs (1900 hrs in winter). The petrol stations on the autobahn are open 24 hours.

STOLEN AUTOMOBILES

One can reach the department for stolen cars (Italian *Macchina rubata*) under the number 5222999 or the Zrentale of the Questura Tel: 5203222, or the emergency number 113.

If the car has been towed away one should contact the local traffic police (*Vigli Urbani*) or their central offices in the Palazzo Loredan, Riva del Carbon (Rialto) San Marco, Tel: 5224063 or 5236010.

WHERE TO STAY

HOTELS

Since prices in Venice vary according to the season, we can only give the category of the hotel. Those who require price details can obtain a hotel list from ENIT or the annual *Michelin Guide* for Italy.

High season is from April 1 to November 1, plus Carnival (10 days, middle to end of February, until beginning of March) and December 22 to January 3.

Off-peak season is from November 3 to March 31, the exception being for Carnival and Christmas.

LUXURY CLASS

Hotel Bauer-Grünwald
Campo San Moisé 1459, San Marco
Tel: 5231520.
213 rooms. An outstanding hotel in the center of the city with first-class service.

Hotel Cipriani
Isola La Guidecca, 10
Tel: 5207744.
One of the most exclusive hotels in Venice. The founder, Guiseppe Cipriani, developed the old wharf buildings first into a restaurant then into a hotel. The hotel has its own tennis courts, swimming pool and yacht marina, a hectare of parkland and a 24-hour boat service from the island to the Piazza San Marco. The cuisine is outstanding. There are courses in cookery before the season begins.

Hotel Danieli
Riva degli Schiavoni, 4191, Castello
Tel: 5226480.
238 rooms. In 1822 the gothic palace of the Doge Enrico Dandolo from the 15th century was made into a luxury hotel. Its position is one of the finest in the city with a beautiful view of the whole lagoon, especially from the terrace restaurant on the top floor. Diet and kosher meals on request. The list of prominent guests of the hotel would fill a whole book. The hotel arranges golf and tennis and can provide equipment for water sports. It also has its own parking house at the Piazzale Roma. In room 13 in 1832, George Sand, the French authoress stayed with her lover Alfred de Musset, the poet. In 1900 Marcel Proust was a guest at Danieli's and in 1915 Gabriele d'Annunzio frequented the hotel.

Hotel des Bains
Lido. Lungomare Marconi, 17
Tel: 768800.
The hotel which stands right on the beach has become well known as the setting for Lucchino Visconti's film of *Der Tod in Venedig* by Thomas Mann. It has tennis courts, a golf course, bathing cabins on the beach and a sea water swimming pool.

Hotel Excelsior

Lido, Lungomare Marconi 41
Tel: 5260201.
A splendid Belle-Epoque building, right on the beach. Its opening celebration for 30,000 guests in 1907 is legendary, also its masked balls in the style of the Arabian Nights. Mussolini was a guest here in 1934 and the Egyptian King Farouk brought his second wife Nariman here on their honeymoon. From 1951 Winston Churchill was a regular patron. The hotel has an 18-hole golf course, tennis courts, beach cabins, a pool and a nightclub.

Hotel Gritti Palace

Campo Santa Maria del Giglio,
2467, San Marco
Tel: 5226044.
88 rooms. Former palace of the Doge Andrea Gritti, from the 16th century. Hemingway describes the hotel in "Across the River and Into the Trees". A marvelous view of Santa Maria della Salute from the terrace. Provides excellent Italian cookery courses in summer.

FOUR STAR HOTELS

La Fenice et des Artistes

Campiello della Fenice, 1936
Tel: 5232323.
67 rooms. Artists have always resided at the hotel which is conveniently located near the Teatro La Fenice. The exclusive Taverna La Fenice restaurant belongs to the hotel.

Hotel Londra Palace

Riva degli Schiavoni, 4147 Castello
Tel: 5200533.
69 rooms. A plaque over the entry tells us that Tchaikovsky composed his Fourth Symphony here. A very elegant hotel with British atmosphere.

Hotel Saturnia e Internationale

Calle Larga XXII Marzo 2398
Tel: 5208377.
99 rooms. Centrally situated hotel in the 14th-century palace of the Pisani family. Vittore Pisani (1324-1380) was admiral of the Republic during the struggle with Genoa for mastery of the Mediterranean. The restaurants "Il Cortile" and "Caravello" belong to the hotel. During periods of high water the hotel provides gumboots.

THREE STAR HOTELS

Accademia-Villa Maravegie

Fondamenta Ballani, 1058 Dorsoduro
Tel: 5210188.
Art lovers stay at this hotel near the Accademia, a former 17th-century palazzo. The hotel is very central but also very peaceful, with a small garden.

Hotel Ala

Campo Sta Maria del Giglio, 2494 San Marco
Tel: 5208333.
77 rooms. A stylishly decorated hotel with good service; the restaurant "Al Giglio" belongs to the hotel.

Hotel Ateneo

Calle San Fantin 1876, San Marco
Tel: 5200588..
23 rooms. A centrally situated hotel near the Teatro La Fenice, with a romantic little garden.

Hotel Bonvecchiati

Calle Goldoni 4488, San Marco
Tel: 5285017.
86 rooms. Right next to the Piazza San Marco. Known for its collection of modern paintings.

Hotel Castello

Campo SS Filippo e Giacomo, 4365 Castello
Tel: 5230217.
Situated in a quiet area, only 100 yards from the Piazza San Marco. Charming Venetian decor.

Locanda Cipriani

Isolo di Torcello, 29
Tel: 730150.
6 rooms. Founded by Cipriani, proprietor of the luxury hotel on La Guidecca Harry's Bar and Harry's Dolci. For those with romantic souls, this idyllic little hotel is just right. Closed from November 1 to March 20.

Hotel San Marco

Ponte dei Dai 877 San Marco
Comfortable and friendly hotel, very centrally situated near the Piazza San Marco.

Hotel Savoia e Jolanda

Riva degli Schiavoni 4187 Castello
Tel: 5224130.

In the same area as the Hotel Danieli but much more reasonably priced.

Hotel Torino
Calle delle Ostreghe, 2356 San Marco
Tel: 5205222.
This hotel lies in the heart of Venice in a former 15th-century palace near the church of Sta Maria del Giglio. Open all year round.

TWO STAR HOTELS

Hotel Campiello
San Zaccaria, 4647 Castello
Tel: 5205764.
15 rooms. Plain, friendly hotel with well furnished rooms, a bar and a restaurant. Near the church of San Zaccaria.

Hotel Cittá di Milano
Campiello San Zulian 5890 San Marco
Tel: 5227002.
26 rooms in a quiet location near the Piazza San Marco and the Rialto.

Hotel Madonna dell' Orto
Fondamenta Madonna Dell' Orto,
3499 Cannaregio
Tel: 719955.
There is no mass tourism in the simple and friendly suburb of Cannaregio. The hotel is a palazzo built by a merchant of the 16-17th century. The 41 rooms, some with shower and bath, are spread over three stories, some looking on to a small canal. This very romantic park has old grottos, trees and a statue of the Madonna. The rooms with wooden floors, plaster mouldings and heavy beams have a homely atmosphere.

Hotel San Gallo
Campo San Gallo, 1093/A San Marco
Tel: 5289877.
A typical Venetian hotel, 5 minutes from the Rialto bridge, open all year round. Comfortable rooms with bath and shower.

HOLIDAY APARTMENTS

Those who would like something more individual than a hotel can rent a holiday apartment in Venice. The Venetian architect Antonio Lorenzo, known for many years as a restorer of old palaces, has done a range of apartments and holiday flats which he rents by the week. They are in suburbs such as Sant' Alvise, San Giobbe and San Lio where there are no tourists but many Venetians. You have a greater chance to get to know the local people and the apartments are close to public transport. They have kitchens or kitchenettes so that you can do some cooking – a good plan in a city full of expensive restaurants. The apartments are available in three categories, from simple one room apartments to luxury apartments in an 18th-century patrician house. The prices range from about $275 a week for two persons to $600 a week. There is a charge for towels and linen of about 30,000 lire per person and other extra charges, plus a cleaning fee of 50,000 lire.

A similar range of apartments is available in Florence. Enquiries in West Germany can be addresses to:

Frau Andrea Eiler
Lachnerstr. 30
8000 München 19
Tel: Germany/089/1 78 34 55.

or contact:
Antonio Lorenzo
Santa Croce 2059
30125 Venice.

CAMPGROUNDS

Camping Venezia
(2 miles or 4 km east of Mestre)
Tel: 975928.

Camping Barche
Via Forte Margherita, Mestre.

Assocamping
Cavallino, Via Fausta 89
Tel: 968071.
Here information is given over as many as 30 camping places that lie on the Littorale di Cavallino, the tongue of land below Jesolo.

Campeggio Marco Polo
Via Triestina, Tessera (near the airport)
Tel: 5415346.

Camping Fusina
Tel: 969055.

Camping Jolly Piscine
Marghera
Tel: 920312.

Camping Adriatico
Via Sandro Gallo 215 Lido
Tel: 966770.

Reserve early for the summer because bookings are heavy. The West German motorists association ADAC puts out a Camping Guide every year.

YOUTH HOSTELS

Ostello A.I.G.
Isola La Guidecca
Tel: 5238211;
Fondamenta Zitelle 86.
Open February 1 to December 15.

In summer accommodation for young people is available in the following places:

Domus Cavanis
Accademia, 912 Dorsoduro
Tel: 5287374.
This dormitory belongs to a religious institution and offers simple and cheap quarters for male tourists of all ages.

Domus Civica
Calle delle Sechere 3082 (by the Campo San Rocco) San Polo
Tel: 721103.
This building is normally a school but in summer it offers accommodation for girls, family groups and, occasionally, single rooms for men.

Convento San Francesco dell Vigna
Castello
Tel: 5222476.
Boat line 5, Station Tana Celestia.

Young people can obtain information on cheap accommodation from the E.P.T. (see information).

FOOD DIGEST

WHAT TO EAT

Italian cookery and eating-habits are different from those of other lands. Breakfast (Italian *Prima Colazione*) in the English, American or even the German tradition is scarcely known, although by now almost all hotels offer a "Continental Breakfast". The Italian is more likely to take a quick Expresso or Capuccino, perhaps with a croissant, at a coffee bar on the way to work. For this reason dinner, at midday or in the evening, is an important meal with several courses. (*Pranzo, Cena*) The appetiser (*antipasto*) is followed by a first course (*primo piatto*) of pasta or a rice dish (*risotto*). Then comes the main dish (*secondo piatto*) with fish or meat. Side dishes (*contorni*) of vegetables or salad are ordered separately. Cheese (*formaggio*) and fruit (*frutta*) or a dessert (*dolce*) end the meal and one drinks coffee or a *grappa*, the spirit distilled from grapeskins from Bassano, which is alleged to help the digestion.

The Venetian cuisine is rich in fish dishes but today they are among the most expensive ones on the menu because the fish are no longer so plentiful in the lagoon. It is best not to eat fish on Mondays because the fish market is closed on this day and restaurants fall back on deep frozen supplies.

VENETIAN SPECIALITIES

• **Soups**
Brodetto di pesce
Venetian fish soup made from fish, onions, tomato juice, white wine, parsley, bay leaves and oil.

Broéto
Eel soup.

Risi e lunganega
Rice soup with pork sausages.

Primo
First Course

Cannelloni ripieni
Pasta rolls with a filling of meat and tomato sauce baked in the oven.

Gnocchi alla Fontina
Small semolina dumplings with grated Fontina cheese.

Gnocchi di patate
Small potato dumplings with cheese.

Pappardelle con funghi
Flat ribbon-shaped pasta with mushrooms.

Risi e bisi
Venetian national dish: rice with peas, ham and herbs.

Risotto dei peoci
Rice with mussels.

Spaghetti con vongole
Spaghetti with baby mussels.

Peoci salati
Mussels cooked in the pan with parsley and garlic.

Castraúra
Artichoke hearts.

Bigoli
Spaghetti made with dark flour.

Turtufi di mare
Sea truffle.

Grancevola or granseola
Tender, baked sea spider.

Cicchetti
Small delicacies eaten with wine. Small fried squid, onions, cheese, ham, sliced polenta.

Risi e bisato
Rice with eel, a typical Christmas dish.

Pasta e fasioi
Pasta and beans with celery, carrots, onions, rosemary, basil, sage and olive oil.

Lasagne
Flat squares of pasta baked in the oven with a filling of meat and vegetable and a creamy sauce.

Risotto nero
Rice with squid – the ink of the squid colors the dish black.

Bigoli in salsa
Dark spaghetti in a piquant sauce.

• Secondo
Second Course: Fish

Sepe in tecia
Squid steamed in its own ink.

Cape lunghe
Winkles.

Cape Sante
Scallops.

Fritto Misto
Fried sea-food.

Moleche
Crabs, caught as they change their shells in spring or autumn and fried in oil with garlic celery or herbs. The crabs, helpless without their shells, hide in the sand and are caught by the fishermen.

Anguile alla griglia
Grilled eel.

Asia bollito
Boiled whitebait.

Baccala Montecato
Dried cod cooked with milk and cream and made into a creamy paste.

Coda di rospo ai ferri
Grilled angler-fish.

Dorate
An Adriatic fish, golden bream.

Mansanete
Shrimps baked in oil.

Calamare fritti
Fried rings of squid.

Filetti di San Pietro fritti
Baked filets of the delicious John Dory.

Go
Venetian lagoon fish.

Seppie ai ferri
Grilled squid.

Triglie con risi
Seabass with rice.

Sogliola alla casseruola
Fillets of sole in a casserole with champignons.

Datteri di mare
Sea dates – a kind of mussel that looks like a date.

Aragosta
Lobster, languoste.

Cozze or *peoci*
Mussels cooked in white wine stock.

Second Course: Meat

Fegato alla Veneziana
Veal liver with onion rings.

Castradina alla griglia
Grilled lamb; traditionally eaten on November 21, Feast of the Salute.

Trippa alla trevisana
Savory tripe, browned in the oven.

Contorni
Side-dishes

Polenta
A maize dish.

Radicchio ai ferri
This red and white plant belongs to the artichoke family and has a typically bitter taste. This bitterness stimulates the secretion of the stomach juices. "Ai Ferri" are *radicchi* fried in oil and pepper.

All sorts of vegetables are available in season, also salads, grown on the island of Sant' Erasmo, Venice's market garden.

Dolci
Desserts

Tiramisu
A dessert made of sponge cake in liqueur with a filling of cream cheese, sprinkled with mocca powder. Resembles English trifle.

Mecedonia
Fruit salad.

WHERE TO EAT

Venetian restaurants are, as a rule, extremely expensive, especially during the high season and round about the Piazza San Marco. The prices become more reasonable as one moves away from the Piazza. Many restaurants offer a Tourist Menu (*Menu Turistico*) at a flat rate, usually with three course service, bread and wine mostly included in the price. You should not forget to add in the usual Italian charge for bread and cutlery (*pane e coperto*) and a service charge of 10-15 percent plus a tip of 10 percent when calculating the cost of a meal. Remember to keep the bill because the tax department sometimes makes a raid in the vicinity of a restaurant and you must pay a fine if you cannot produce a restaurant check.

Lunchtime in Venice is between 1230 and 1400 hrs and in the evening between 1900 or 1930 until 2200 hrs. Restaurants and bars seldom stay open after midnight. The Venetians go to bed early.

FIRST CLASS RESTAURANTS

Antico Martini
Campo San Fantin, near the Teatro La Fenice Tel: 5224121.
Daily except Tuesday and Wednesday. Open from 1200-1430 hrs and 1900-2400 hrs.
Generally regarded as one of the best and most elegant restaurants with excellent cuisine. One can dine on the terrace in summer but the interior is very charming. Pietro Mascagni composed an opera here and it is patronized by many of the artists from the Teatro La Fenice.

Danieli Terrace
Riva degli Schiavoni 4196 Castello
Tel: 5226480.
From the top floor of the Palace Hotel Danieli

Excelsior there is an enchanting view over the lagoon, especially at night. Prices begin at about $50 per person.

Gritti
Campo Santa Maria del Giglio 2467 San Marco, opposite the Salute Church.
Jean Cocteau regarded this terrace of the luxury hotel Gritti Palace as the most beautiful in the world. Specialities of the house are fish dishes made from old recipes out of the splendid days of the Doges. Festive dinners are served during the *Regatta Storica* and the Festival of the Redentore.

La Colomba
Piscina Frezzeria 1665, in a small courtyard. Closed on Tuesday and in November. The main attraction of the restaurant, besides the exquisite cuisine is the valuable collection of works by Picasso, Chagall and Hundert–wasser. You must pay a high price for this display.

La Regina
Calle della Regina 2330 Santa Croce
Tel: 5341402.
Closed on Monday and at the beginning of August.
Also very expensive. The former Trattoria, situated in an 18th-century palace, has become a gourmet restaurant. Named after Caterina Cornaro (1454-1510), Queen of Cyprus, whose palace is nearby.

Taverna La Fenice
Campiello Fenice 1938 San Marco
Tel: 5223856.
Open daily except Sunday.
Right next to the opera house. A popular meeting place for artists with lots of atmosphere and excellent fish dishes. Exclusive and expensive.

MIDDLE CLASS RESTAURANTS

In contrast to the elegant luxury restaurants, the simpler *trattorie, ristoranti* and *osterie* give the visitor the opportunity of seeing the Venetians and appreciating their way of life. Simpler but very tasty Venetian dishes are served. Unlike the *Ristorante*, the *Trattoria* is usually a family business, where the wife of the proprietor does the cooking herself from old family recipes.

Alla Madonna
Calla della Madonna 594 Rialto
Closed on Wednesday and mostly in the first week of August, Christmas and January.
Reasonably priced restaurant with excellent fresh fish dishes and large helpings. A very large restaurant with room for 220 people which is unusual in Venice where most restaurants are very tiny.

Altanella
Guidecca 268
Tel: 5227788.
Closed Monday evenings, Tuesdays and in August.
A friendly family business on the island of Guidecca where one can eat in comfort at reasonable prices. Gabriele D'Annunzio loved this restaurant where one can sit on the terrace (altanella) in the open air in summer.

Antica Trattoria Poste Vecchie
Mercato del pesce 1608 (behind the Fish Market)
Closed on Tuesday.
The restaurant is named after the old Venetian post station of the 16th century which once stood here. It is colorfully decorated but not a "tourist trap". Inside it is very cosy with a big open fire which is very welcome in winter. There is always good fresh fish and seafood available with it being so close to the Fish Market.

Trattoria Cittádi Vittorio
San Marco 1591, in a side street off the Frezzeria.
Gondolieri eat here. The meals are simple but delicious.

Trattoria da Arturo
Calle dei Assassini 3656 San Marco
Daily except on Sundays, from 1230-1430 hrs and 1930 to 2230 hrs.
This restaurant which is known for its fantastic salad creations and its warm friendly atmosphere is in Murderers' Alley, near the Teatro La Fenice. There are only 22 places so it is advisable to book ahead.

Trattoria da Ignazio
Calle dei Saoneri 2749 (near Campo San Polo
Closed Saturdays
Has a pretty little garden. Offers other

Italian specialities besides the Venetian dishes.

Locanda Montin
Fondamenta della Eeremite (also *Romite*) 1142 Dorsoduro (near Campo San Barnaba)
Closed Wednesdays and in August and the beginning of February
The actress Eleonora Duse and the poet Gabriele D' Annunzio had one of the upstairs rooms. Ezra Pound also came regularly to the Locanda. Specialities are the spaghetti with seafood, fillets of John Dory, and the *Tiramusú*.

Shuang Hsi
Campo Santa Margherita 2894 Dorsoduro
Tel: 5338366.
Closed on Mondays.

Tempio del Paradiso
San Marco 5495, Calle della Bissa, near the Campo San Bartolomeo
Tel: 5224673.
Closed on Mondays.
These two Chinese restaurants are the only foreign speciality restaurants found in Venice. The Tempio del Paradiso adds touches of eastern mystery with its red-lit "temple entrance" and menu in Chinese and Italian.

Trattoria Roma di Poveledo
Lista di Spagna 122
Closed Fridays.
A very good place for a last meal before catching the night train – it opens earlier than usual and is near the Railway Station.

Trattoria La Furatola
Calle Lunga San Barnaba 2879A
Tel: 5208594..
Closed Wednesday evenings, Thursdays, July and August.
The speciality of this small restaurant, where tourists are hardly seen, are the *moleche*, crabs caught when they change their shells in spring and autumn. Cooked in oil they are a Venetian delicacy and so is the *pasticco di pesce*, fish pasty.

PLAIN RESTAURANTS

Al Mascaron
Calle Lunga Santa Maria Formosa
5225 Castello
Tel: 5225995.
Closed Sundays and in December.
A good, reasonably priced meal with large helpings can be had here among the locals. Do not fear or be put off by the rather dark atmosphere.

Trattoria Corte Sconta
Calle Pestrin, 3886 Castello (near Campo Bandiera e Moro)
Closed Mondays and Tuesday afternoons.
Plain restaurant with excellent dishes; in summer one can sit in the courtyard. Hardly a tourist to be seen, the host speaks German but who knows what his English is like?

Trattoria Da Pinto
Calle Racchetta 3728 Cannaregio
Closed Sunday evenings and on Mondays.
Here the Venetians enjoy reasonably priced seafood, fresh fish and good wine.

Al Milion
Corte al Milion 5841 Cannaregio
Closed Sundays and in August.
Located behind the Church of San Giovanni Crisostomo. One of the oldest wine taverns in Venice. The house in which Marco Polo was born is supposed to have stood in its courtyard. Large selection of wine and a good self-service buffet. Reasonable prices.

Trattoria Ai Tosi
Ponte delle Spade 1586 (on the way from the Fish Market to the Ca' Pesaro)
Closed Saturday evenings and Sundays.
A very friendly, homelike restaurant with excellent fish dishes. The great-grandfather of the owner called his restaurant proudly after his children. (*Toso* = boy, child).

RESTAURANTS ON THE ISLANDS

• Burano
The restaurants on Burano are all very good but expensive, because the Venetians visit them at weekends. It is wiser to visit the island during the week when it is not so crowded.

Gatto Nero
Fondamenta Guidecca
Very full at weekends.

Da Forner
Fondamenta Terra Nuove
Really a middle-class restaurant but always full and therefore expensive.

Trattoria Graspo de Ua
Via Bassaldare Galuppi
A restaurant which is often visited by tour groups – when this happens the place is too full and there is only one menu. Simple rooms for rent.

Tre Stelle-Da Romano
Via Bassaldare Galuppi 221
Closed Tuesdays.
The best culinary address on the island but overcrowded and expensive. It looks like an old ballroom with many pictures on the walls. Specialities are grilled fish, fish soup and Go, a lagoon fish.

Trattoria Dei Pescatori
Via Bassaldare Galuppi
Closed Mondays.
Also an excellent fish restaurant but not so well known and therefore cheaper than Da Romano.

• Murano
All four of the restaurants listed below are simple places, with good fish dishes and reasonable prices.

Al Corallo
Fondamenta dei Vetrai 73
Closed Tuesdays.

Ai Frati
Fondamenta Venice 4
Closed Thursday evenings.

Busa alla Torre
Campo Santo Stefano 3
Closed Sundays.

Ai Vetrai
Fondamenta Manin, 29
Closed Wednesdays.

Pellestrina Da Nane
San Pietro in Volta 282
Closed Mondays and in February.
Known to the local people for its fresh fish. Hardly any tourists find their way here because it is difficult to reach. (See "Things To Do".) The restaurant has a wonderful view of the lagoon.

• Torcello
Locanda Cipriani
Daily except Tuesday. Remains open all week during July, August and September.
One of the most famous restaurants in Venice; the Cipriani family own Harry's Bar in the city and Harry's Dolci on La Guidecca. The food is excellent but expensive. One can also rent accommodation in this exclusive country hotel; prominent guests include Queen Elizabeth (the Second) and Winston Churchill. It is one of Hemingway's old haunts.

Al Ponte del Diavolo
Closed Thursdays and every evening except Saturday.
Not a very large menu but the food is good. The restaurant is on the small canal that leads to the center of the island.

Villa '600
A country style Trattoria with simple dishes. Very friendly atmosphere. Plenty of rooms to rent.

SELF-SERVICE RESTAURANTS

Chat qui rit
Calle del Salvadego 1131/Angolo Frezzeria
San Marco
Tel: 5229086.
The advantage in all self-service restaurants is that there is no charge for bread, cutlery and service.
The "Chat qui rit" is one of the best of these restaurants in the city. There is a wide choice of good pizzas and other dishes at reasonable prices. Crowded at rush hours.

Gianni
Zattere 918, Dorsoduro.
Specializes in many varieties of pizza. It is very pleasant to sit on the terrace built out on piles into the Guidecca Canal.

Mario e Emilio
Calle delle Madonna 1463 San Polo.
Pizzas to eat there or take away.

Piccolo Martini
Frezzeria 1501 San Marco.
A good, cheap stand-up food bar with tasty
meat, fish and vegetable dishes. There is a
restaurant adjoining with tables and service
but the prices are much higher.

Tiziano
San Giovanni Crisostomo 5747 Canna regio
Closed Fridays.
A very good stand-up food bar with attrac-
tively displayed food. Inexpensive.

DRINKING NOTES

Wine: Italians drink wine with their meals,
red or white according to the dishes served.
There is a large selection of bottled wine
from the Veneto or Friuli. Every restaurant
also has its own house wine, *vino della casa*,
sold by the glass and mostly very good.

White wines
Very dry (*asciutto*)
Breganze bianco, Prosecca, Garganega,
Ribolla.

Dry (*secco*)
Bianco di Conliano, Gambarella, Verduzzo,
Sauvignon.

Flowery (*abbocato*)
Barbarano bianco, Tocai, Verdiso.

Semi-sweet (*Soave*)

Sweet, mellow (*Recioto*)

Red Wine
Very dry
Barbarano Rosso, Breganze, Friularo,
Cabernet di treviso.

Dry
Valpantena, Merlot, Ricioto Amarene,
Bardolino Rabeso (8 or 10 years old.)

Flowery
Rubino della Marca, redioto rosso, Rubina
del Piave.

Sweet Desert Wines
Moscato di Arqua, Vino Santo.

BARS

An Italian bar is not a counter in a pub or a
place where only alcohol is sold or even a
nightclub. It is a coffee stand where one can
also get a bite to eat and meet for a chat.
There are bars on every corner; here are two
highly recommended Venetian bars.

Al Volto
Calle Cavalli, 4081, San Marco.
1200 different varieties of wine from all over
the world attract many Venetian customers
who keep the place very full. In August,
when Italians go on holiday, the bar is shut.

Harry's Bar
Calle Vallaresso 1323 San Marco
Open daily from 1200-2300 hrs (restaurant)
and 1030-2300 hrs (bar). Closed on Mondays and in January.
The most famous bar in Venice, it is located
on one of the best and most expensive addresses in town. It is one of the meeting
places of the jet set and those from the
cultural scene. Hemingway's ghost appears
on moveable feast days. Specialities are:
Bellini Champagne with peach juice; *Tiziano*
Champagne with grapefruit juice; *Risotto di
seppie,* black rice with squid; *Fegata alla
veneziana,* veal liver with onions and the
invention of the founder; Giuseppe Cipriani:
Vero Carpaccio Cipriani wafer thin slices of
raw beef fillet with a special sauce.

CAFÉS

Chioggia
Piazzetta San Marco 11.
Under the portico of the St. Mark's Library
on the Piazetta. The best place to admire the
facade of the Doge's Palace, St. Mark's
church and the Bacino San Marco.

Caffè Florian
Piazza San Marco 56/59.
Right on the Piazza San Marco. Founded
1720, the oldest coffeehouse not only in
Venice but in all Italy. Tastefully decorated
inside…a meeting place for artists and jour-
nalists. Many famous personages met here:
Goethe, Mark Twain, Honoré de Balzac,

Marcel Proust, Thomas Mann and Ernest Hemingway. The Caffè Florian is very expensive but a must for all visitors to Venice. Closed on Wednesdays, but open all the time during the season from July to September.

Quadri
Piazza San Marco 120.
The café's own orchestra plays music and gives Quadri the air of a Viennese coffee house. There is a beautiful view of the Piazza and St. Mark's Church. In summer, there is an elegant restaurant on the first floor.

Foscarini
Accademia 878, Dorsoduro.
Next to the Accademia, right on the Grand Canal. Many artists meet here.

Penasa
Calle delle Passe, 4587 Castello.
Popular with Venetians who give the café a typical Venetian atmosphere.

Zorsi
Calle dei Fuseri 4357 San Marco.
An address that the Venetians keep to themselves. More of a Milk Bar than a café, situated between the Campo San Luca and St. Mark's Church. Very fine cappucino and hot chocolate and delicious pastries.

ICE CREAM PARLORS

There are many of them in Venice and the best are found on the Zattere: Aldo, Cucciocle, Nico and Franco.

Causin
Campo Santa Margherita, 2996 Dorsoduro.
Many Venetians regard this as the best ice cream parlor in the city. Do not be put off by the homely exterior.

Paolin
Campo San Stefano.
Famous for homemade ices. The oldest ice cream parlor in Venice.

THINGS TO DO

CITY

BASSANO
37.2 miles (60 km) west of Venice: 35,000 inhabitants.
A small town at the foot of the Alps where the summit of Monte Grappa was the scene of fierce fighting between Austrians and Italians during the First World War. Bassano lies in a strategically important place on the left bank of the Brenta which is spanned by a roofed wooden bridge from the 13th century, trademark of the town. Bassano is famous for the grape-skin spirit *grappa* which is distilled here and for its ceramic industry, established in the 17th century. The town, first mentioned in the 10th century, belonged to the Republic of Venice since 1400.
   How to get there: By car on the SS 11 and 245 or by train from Venice.

THE BRENTA VILLAGE
In the 15th century Venice extended her dominion to the nearby mainland, the *terra firma*. In the following years a great many splendid summer residences were built in this area for the Venetian nobles by the foremost architects of the time. The architectural style of these villas influenced the whole of Europe and even served as a model for the mansions of the southern states of America.
   The villas of Brenta are mostly in private hands and visitors should telephone before making a tour.

VILLA FOSCARI (La Malcontenta)
Luigi and Niccoló Foscari had the villa built between 1550 and 1560 by Andrea Palladio, the fashionable architect of the day, who put up many similar villas near Venice and Vicenza. The story goes that a high spirited lady of the house of Foscari who led a life of pleasure was banished to this villa by the

family, hence its name: the discontented woman.

Opening times: Tuesday, Saturday and the first Sunday of the month 0900-1200 hrs, from May to October. In April by appointment only. Tel: 969012. Entry fee: 5,000 lire. The villa is privately owned.

How to get there: "La Malcontenta" lies between Marghera and Fusina and can be reached on the SS 11. At the town of Mira, just before Oriango, turn off in the direction of Fusina and the sea.

VILLA PISANI (also called the Villa Nazionale)

Alvise Pisani had the villa built in 1735 after he was elected Doge. Its buildings and park make it one of the most beautiful estates in the area. The ceilings painted by G.B. Tiepolo from 1761-62 should not be missed. In 1807 Napoleon confiscated the villa and gave it to his stepson Eugéne Beauharnais, the Viceroy of Italy. Since 1882 the villa is a national monument, open to the public. The park is not in its original state, it was landscaped in the 19th century. In the park there are stables, a belvedere, a labyrinth and an orangery.

In the Villa Nazionale, Hitler and Mussolini met for the first time on July 14, 1934.

Opening times: In summer, daily except Monday, 0900-1330 hrs (villa), 0900-1800 hrs (park). Entry fee 3,000 lire. Tel: 049/ 502074.

How to get there: On the SS 11 to Strá. Near this town there are two smaller villas, the **Villa Soranza** near Fiesso Artico and opposite the **Villa Lazzara-Pisani**, called "La Barberiga". Both buildings are right on the banks of the Brenta.

It is possible to take a very romantic trip from Venice and visit the Brenta villas by ship. The **Burchiello** (an "old-time Post boat") leaves from San Marco (Giardinetti) every Tuesday, Thursday and Saturday at 0920 hrs, the return trip by bus leaves Padua every Wednesday, Friday and Sunday at the same time from the Pontile Bassanello Stop. The boat travels through the Brenta Canal past the villas. The excursions run from the middle of April to the middle of October. Cost: 95,000 lire for lunch, tours of the Villa Foscari and the Villa Pisani and return by bus from Padua.

The way through the Brenta Canal was used by travelers in other days: Goethe came to Venice in this way.

For further information, contact:

Burciello Excursions
CIT San Marco 4859
Tel: 85480.

SIAMIC Express
Via Trieste, 42 35100 Padua
Tel: 049/664755.

Trips to the Brenta villas:
Wagon-Lits/Cook
Piazzetta dei Leoncini 286-305, Venice
Tel: 23405.

American Express
Salizzada San Moisé, Venice
Tel: 700844.

Ventana
Piazzetta dei Leoncini 4843, Venice
Tel: 2 5449.

General information on the Brenta villas can be obtained at:

Proloco Riviera di Brenta
Via Venezia 19, 30030 Oriago
Tel: 041472255.

CASTELLFRANCO VENETO

24 miles (40 km) northwest of Venice, 27,000 inhabitants. The **Castle** was built in 1199, with moat, fortress walls and historical old town. Within the castle walls is the cathedral from the 18th century with an early work of Giorgione, from the Venetian renaissance. Giorgione was born in Castellfranco Veneto in 1477.

Near the little town is the **Villa Revedin-Bolasco**, built by Vincenzo Scamozzi in 1607. Visitors should see the park, decorated with statuary.

VILLA REVEDIN-BOLASCO

Borgo Treviso, 59
Tel: 04 23/494112.
Open Tuesday, Saturday and first Sunday in the month 1530-1830 hrs (May to October), 1400-1700 hrs (October to end of April).

How to get there: By car on the SS 11, 245 and 307. By train from Venice.

PADUA

21 miles (35 km) west of Venice,
pop. 232,000.

Padua was the spiritual and artistic heart of the Veneto until well into the 15th century. Galileo taught at its venerable University from 1592 until 1610.

Things to see: The frescoes by Giotto in the **Scrovegni Chapel** (1305).

– The Roman-gothic **Basilica of St. Antony** with a statue by Donatello. The High Altar is also done by Donatello (15th century).

– The **Caffè Pedrocchi** a famous Italian coffee house, rich in tradition. The Botanical Gardens, among the oldest in Europe, open daily except Mondays 0900-1300 hrs (October to April) and 1500-1800 hrs (May to September).

How to get there: By car on the SS 11 or the A4 (autobahn), with the train from Venice or by ship with the Burchiello. Buses leave Venice for Padua on the hour at the half hour.

COUNTRY

BURANO

This island, home of the fishermen, with 6,000 inhabitants today, lies northeast of Venice and its attractive brightly painted houses have made it into a popular artists' colony. Until the 18th century and even later, costly stitched lace was made in Burano, and it is again becoming popular.

Things to see: Lace School and display: Consortio Merletti in the **Palazzo del Podestá** Piazza Galuppi. Daily except Tuesday, 0900-1800 hrs. (Entry fee 5,000 lire)

– Convent and Church of **San Martino** with an early work of Tiepolo, (*The Crucification*) in the St. Barbara Chapel.

How to get there: By ship Line 12 from the Fondamenta Nuove to Murano and Burano.

CHIOGGIA

This old fishing center, (pop. 52,000) lies 31 miles (50 km) from Venice on the southern edge of the lagoon and was once the seat of the Venetian salt industry. Today it is the largest fishing port in Italy and has a popular bathing beach at Sottomarina. Its name comes from Pliny the Elder who called the narrow navigable channel between Sottomarina and the island Pellestrina "fossa Claudia".

Claudia became Cloda, then in dialect Chioggia.

Things to See: Cathedral Cloe, founded in the 11th century, renewed in 1662-74 by Bassaldare Longhena.

– Next to the Cathedral the small **Church of San Martino** (14th century) with an altar picture to Paolo Veronese with scenes from the life of St. Martin (1349).

– At the end of the main street, **Corso del Popolo**, is an old granary from year 1322.

– From the island there is a good view of the massive **Murazzi**, a 3-mile (5-km) long dam with walls 14 feet (4 meters) high and 50 feet (15 meters) thick, of blocks of istrian stone, built by the Republic between 1744 and 1782, as a protection against the sea.

Chioggia can be reached by ship and bus over Lido and Pellestrina (*see* under Pellestrina).

LIDO

During the rule of the Doges, many patrician families built summer villas on the 7-mile (12-km) long island. Since the beginning of the 20th century, the Lido has been a sophisticated bathing resort with many elegant Hotels. The long beach with its fine sand still attracts many tourists every year. The Lido was so famous that its name has become a synonym for "beach".

In the Hotel des Bains, directly on the beach, Visonti filmed a version of *Der Tod in Venedig*, the famous novel written by Thomas Mann.

MURANO

Center of the Venetian glass production since the 13th century. In the 15th century, noble Venetian families built many villas with parks, but very little remains from this time. There were 30,000 inhabitants in those days, today barely 10,000. The famous family of painters, the Vivarini, lived in Murano.

Things to See: Guests are welcome to watch the glass-blowers. The glass objects offered for sale are mass produced for tourists and sometimes they are not even from Murano. Better quality wares can be found in the city center in the expensive establishments of Pauly, Barovier, Venini, Salviati, Cenedese, Moretti, Seguso and others. (See "Shopping".)

– The glass museum (*Museo Vetrario*) founded in 1862 and housed in the Palazzo

Giustinian, former seat of the Bishop of Torcello, built in 1689, gives a good survey of the history of Venetian glass. In Room X the most beautifully crafted pieces from the 15-18th centuries are to be found, including the wedding bowls of the Barovier, the most famous family of glass blowers.

Opening times: Monday, Tuesday, Thursday, Saturday 1000-1600 hrs. Sundays and public holidays 0900-1230 hrs. Entry fee: 3000 lire.

– **San Pietro Martire**, founded as a monastery church by the Dominicans in 1348, was originally dedicated to St. John and destroyed by fire in 1474. The rebuilt church (1511) was dedicated this time to Peter the Martyr, one of the main saints of the Dominicans. The church contains precious glass lusters and paintings by Bellini and Veronese.

– **SS Maria e Donato**, founded in 999 and dedicated to the Virgin Mary, received the extra title "San Donato" in 1125 when the relics of Saint Donatus were brought here from Sicily.

– **Palazzo da Mula** on the Fondamenta Vetrai is from the 14th century and **Palazzo Trevisan** from the 16th century, is on the Fondamenta Nivigero, opposite SS Maria e Donato. They are not open to the public.

How to get there: Ships are available on Line 12 from the Fondamente Nuove to Murano, Burano, Torcello and back.

Line 13 from the Fondamente Nuove to Murano, Le Vignole, San Erasmo and back.

PELLESTRINA
This island, adjacent to the Lido, has retained much of its original character; tourists seldom come here and there are no historical buildings. Venetians who are in the know go to the restaurant **Da Nane** in the little fishing village of San Pietro in Volta for fresh and delicious fish dishes.

How to get there: Pellestrina is crossed on the way to Chioggia. From the Lido (Bus Stop Santa Maria Elisabette) the bus No 11 goes to Alberoni. The bus now takes the vehicular ferry to Pellestrina, drives to the other end of the island and connects with the ship to Chiogga.

SAN FRANCESCO DEL DESERTO
According to legend, St. Francis of Assisi was shipwrecked here in 1200. When he arrived on the island a spring bubbled up in his path and his pilgrim's staff suddenly began to blossom. Today there is a Franciscan monastery here with cloisters from the 14th century and an idyllic garden. The monastery is open daily from 0900-1100 hrs and 1500-1730 hrs, for a donation.

How to get there: By ship, Line 19 (only in summer) from the Riva degli Schiavoni to San Francesco del Deserto, Torcello and Burano.

Line 12 from the Fondamente Nuova to Burano. Behind the church of San Martino there are boats waiting to take visitors on a half hour journey to San Francesco. It is easier with the Line 8 ferry from San Zaccaria via San Giorgio Maggiore and La Guidecca.

SAN LAZZARO DEGLI ARMENI
During the middle ages plague victims were cared for on this island. In 1717 the Armenian monk, Petrus Mechithar, founded a monastery which gave asylum to Armenian refugees. The Venetian government gave the Monk this island, twice the size of the Piazza San Marco. Today it is the center of their religion for the more than 2 million Armenians who live dispersed throughout Europe and the USA. Armenian culture is preserved by the 15 monks who live here today and they are especially proud of their library which contains 40,000 volumes on Armenian history and culture, together with 4,500 ancient handwritten documents, the oldest from the 8th century. In the monastery's printing workshop books were printed in 36 languages and in eight different alphabets. In 1816 Lord Bryon spent a long time in the monastery learning Armenian. The Monks call themselves Machitharists, after their founder, and use a Catholic-oriental ritual.

Opening times: Thursday and Sunday, 1500-1700 hrs, after the visit has been arranged by telephone. Tel: 5260104.

How to get there: By ship Line 20 San Zaccaria to San Servolo and San Lazzaro degli Armeni.

SAN MICHELE
Venice's cemetery island is about a mile from the Fondamenta Nuove, half way to Murano. In the 13th century the island was the home of Camaldulan Monks (from the monastery at Camaldoli, in Tuscany) whose monastery was closed at the beginning of the

19th century. Afterwards the place became a graveyard. Since there is very little room Venetians can only have a personal grave for 12 years, after which the remains go into a common grave.

The cloisters of the monastery (15th century) and San Michele (1469-78) built by Mauro Codussi, and one of the earliest renaissance churches in the Lagoon, are well worth seeing.

In the Protestant cemetery lies the American poet Ezra Pound (1885-1972); in the Russian Orthodox section Igor Stravinsky (1882-1971) and the ballet impressario Serge Diagilev (1872-1929), who gave the world *Petrushka* and *The Firebird*. A plan of the cemetery is available from the porter and helps visitors to find their way.

During the Counter Reformation the scholarly monk, Paolo Sarpi (1552-1623), who boldly defended the rights of Venice against the attacks of Rome, lived on San Michele. One of his famous sayings was: "I never, *never* tell a lie, but the truth not to everybody."

How to get there: By ship Line 5 (Circolare) to San Michele.

TORCELLO

Torcello, which lies in the northern lagoon, was founded in the 7th century and from the 9th to the 12th century was a flourishing trading city until its population was decimated by plague and malaria. The island lost its place to the rising city of Venice. Torcello was the seat of a Bishop from 538.

Things to See: The early Christian church of **Santa Maria Assunta**, dedicated in 639, is the finest example of Venetian-Byzantine style, with beautiful mosaics from the 11th and 12th centuries. Open daily 1000-1230 hrs and 1400-1800 hrs. Entry fee: 1,000 lire.

– **Santa Fosca:** A Byzantine church from the 11th century, with its central building surrounded by a five-sided arcade. The interior, with its harmonious use of space, is greatly valued by art historians. The church was built as a memorial to Saint Fosca, a female martyr from Ravenna.

– **Museo dell' Estario** (The Museum of the Lagoon): Contains a collection of marble sculptures, church vessels and old artifacts from the history of Torcello. Open daily except from 1000-1230 hrs and 1400-1600 hrs. Entry fee: 100 lire.

Restaurants:

Locanda Cipriani
Hemingway slept here. Rooms can still be rented. Closed from November 1 to March 20 and every Tuesday.

Villa '600
Closed on Wednesdays.

Al Ponte del Diavolo
Closed on Thursday and every evening except Saturday.

How to get there: By Ship Line 12 from the Fondamenta Nuove via Murano and Burano to Torcello.

TRAVEL AGENTS

Tours of the city, excursions to the islands etc. can be booked at the following agencies:

ACITOUR Veneto
Piazzale Roma, 540/b
Tel: 5208828.

Adriatic Shipping Company
San Marco, 2089
Tel: 5205533.

American Express Company
San Marco, 1471
Tel: 5200844.

Bucintoro
San Marco 2568
Tel: 5210632.

C.I.T. (Compagnia Italiana Turismo)
San Marco, 4850
Tel: 5285480.

Doge Gritti
Via Fausta, 122, 30010 Treporti
Tel: 658312.

Fantasy Tours
Lido, Via Lepanto, 7
Tel: 5261991.

Gondola Viaggi
Calle Avogaria, D.D. 1621/A
Tel: 5222808.

Guetta Travel
San Marco, 1289
Tel: 5208711.

ITAL Travel
San Marco, Ascensione, 72/b
Tel: 5229111.

Marco Polo
San Zaccaria, 4682/b
Tel: 5203200.

Waggons Lits/Turismo
San Marco, 289/305 Piazzetta dei Leoncini
Tel: 5223405.

Travel Agencies offering reasonably priced transport, language course and study trips:

A.T.G.
Calle Lerga Foscari, 3856, Dorsoduro.

C.T.S.
Fondamenta Taglia Pietra, 3252, Dorsoduro.

Duty Free
Crosera San Pantalon, 3943, Dorsoduro.

CULTURE PLUS

MUSEUMS

On the way to many museums, churches and palaces, illustrated brochures are sold: these are mainly very good and give an authoritative survey of the various displays. The publications are in many languages and not very expensive. The best ones are published by Edizione Electa of Milan (Gruppo Editoriale Electra) and cost between 6,000 and 15,000 lire.

There are sometimes local alterations to the opening times given here, as often happens in Italy. Museums, palaces and other places are sometimes shut for restoration.

Accademia
Canal Grande/Ponte dell' Accademia, Line 1, Stop: Accademia
Opening times: Work days 0900-1400 hrs; Sundays and holidays 0900-1300 hrs. Entry fee: 4,000 lire

The most popular works in the Accademia
1. Paolo Veneziano, Polyptych
2. Niccolódi Pietro, Madonna and Child
3. Jacobello Alberegno, Polyptych
4. Giovanni Bellini, Madonna enthroned with Saints
5. Cima da Conegliano, Madonna of the Orange Tree
6. Lorenzo Veneziano Polyptch
7. Andrea Mantegna, St. George
8. Piero della Francesca, St. Jerome
9. Cosmé Tura, Madonna
10. Giovanni Bellini, Madonna and Child
11. Giovanni Bellini, Madonna
12. Giovanni Bellini, Madonna and Child
13. Giorgione, La Tempestá
14. Giorgione, La Vecchia
15. Paris Bordone, The Giving of the King
16. Titian, John the Baptist
17. Girolamo Savoldo, SS Antonio e Paolo Eremita

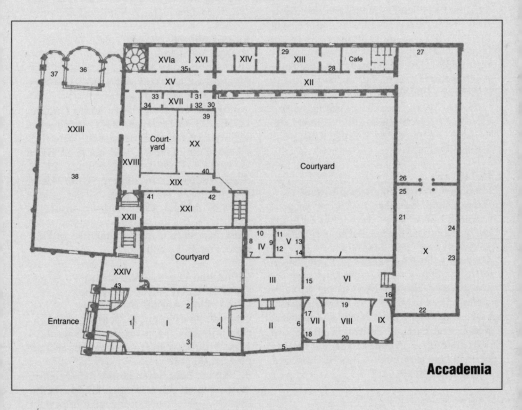

Accademia

Aquarium di Venezia
Calle Albanesi
Opening times: Daily 0900-1900 hrs, closed on Tuesdays. Entry fee: 1,500 lire

Museo Archeological
(Archeological Museum)
Piazza San Marco
Line 1, Stop: San Marco. Entrance in the Bibliotecá Marciana (Library of St. Mark) building.
Opening times: Work days 0900-1330 hrs; Sundays and holidays 0900-1230 hrs. Entry fee: 2,000 lire

Ca'd' Oro-Galleria Franchetti
Canal Grande
Line 1, Stop: Ca'd' Oro
Opening times: Work days 0900-1400 hrs; Sundays and holidays 0900-1200 hrs. Entry fee: 2,000 lire
Finest example of a Venetian gothic palace. It received the name "Golden House" because of the original blue and gold painting of the facade, today only the marble filigree decoration remains. It was built between 1421 and 1440 and is among the most beautiful of all palace facades in Venice. The museum gives a good impression of the domestic life of the Venetian patricians in the middle ages. Also displayed here is the art collection of Giorgio Franchetti who left it to the city in 1922. The collection contains works by Titian, Van Dyck, Mantegna, and also bronzes, sculptures and terracotta figures by Giambologna, Bellini, Riccio and Tullio Lombardi.

Ca' Pesaro
Fondamenta Mocenigo/Canal Grande
Line 1, Stop: San Staé
Opening times: Work days 0900-1400 hrs except Monday, Sundays and holidays: 0900-1300 hrs. Entry fee: 2,000 lire
The palace, built by Baldassare Longhena in the 17th century, houses the Museums for Modern and Oriental Art. In the Modern section are works by Franz von Lenbach, Franz von Stück, Marc Chagall and Auguste Rodin. The Oriental collection on the 3rd floor contains work from India and the Far East: Indian sculptures, Chinese vases and Japanese paintings.

Ca' Rezzonico:
Rio di San Barnaba/Canal Grande
Line 1, Stop: Ca' Rezzonico
Opening times: Work days except Friday 1000-1600 hrs; Sundays and holidays 0900-1230 hrs. Entry fee: 3,000 lire
This palace, built for the Rezzonico family in about 1600 is today a museum for the history of Venice in the 18th-century. In over 40 rooms there are charming examples of chinoiserie, lacquer furniture and Venetian china, beloved during the Rococo period. There are also original 18th century costumes, Flemish tapestries, silk carpets and Rococo furniture. On the third floor there are detailed reconstructions of an apothecary's shop and a theater of the day.

Campanile di San Giorgio Maggiore
Isola di San Giorgio Maggiore
Open daily 1000-1230 hrs and 1400-1630 hrs. Entry fee: 1,000 lire.

Campanile di San Marco
Piazza San Marco
Opening times : daily 1000-1600 hrs. Entry fee: 1,500 lire.

Casa Goldoni
Campo San Tomá, San Polo
Line 1, Stop: San Tomá.
Opening times: Work days 0830-1330 hrs. Closed Sundays and holidays.
Birthplace of the dramatist Carlo Goldoni (1707-1793) who developed in his comedies the style of the Commedia dell' Arte. Because of the quarrels with his rival Carlo Gozzi (1720-1806) he left Venice full of disappointment and went to Paris. Here, until his death, he wrote plays for the famous Theatre Itlien. The Museum contains momentos, documents, first editions of his work and there is also an Institute of Dramatic Art in the building.

Collezione Peggy Guggenheim
Canal Grande/Fondamente Venier
Line 1, Stop: Accademia or Salute
Opening times: April to October, daily except Tuesday 1200-1800 hrs; Saturdays 1800-2100 hrs (entry free). Entry fee at other times: 5,000 lire.
In Venice, her chosen home, the eccentric American art lover Peggy Guggenheim, brought together one of the most important

collections of modern art. The museum in the Palazzo Venier dei Leoni contains works by Kandinsky, Klee, Chagall, Picasso, Magritte, Tanquy, Léger, Schwitters and Rothko. There are many works of Max Ernst, who was married to Peggy Guggenheim, and of Jackson Pollock, whose work she encouraged.

Museo Diosesano di Arte Sacra (Diocesan Museum of Sacred Art)
Fondamenta Sant' Apollonia, Chiostro Sant' Apollonia, Castello (behind the Basilica San Marco)
Line 1, Stop: San Zaccaria.
Open on work days 1030-1230 hrs. Closed on Sundays and holidays.
This museum for religious art is housed in a cloister of the 12th century. It contains a collection of the work of Venetian goldsmiths over several centuries including monstrances, chalices, and tabernacles, as well as standards and precious illuminated manuscripts from the 15th century. There are four organ wings painted by Gentile Bellini (from the Basilica) and work by Palma the younger, Tintoretto and Titian.

Palazzo Ducale (The Doge's Palace)
Piazza San Marco
Line 1, Stop: San Marco
Opening times: daily 0830-1300 hrs. Entry fee: 5,000 lire.
The small **Museo dell' Opera** is attached to the palace and contains decorations from the building which were endangered by air pollution and have been replaced by copies.

Galleria Basilica di San Marco
Opening times: Work days 1000-1600 hrs, Sundays and holidays 1330-1600 hrs. Entry fee: 500 lire
Until 1981 the four bronze horses of St. Mark, which Enrico Dandolo seized from the Hippodrome of Constantinople in 1204, stood here. Napoleon shipped them off to Paris in 1797 but they were returned in 1815 following the protests of the outraged Venetians.

The Glass Museum (Museo Vetrario di Murano)
Isola di Murano
Open work days 1000-1600 hrs, except Wednesday, Sundays and holidays 0900-1230 hrs. Entry fee: 3,000 lire.
The Glass Museum is in the Palazzo Giustinian, the former seat of the Bishop of Torcello. It is one of the largest and most important collections, showing the history of glass making from Roman times to the present day with ca. 4,000 exhibits.

Museum of Jewish Culture and the Synagogues (Museo Communitá Israelitica)
Campo Ghetto Nuovo, Cannaregio
Line 1, Stop: Ferrovia or San Marcuola Line 5, Stop: Ponte Guglie.
Opening times: Work days 1030-1300 hrs. Closed on Saturdays, Sundays and Jewish holidays. Entry fee: 2,000 lire.
The Museum contains documents, cultural objects and manuscripts relating to the history of the Jewish community in Venice. Above the Museum is the Scuola Grande Tedeschá, and the other synagogues of the ghetto are all nearby on the Campo delle Scuole. They include the Scuola Canton, the Scuola Italiana, Scuola Levantina (17th century) and the Scuola Espagnola.

The Lagoon Museum (Museo dell' Estuario)
Isola di Torcello
Open work days except Monday 1030-1230 and 1400-1600 hrs. Entry fee: 2,000 lire.
Here one can see archaeological pieces from the early history of Venice: Roman tombs, fragments and inscriptions from Altinum and the lagoon, also hellenistic lamps and sculptures. In the adjoining Palazzo del Podestá there are the works of goldsmiths of the 11th-13th centuries, following Byzantine models, - very beautiful examples of such handwork. There is also a fragment of the Pala d' Argento, altarpieces from the Cathedral of Torcello.

Museum of Byzantine Art (Museo Dipinti Sacri Bizantini)
Salizzada dei Greci, Castello, (near the church of San Giorgio dei Greci)
Line 1, Stop: Riva degli Schiavoni.
Opening times: work days 0900-1230 and 1430-1700 hrs, Sundays and holidays 0900-1230 hrs. Entry fee: 2,000 lire.
In the 16th century there were about 5,000 Greeks living in Venice who built San Giorgio dei Greci for their community. The Museum of Byzantine Art contains treasures

from this small church, including important icons of the 14th-18th centuries, church utensils and splendid vestments. The museum and the Institute Ellenico di Venezia, the Institute for Greek Culture, are housed in a 17th-century palace built by Longhena.

In San Giorgio dei Greci there is an Orthodox church service every Sunday at 1100 and at 1200 hrs. (See "Religious Services".)

Museo Civico Correr and Museo di Risorgimento'
Piazza San Marco, entrance in the passage of the Napoleonic wing.
Open work days except Tuesday 1000-1600 hrs; Sundays and holidays: 0900-1230 hrs. Entry fee: 3,000 lire.
This museum gives a survey of the urban and cultural history of Venice, as well as a history of the Doges and the political institutions of the Republic. It contains gorgeous robes of the Doges and the nobles from the 14th-17th centuries and paintings by Carpaccio, Vivarini, the Bellini brothers, Pieter Breughel and other Flemish painters. The Museo di Risorgimento contains documents on 19th-century Venetian history including the fight for Italian unity, the resistance against Austrian rule and the Revolution of 1848.

Museo Fortuny
Campo San Benedetto, San Marco
Tel: 5200995.
Open Tuesday-Sunday 0900-1300 hrs.
In a gothic palace lived the painter, inventor, designer, couturier, photographer and architect Fortuny; now his rooms house a curious museum. Fortuny, a Spaniard by birth, was best known as a designer of textiles, which he printed with special dyes, and as a designer of dresses, worn by theatrical personalities such as Isadora Duncan, Eleanora Duse and Sarah Bernhardt. The museum contains a collection of his textiles, theater costumes, paintings, and set designs. Now and then exhibitions of photography and graphics are held here.

Museo Marciano (Church museum from the Cathedral of St. Mark's)
Inside the Cathedral
Open daily 1000-1700 hrs.
Here there are Byzantine sculptures from the 12th century, tapestries from the 13th-16th centuries and St. Mark's original bronze horses. Important pieces include the legendary chair of St. Mark, the Doge's throne and Byzantine shrine, reliquaries and icons.

Museo del Tessuto e del Costume (Textile and Costume Museum)
Bibliotheca Ca' Mocenigo-San Staé
Opening times 0900-1300 hrs Tuesdays and Saturdays .

Natural History Museum (Meseo di Storia Naturale)
Fondeco dei Turchi. Fondamenta del Megio/ Rio Fortego dei Turchi, Santa Croce
Line 1, Stop: San Staé.
Opening times: Work days 0900-1330 hrs; Sundays and holidays 0900-1300 hrs. Entry fee: 3,000 lire.
This palace was the residence of the Dukes of Ferrara from the 13th to the 15th centuries. In the years 1608-1621 it was used by the Imperial Ambassador Czorg Fugger until he moved into the Fondaco dei Turchi, former home of the Turkish merchants in Venice. Since 1880 it houses the Natural History Museum which provides an interesting survey of the marine fauna of the Adriatic, as well as zoological and mineral collections. On the ground floor there is a display of Venetian fountains and wells.

Oratorio dei Cruciferi (Oratory of the Order of the Cross)
Campo dei Gesuiti, Calle dei Cruciferi, Castello
Line 5 Stop: Fondamenta Nuove.
Opening times: Friday, Saturday, Sunday 1000-1200 hrs.

Pala d'Oro
In the Cathedral of St. Mark.
The famous altar piece is displayed on work days 1000-1600 hrs; Sundays and holidays 1330-1600 hrs. Entry fee: 500 lire.

Treasury, Cathedral of St. Mark
Open work days 1000-1600 hrs; Sundays and public holidays 1330-1600 hrs. Entry fee: 500 lire.
Basis of the church's treasure is the loot from the sack of Constantinople, 1204.

Marine Museum (Museo Storico Navale)
Riva San Biagio, Castello
Line 1, Stop: Arsenale
Opening times: work days 0900-1300 hrs; Saturday 0900-1200 hrs. Closed on Sundays and holidays.
The museum shows trophies from Venice's sea fights, also ship's models, documents and momentos to do with ship-building and types of ships. There is a model of the Doge's ship of state, the *Bucintoro*.

Lace Museum (Consorzio Merletti)
Isola di Burano
Opening times: work days except Tuesday 0900-1300 hrs; Sundays and holidays 0900-1300 hrs. Entry fee: 3,000 lire.
Old and new examples of the famous Burano stitched lace.

Clock Tower (Torre dell' Orologico)
Piazza San Marco
Open Tuesday-Saturday 0900-1200 hrs and 1500-1700 hrs; Sundays and holidays 0900-1200 hrs.
The tower, built by Mauro Codussi, shows a lion, symbol of St. Mark the Evangelist and of the Republic of Venice itself, on a blue field, strewn with golden stars. Every full hour the two Moors strike the bronze bell, the clock shows, besides the hours, the position of the sun in the zodiac and the phases of the moon. The Moors and the clock are the work of the artist Paolo Raniero and his sons, who poured them in bronze. Under the clock tower is an entrance to the Merceria, Venice's main shopping street.

CHURCHES

Churches, as a rule, open for early Mass from 0700 or 0800 hrs until noon and from 1700-1900 hrs, or until sunset. Different opening times will be given below. During services sightseeing and tours are not permitted. Photographers are usually not permitted to use flashlights. Look for directions in the individual churches! Visitors should be suitably dressed when they tour a church; Italians can be very conservative about this.

I Frari (Santa Maria Gloriosa dei Frari)
Campo San Rocco, Vaporetto 1
Stop: San Tomá.
Open daily 0930-1200 hrs and 1430-1700

hrs; Sundays and holidays 1500-1700 hrs. Entry fee: 500 lire.
In 1338 the Francescans – locally known as *Frari,* the Venetian for *Frati* (= Friars), Brothers – built their first church which stood until 1415. The land was given to them in 1250 by the Doge Jacopo Tiepolo. The building of the second church which we see today began in 1420. It follows the plan of a north Italian church of the mendicant friars: a pillared basilica with three naves, a vaulted transept, six small and one large, and a central Choir Chapel. The master builders of the two Frari churches are unknown but Peter Scipione Bon is regarded as the architect of the nave.
The following works of art make the Frari Church one of the great sights to be seen in Venice.

– The tomb of Claudio Monteverdi (1567-1643) in the most northerly side chapel, seen from the Presbytery.
– Titian's tomb, presented by the Emperor Ferdinand I of Austria, then King of Lombardo-Venetia.
– The tombs of the Doges Francesco Foscari (1423-1457), Niccoló Tron (1471-1473) and Giovanni Pesaro (1658-1659) by Bassaldare Longhena.
– The tomb of the neo-classical sculptor Antonio Canova (1757-1822). Only his heart is buried here, the rest of his remains are in his home town Possagno.
– The most famous painting in the Frari Church is Titian's *Assunta* (Assumption of the Virgin Mary) at the High Altar. It was completed in 1516 and 1518 and measures 22 feet by 11 feet (6.90 meters by 3.60 meters).
– In the apse of the Sacristy there is *The Madonna Enthroned* by Giovanni Bellini. On the north wall of the central nave, just before the chapel of the Emiliani, is another Titian: *Madonna di Ca' Pesaro.*
– Donatello's wood carving of John the Baptist (1451) and Jacopo Sansovino's sculpture of the same saint (1550) in the Cappella Cornaro are also among the important works in the church.

Chiesa dei Gesuiti (Santa Maria Assunta)
Campo dei Gesuiti, Cannaregio, Vaporetto 1
Stop: Ca' d' Oro.
In 1657 the Jesuits settled in Venice in place

of the forbidden order of the *Crociferi* and took over their monastery from the 12th century. From 1714-1729 the church was renovated and is still impressive today with its rich interior decoration of white-green marble encrustation, plaster mouldings and gilt. The massive baroque facade, the gift of the Manin family, recalls Roman models. The building and decoration of the presbytery was also made possible by the family Manin, whose grave is inside the church. In the left side-chapel is the tomb of Doge Pasquale Cicogna (1585-1595).

One of the greatest treasures here is the *Martydom of St. Lawrence* by Titian, in the last chapel on the left, and so is the wall and ceiling painting of Palma the younger in the Sacristy. In the left arm of the transept is Tintoretto's *Assumption of the Virgin*.

In Redentore (the Redeemer)
Isola La Guidecca
Lines 8 & 9 to "Redentore".
The name of La Guidecca comes probably from the Jews who settled here in the middle ages before they moved to the ghetto. Formerly noble Venetians had fine summer villas on the island, today La Giudecca is the home of working class people, handworkers and small businessmen.

The Church of the Redeemer is one of the main works of Andrea Palladio (1598-1580). In 1576 the Council promised to build a votive church if the city was freed from the plague. The contract went to Palladio, who had already built the Church of San Giorgio Maggiore in 1566 on the island of the same name. After the dedication of Il Redentore the Signoria went to La Giudecca on the 3rd Sunday in July, for a thanksgiving service. This festival is still celebrated by the Venetians (*see* "Festivals").

Le Zitelle (Santa Maria della resentazione)
Isola La Guidecca
Lines 8 & 9, Stop: "Zitelle".
Probably another work of Andrea Palladio from the 16th century. Similar in style to the Redentore church but smaller and plainer.

Madonna dell' Orto
Fondamenta Madonna dell' Orto
Line 5, Stop: Madonna dell' Orto.
The painter Tintoretto (1518-1594), whose name was really Jacopo Robusti, lived and worked in this suburb of Cannaregio, in the house no. 3399 on the Fondamenta dei Mori. His father was a dryer (*il tintore*) and this became his nickname, Tintoretto, the little dryer. The church contains 10 important paintings by the master and his son Domenico, who is also buried here, like his father. In the right aisle is the *Presentation of the Virgin*, left in the Choir is *The Worship of the Golden Calf*, and on the right is *The Last Judgement. The Awakening of Kicinius* by St. Agnes is on the fourth side of the chapel on the left. The church was originally dedicated to St. Christopher, later it became a church dedicated to the Virgin Mary.

Sant' Alvise
Campo Sant' Alvise, Cannaregio
Line 5, Stop: Sant' Alvise.
Formerly a convent church built in 1388 and dedicated to Saint Aloysius of Toulouse. The facade is one of the plainest in all Venice. The interior was changed in the 17th century into a hall church, without aisles, popular since the renaissance. The main sights include: three paintings by Tiepolo (1696-1720): *Christ on the way to Calvary* in the presbytery on the right, and two early works of this same artist, *The Crowning with Thorns* and *The Scourging*, on the south wall.

San Bartolomeo
Campo San Bartolomeo, San Marco
Line 1 Stop: Rialto.
Open on working days 0900-1100 hrs.
This was the church adopted by the German merchants in Venice whose trading depot in the Fondaco dei Tedeschi was nearby. The church was built in the 12th century, the present building is from the 18th century. It is famous for a painting which is no longer there: Albrecht Dürer's *Rosenkrantzfest* (Feast of the Rosary) painted for San Bartolomeo and later carried off the Prague, where it still hangs by the Emperor Rudolph II. In the sanctuary are the *Four Saints* by Sebastiano del Piombo (1507/09) and at the High Altar *The Martyrdom of Saint Bartholomeo* by Palma the younger. See also gravestones and epitaphs of many German merchants who were buried here.

San Francesco della Vigna

Campo Dan Francesco della Vigna, Castello
Line 5, Stop: Celestia.

This is the second monastery church of the
Franciscans in Venice. It is named after the
vineyard of Marco Ziani, son of the Doge
Pietro Ziani (1205-1229), who presented the
land to the Friars in 1253.

In 1534 Doge Andrea Gritti (1523-1538)
laid the foundation stone of the second church
(nothing is left of the first), designed by
Jacopo Sansovino. Forty years later Palladio
finished the building and erected the impressive facade (1568-72).

Things to see: A *Madonna* by Veronese,
a triptych by Antonio Vivarini (15th century)
in the sacristy, the *Madonna Enthroned*
painted by the lay brother Antonio da
Negraponte (1450) in the right transept, and
Giovanni Bellini's *Madonna with Saints*.

San Giacomo dell' Orio

Campo San Giacomo dell' Orio, Santa Croce
Line 1, Stop: Riva di Blasio or San Staé.

The main entrance to this parish church from
the 9th century is on the Rio San Giacomo
dell' Orio; its name may have in reference to
a sacred bay tree. The present form of the
church is from the 15th century. It is noted
for the richly carved wooden ceiling of the
nave, transept and choir as well as the carved
and gilded wooden panelling of the closed
wall sections between the arcades and the
clerestory, work from the 16th and 17th
centuries. In the new sacristy, which is outside the church building, there are wonderful
ceiling paintings by Veronese and Palma the
younger. The Campanile has kept its
romanesque form.

San Giacomo di Rialto

Campo San Giacomo di Rialto, San Polo
Line 1, Stop: Rialto.

This little church is popularly supposed to be
the oldest in Venice, founded in the 5th
century, but is more likely that it was actually founded in the 7th or 8th century. On
Maundy Thursday the Doge made a festive
procession to this church, for it had been
granted special indulgences by Pope Alexander III in 1177. After the Rialto fire of
1513 the church was completely rebuilt.

San Giobbe

Campo San Giobbe, Cannaregio
Line 5, Stop: Ponte Tre Archi (a rare example of one of the pier bridges with more than
one arch in Venice).

A monastery church of St. Job from the 15th
century. Its patron was the Doge Cristoforo
Moro (1462-71) who is buried here with his
wife. His fine grave stone lies before the
High Altar.

The church was originally supposed to
have been dedicated to St. Bernadin of Sienna, whom Moro knew and honored. Later
the figures of Job, St. Antony, St. Louis and
St. Francis of Assissi were set up on the
facade near St. Bernardin. The remains of an
old cloister can be seen on the Campo.

San Giorgio Maggiore

Opening times: 0900-1230 hrs and 1430-
1600 hrs, daily.

Already in 990 there was a Benedictine
monastery on San Giorgio Maggiore, the
island beside La Guidecca, and its church
was 200 years older. Both buildings were
destroyed by an earthquake. In 1566 San
Giorgio Maggiore was erected on the site of
the old church, to the design of Palladio; the
building was not completed until 1610. Important paintings in the interior are
Tintoretto's *Rain of Mann*, also his *Last
Supper* and the *Martyrdom of St. Stephen*. The
High Altar from the 16th century is by the
pupil of Sansovino, Girolamo Campagna.

From the 200-feet (60-meters) high
Campanile (18th century) there is a marvelous
view of the lagoon, in clear weather. The
Campanile is reached by a door left of the
monk's choir by a lift.

In 1800 there was a papal conclave on this
island which elected Pope Pius VII. Rome
was occupied by French troops at the time.

In 1951 the rich industrialist, Vittorio Cini,
endowed the Fondazione Giorgio Cini, in
memory of his son. It comprises an international study center, with a scientific department, a library, an art and graphic school and
a naval academy with a ship-building
workshop. The foundation is housed in a
former monastery; congresses and exhibitions are also held here.

The two cloisters of the monastery,
Palladio's refectory, the library, the open air
theater (**Teatro Verde**) and the **Centro
Marinaro** are open to the public.

How to get there: By Ship Line 5 (Circolare). This ferry line goes round the city in two directions. The Circolare sinistra (left) goes from the Piazzale Roma to La Guidecca, San Giorgio Maggiore, San Zaccaria, Arsenale, F. Nuove, Cannaregio-Canal, Railway Station, back to Piazzale Roma. The Circolare destra (right) goes the same way but in opposite direction. Line 8 is from San Zaccaria to San Giorgio Maggiore.

San Giovanni Crisostomo
Campo San Giovanni Crisostomo,
Cannaregio
Line 1, Stop: Rialto.
This church is the last work of the renaissance architect Mauro Codussi (1440-1504), and his masterpiece. The same artist designed and built the Church of San Michele in Isola, the clock tower on the Piazza San Marco, the facade of the Church of San Zaccaria, and the Palazzo Vendramin-Calergi. This church was built in 1497 and dedicated in 1504, the year Codussi died. It is dedicated to St. John Chrisostom and stands on the foundations of an earlier church. High points of the interior are: **Three Saints** by Giovanni Bellini (1513) and a monumental early work of Sebastiano del Piombo (1509) in the first side chapel on the right.

The building is a typical example of a Venetian church of the renaissance, with transept domes.

San Lio (San Leone)
Salizzada San Lio, Castello
Line 1, Stop: Rialto.
The church was built and decorated by Pietro Lombardi and his sons. It is named after the canonized Pope Leo IX, to whom it was dedicated in the 11th century. It was renovated in the 15th century (new presbytery); in the 17th century it was remodeled into a church hall, and in the 18th century it was further remodeled. The church no longer tallies with its original plans and its state before 1600 is known from views and paintings from this time.

At the High Altar there is a painting by Palma the younger, *The dead Christ carried up to heaven by angels* and Titian's painting of *The Apostle James* in the last side chapel on the left. The picture on the ceiling of the organ loft is by Domenico Tiepolo (1783).

Basilica di San Marco
Piazza San Marco, San Marco
Line 1, Stop: San Marco.
At first the church beside the Doge's Palace was only the private chapel of the reigning doge. It became important as a state church and the spiritual center of Venice with the transfer and burial of St. Mark's relics from Alexandria in 829; thereafter Venice called itself the Republic of St. Mark. The celebrated mosaics, modeled on Byzantine work, cover 47,111 sq feet (4,240 sq meters) of the interior and have brought the Cathedral the name of the Golden Basilica. Visitors are also impressed by the beauty of the architectual forms and the changing vistas in the interior of the great church. The building's interior measures 252 feet (76.5 meters) long and 170 feet (51.8 meters) wide and is built in the form of a Greek cross. (See chapter on "The Cathedral of St. Mark".)
Opening times:
Basilica: Monday-Saturday 1000-1800 hrs; Sundays and holidays 1400-1800 hrs.
Gallery: Workdays 1000-1600 hrs; Sunday and holidays 1330-1600 hrs.
Treasury: Monday-Saturday 1000-1600 hrs; Sundays and holidays 1330-1600 hrs.
Palau 'Oro (Altarpiece): Monday-Saturday 1000-1600 hrs; Sundays and holidays 1330-1600 hrs. Campanile: daily 1000-1600 hrs.

San Marcuola (SS Ermagora e Fortunato)
Campo San Marcuola, Cannaregio
Line 1, Stop: San Marcuola.
The name of the church is another of the "portmanteau words" which often occur in Venetian dialect; the two saints Hermagoras and Fortunatus have been placed together.

The well known architect Giorgio Massari erected the church in the years 1728-1736; the facade of the Grand Canal is incomplete.

The church is mainly famous for two paintings by Tintoretto, the *Last Supper* in the presbytery (1547) and opposite a copy of his *Christ washing the feet of the Disciples.* The original was taken to Spain in the 17th century and is now in the Escorial. It is interesting to see that the altars in this church are decorated with sculpture, and not with pictures.

Santa Maria Formose
Campo Santa Maria Formosa, Castello
Line 1, Stop: Rialto, San Zaccaria.
This church was built in 1492 by Mauro

Codussi and in its lovely, rather Byzantine interior there are many important works of art. Leandro Bassano's *Last Supper*, a polyptych by Palma the Elder and Bartolomeo Vivarini's *Mater Misericordiae*.

Traditionally the Doge visited this church every year at Candlemas, the Feast of the Purification of the Virgin Mary. According to legend, in the year 944 a group of young girls had been seized by pirates and rescued by gallant lads from the Cabinet Makers' Guild. They asked the Doge to visit the church at Candlemas for their reward.

The name of the church refers to a beautiful vision of the Virgin, seen by a Bishop in the 7th century. (*Formoso* = beautiful.) On the campo before the church there were once plays, festivals and bullfights.

Santa Maria del Giglio (Santa Maria Zobenigo)

Campo Santa Maria del Giglio, San Marco
Line 1, Stop: Santa Maria del Giglio.
The name comes from the founding family Zubanico, who lived in the 9th century. The present building stems from the 16th and 17th centuries and was made possible by donations from the Barbara family. The creator of the facade, Giuseppe Sardi, placed a likeness of himself on the outside of the church, over the main doors. Underneath there are reliefs of all the towns in which Antonio Barbara had served as a sea captain for Venice: Split, Cjania (Crete), Padua, Rome, Zadar and Corfu.

A special treasure in the interior is the fragment of a *Holy Family*, which may be the only Rubens painting in Venice. In the presbytery there is a painting of the *Four Evangelists* by Tintoretto and also a painting by him dedicated to the memory of the victory at Lepanto: *Christ, St. Justine and Francesco di Paola*.

Santa Maria dei Miracoli

Campo Miracoli, Cannaregio
Line 1, Stop: Rialto.
Open Monday-Saturday 0900-1200 and 1500-1800 hrs, Sundays and holidays 0900-1200 and 1500-1900 hrs.
One of the purest and most beautiful examples of Italian early renaissance architecture, built in 1481-89 by Pietro Lombardo and his sons as the votive church for a miracle picture of the Madonna.

The picture, honored since 1477, when Pope Sixtus IV promulgated the cult of the Immaculate Conception, is a work from Niccoló da Venezia and stands today on the High Altar. The interior has a clear, serene architectural form in which the way the light falls is part of the total impression. Marble encrustation and sculpture largely take the place of paintings for decoration. Different colored varieties of marble are also used effectively on the facade.

Santa Maria del Rosario (Chiesa dei Gesuati)

Zattere di Gesuati, Dorsoduro
Lines 5, 8, Stop: Zattere.
The **Gesuati** was an order founded in 1367 who in 1423 erected a church dedicated to St. Jerome. After the community was dissolved, the Dominicans built the present church of Santa Maria del Rosario after a design of Giorgio Massari, between 1726 and 1736.

The facade is strongly influenced by Palladio. Inside there are altar pictures by G.B. Tiepolo, Sebastiano Ricci (1659-1734) and G.B. Piazzetta (1682-1754), also a *Crucifixion*, by Tintoretto and ceiling frescoes from Tiepolo showing the *Virgin Mary Institutes the Use of the Rosary* and *St. Dominic Ascends into Heaven*. Also worth seeing is the richly carved choir stall from the 18th century in the monk's choir.

Santa Maria della Salute

Campo della Salute, Dorsoduro
Line 1, Stop: Salute.
Open daily 0800-1200 and 1500-1700 hrs.
The church was built as a votive offering, after the city was freed from a bout of the plague in 1630 which had cost 40,000 lives. The vow of the Signoria is remembered every November, at the festival of the Salute (see "Festivals"). Twelve designs for the church were considered but Bassaldare Longhena's was chosen because "it achieves an extremely decorative effect, without costing very much". The building was completed in 1687, after the architect's death. It was dedicated to the Virgin Mary both as Venice's saviour from the plague and as ruler of the sea (Capitana del Mar). This is the explanation of the statue on the summit of the dome which shows the Virgin Mary holding a Venetian admiral's baton. Inside

the church the paintings in the great Sacristy are interesting: *The Marriage at Cana* by Tintoretto, Titian's ceiling paintings of *Cain and Abel*, *Abraham's Sacrifice*, and *David and Goliath*, as well as one of Titian's early masterpieces, an altar picture from 1511-12 showing the Saints Mark, Sosmas, Damian, Sebastian and Roche.

San Moisé
Campo San Moisé, San Marco
Line 1, Stop: San Marco.
The building is a foundation from the 8th century, renovated in its present baroque style in 1688 by Alessandro Tremignan and the Flemish artist Meyring. His sculptures of fantastic creatures, figures of women and animals, crowd the facade which looks like a theatrical setting.

At the High Altar is a painting by Antonio Pellegrino showing Moses, the patron of the church, receiving the tables with the 10 commandments on Mt. Sinai. On the organ are further scenes from the life of Moses.

San Niccoló di Lido
Lines 1, 2, 6, 11, Stop: San Niccoló.
This little church, founded in 1044 and renovated in baroque style in the 17th century, takes its name from St. Nicholas, Bishop of Myra in Asia Minor, which then still belonged to Byzantium. Venetian sea farers seized his bones – as they thought – and brought them to Venice. Later it was discovered that the saint's real remains had been taken to Bari…someone had stolen a march on the Venetians.

Every year on the feast of the Ascension the Doge used to hear mass in this church after the **Wedding with the Sea**. Visitors should see the parts of the mosaic floor, from the 11th century, and the cloisters, together with paintings by Palma the Elder and the younger.

San Niccoló dei Mendicoli
Campo San Niccoló, Dorsoduro
Line 5, Stop: San Basilio.
This small church, not visited by many tourists, lies near the old harbor and fishing quarter of Santa Maria. The church was founded in the 7th century, and often renovated from the 12th to the 16th century, but it still retains its simple medieval atmosphere. Old marble pillars divide the interior

into three naves; the gilded wooden decorations over the pillars of the central nave shimmer mysteriously in the dim church. Behind the High Altar is a large wooden statue of St. Nicholas.

San Pantalon (San Pantaleone)
Campo San Pantalon, San Polo
Line 1, Stop: San Tomá (near the Frari church)
This is the church of an old patron saint from Venice whose name is also found in the Commedia dell' Arte character Pantalone, the miserly old merchant. The baroque church is interesting mainly for its painting – allegorical pictures from the life of the saint and biblical stories by Gianantonio Fumiani. There is also an altar picture by Paolo Veronese. The church keeps as a relic, a nail believed by the faithful to have come from the cross of Christ.

Chiesa della Pietá (Santa Maria della Pietá Santa Maria della Visitazione)
Riva degli Schiavoni, Castello
Line 1, 2, Stop: San Zaccaria.
This church belonged to the former Ospedale della Pietá, a conservatorium of music for young girls of good family; it is now known by the Venetians as the **Chiesa di Vivaldi**. The famous musician worked at the conservatorium for many years as a violin teacher and composer. Venice honors his memory with regular concerts of chamber music in the Chiesa della Pietá. The facade of the church forms the center of a building of which the Ospedale also forms a part. The ceiling paintings are by G.B. Tiepolo.

San Pietro in Castello
Campo San Pietro, Isola di San Pietro, Castello
Line 1, Stop: Giardini (near the Biennale grounds.)
On this island far east of Venice (connected with the city today by two bridges) stood **Olovolo**, one of the earliest settlements in the lagoon.

Bishop Magnus of Altinum (7th century) saw St. Peter in a dream, who bade him build a church in the place where he saw *sheep and goats grazing*. Since 775 this was the seat of the Bishop of Venice who bore the title of Patriarch from 1451. The Cathedral of St. Mark was seat of the Bishop and Patriarch only after the fall of the Republic, in 1807.

The present church was built in the 17th century from old plans of Palladio; the Campanile is from Mauro Codussi. The interior has an impressive High Altar from Bassaldare Longhena and the **Cattedra di San Pietro**, the alleged throne of St. Peter, from Antioch.

San Polo
Campo San Polo, San Polo
Line 1, Stop: San Tomá or San Silvestro.
Little remains of the building founded in the 9th century by Doge Pietro Tradenico (836-864). The Campanile (1362), the wonderful side portal (1440) and the main entry, together with the reliefs on the outer walls of the side passages, suggest that this was the original building.

In the interior, only the wooden vaulting of the central nave and the windows of the inner facade walls remain from the gothic triple nave construction of the 15th century.

The paintings in the church are by Tintoretto; *Ascension of the Virgin* and *The Last Supper* are at the first side altar to the right. Two other paintings of the *Last Supper* by this artist are to be seen in San Marcuola and San Giorgio Maggiore. At the second side altar, left, are G.B. Tiepolo's *The Virgin Mary with St. John Nepomuk*, also paintings by his son Domenico (*Stations of the Cross*) and an altar picture by Paolo Veronese showing the *Bethrothal of the Virgin Mary*.

San Salvatore
Campo San Salvatore, San Marco
Line 1, Stop: Rialto
In the 12th century there was a monastery church of the Augustine order of this sire, renovated in 1507-1534 by Tullio Lombardo and Jacopo Sansovino, while the baroque facade was designed by Guiseppe Sardi. From its proportions and its rich design it seems that this church was meant to be a counterpart of the Basilica of St. Mark but it has only three domes while St. Mark's has five. The interior is impressively wide, because of the open baldachins.

Visitors should not miss the grave monuments of the Doge Francesco Venier (1554-1556), the work of the 80-year-old Sansovino, the figure "Hope" is particularly impressive. On the front of the transept and the left wall of the nave are the tombs of the Cornaro family, in particular the tomb of Caterina Cornaro, Queen of Cyprus, burned here in 1510. A third important burial place is that of Doge Lorenzo and Doge Girolamo Priuli, who reigned from 1556-59 and 1559-67.

One should also see the *Annunciation*, painted by the 76-year-old Titian.

San Sebastiano
Campazzo Sebastiano, Dorsoduro
Line 5, Stop: San Basilio.
Opening times: Monday-Saturday 0900-1200 and 1500-1800 hrs, Sundays 0900-1200 and 1500-1900 hrs.
San Sebastiano is a monument to the great painter Paolo Veronese (1528-1588), born Paolo Caliari. He designed and decorated the church almost entirely by himself and he is buried here, his grave marked by a tablet in the floor at the High Altar.

In the nave there are scenes from the story of Esther; the ceiling in the sacristy shows *The Four Evangelists* and the *Crowning of the Virgin*. Both are the earliest known works of the master, from 1555. The splendid gold frames should also be noted. In the Nuns' Choir there is the *Martyrdom of St. Sebastian* and *St. Sebastian before the Emperor Diocletian*; at the High Altar is a late work of Veronese, *The Virgin Mary enthroned with Saints Sebastian, Peter, Catherine and Francis*. The artist also designed and painted the organ.

San Staé (Sant' Eustachio)
Campo San Staé Santa Croce
Line 1, Stop: San Staé.
Built in 1678 by Giovanni Grassi in the form of a Greek cross. Domenico Ross designed the facade of the church, which is highly reminiscent of Palladio but overlaid with baroque ornament.

The interior contains mainly paintings from the 18th century, including *The Torture of St. James*, by Piazzetta, *The Crucifixion of St. Andrew* by Pellegrini and *The Martyrdom of St. Bartholomew* by G.B. Tiepolo.

Santa Stefano
Campo Francesco Morosini-Santa Stefano, San Marco
Line 1, Stop: Accademia or Santa Maria del Giglio.
The most interesting thing about the exterior of this church is the "leaning tower", best

seen from Campo Sant' Angelo. The building itself has a splendid portal, the interior of the gothic church (14th century) contains colored capitals, marble pillars and wooden vaulting.

In the sacristy are three paintings by Tintoretto which originally hung in the Church of St. Margaret. The large cloisters (1532) and the fine chapter house of the former Augustan monastery from the 13th century can still be visited. Today the buildings house the taxation departments.

San Trovaso (SS Gervasio e Protasio)
Campo San Trovaso, Dorsoduro
Line 1, Stop: Accademia or Lines 5, 8 Stop: Zattere.
A very plain church which contains paintings by Tintoretto (*The Last Supper*, *The Temptation of St. Antony*), also *St. Chrysigonus* by Michele Giambono and a beautiful Maddona by Giovanni Bellini. The marble reliefs from the middle of the 15th century which cover the altar are the work of an unknown master.

San Zaccaria
Campo San Zaccaria, Castello
Line 1, Stop: San Zaccaria.
The monastery church of St. Zacharias was founded by the Emperor Leo V in the 9th century; the present building was erected between 1460 and 1500 by Antonio Gamballo, followed by Mauro Codussi. It is a blend of early renaissance and late gothic architectural style. In the 16th century the convent was one of the most highly-spirited in Venice; the gallant adventures and the convent balls of the nuns were known all over town.

Particularly worth seeing is the Cappella Tarasio, the choir section of the old pre-gothic convent church from the 10th century, which was reserved for the private use of the nuns. It is built over the crypt which also stems from the the 10th century. The wonderfully worked capitals of the pillars are worth seeing and the frescoes in the vaulting by the Florentine master Andrea Castagno (1442).

At the right side altar is a picture of the *Doge and the Council visiting the Church of San Zaccaria at Easter*. Besides work by Palma the younger is *The Birth of John the Baptist* by Tintoretto.

San Zanipolo (SS Giovanni e Paolo)
Campo San Zanipolo, Castello
Line 1, Stop: Rialto or Line 5, Stop: Ospedale Civile.
Next to the Frari church and the Basilica di San Marco, the church of San Zanipolo is the most important in Venice. Twenty-seven Doges are built in this church of the Dominicans, including Giovanni Dolfin, Pietro Mocenigo, Niccoló Marcello, Pasquale Malpiero, Sebastiano Venier, Marco Corrier, Andrea Vendramin – his tomb is one of the most important and was made by Tullio Lombardi.

The High Altar is the work of Bassaldare Longhene. Besides many fine paintings, the windows in the right transept, made of Murano glass from about 1500 should not be missed; they show saints of the Dominicans and other figures.

Chiesa di Scalzi (Santa Maria di Nazareth)
Fondamenta degli Scalzi, Cannaregio
Lines 1, 2, 3, 4, 5, Stop: Ferrovia (the Railway Station)
This Carmelite church was built between 1670 and 1705 after plans by Bassaldare Longhene. It is very splendidly decorated with marble encrustation, sculptures and gilt. The church contains the grave of the last Doge of Venice, Ludovico Manin. The ceiling frescoes are by G.B. Tiepolo.

SCUOLA (HOUSES OF THE BROTHERHOOD)

Scuola dei Carmini
Campo Carmini, Dorsoduro
Line 1, Stop: San Tomá.
Opening times: Work days 0900-1200 and 1500-1800 hrs; Saturdays, Sundays and holidays closed. Entry fee: 2,000 lire.
The Scuola are the meeting houses of religious lay brotherhoods whose wealth was displayed in the splendid decoration of their buildings.

The Scuola dei Carmini belonged to the six largest and most high esteemed brotherhoods of the city and the building was designed by Bassaldare Longhene in the 17th century. There are important ceiling paintings by G.B. Tiepolo.

Scuola di San Giorgio Degli Schiavoni

Calle dei Frulani, Castello
Line 1, Stop: San Zaccaria.
Opening times: Work days 1000-1230 and 1530-1800 hrs; Saturday and Sunday 1000-1230 hrs. Entry fee: 3,000 lire.
This was the Scuola of the Dalmatian merchants (Schiavoni = Slavs, Dalmatians) and was decorated by Vittore Carpaccio between 1502 and 1508. His picture cycle shows scenes from the life of St. George (patron of the Brotherhood) and St. Jerome.

Scuola di San Giovanni Evangelista

Campiello San Giovanni Evangelista, San Polo
Line 1, Stop: San Tomá.
Like the Scuola dei Carmini this was one of the most wealthy and important Brotherhoods in Venice and was grounded in 1261. The Scuola's famous paintings, including the *Miracles of the Holy Cross* by Gentile Bellini and Vittore Carpaccio are now found in the Accademia. The Brotherhood was dissolved during the secularization in 1806, but formed again and still exists in the old buildings near the Frari church.

Opposite the Scuola lies its own small church San Giovanni Evangelista from the 15th century. Here concerts of classical music are sometimes performed.

Scuola di San Marco

Campo SS Giovanni e Paolo, Castello
Line 1, Stop: San Marco or Line 5, Stop: Ospedale Civile.
Opening times: workdays 1000-1200 hrs.
Next to the church of San Zanipolo stood the meeting house of the Silk dealers and Goldsmiths. It was built between 1490 and 1500 under the direction of Pietro and Tullio Lombardi. Today it is the city hospital (Ospedale Civile).

Scuola Grande di San Rocco

Campo San Rocco, San Polo
Line 1, Stop: San Tomá.
Opening times: Work days 1000-1300 hrs; Saturdays and Sundays 1000-1300 and 1500-1800 hrs.
The fame of this house was made known by the cycle of pictures by Tintoretto.

PALACES

The Canal Grande is the main thoroughfare of Venice. The Venetian patricians built their splendid palaces on its banks in the 12th to the 19th centuries; their show side is facing the water and they have their own water entrance (*ingresso all' aqua*). The backs of the palaces and their land entrances are often very plain. Boats and gondolas were tied to special mooring-posts (*pali*) in the water that were decorated with the colors and the coats of arms of the noble families. A number of them can still be seen before the palaces. In the 12th and 13th centuries the palaces were built with only two stories; the main architectural motif is the pillar which gives the house the character of a structure that is open to the outer world. In the gothic style of the 13th and 14th centuries this conception altered; the house was increasingly regarded as a private realm, cut off from the outside world, in which the individual could withdraw from the ever-expanding power of the state and keep himself free from its encroachment. This was shown architecturally in the use of large solid expanses of wall, while the pillar, as a light and frail building element, was less used. In the course of centuries other styles developed so that a journey down the Grand Canal can be regarded as an object lesson in art history and city architecture. Here is an alphabetical list of the most important palaces on the Canal Grande and in other parts of the city.

Palazzi Barbara

Canal Grande/Ponte dell' Accademia
Line 1, Stop: Accademia.
Two palaces from the 15th and 17th centuries which once contained precious paintings by G.B. Tiepolo. In fact some of these paintings are still in place, plus an interesting portrait of Giovanni Grimani by Barnardo Strozzi, but visitors cannot see them because the palace is not open to the public.

Palazzo Barbarigo

Canal Grande
Line 1, Stop: Accademia.
The palace is now occupied by the Glass Company of Murano (Compagnia Vetri Muranesi). There are striking mosaics on the facade from the 19th century advertising the work of the glass makers; they depict *The*

Emperor Charles V visiting Titian's Studio and *Henry III of France with the Glass-blowers of Murano.*

Palazzo Belloni-Battagia

This palace lies next to the Deposito del Megio, an old corn storehouse from the 15th century. It is probably the work of Bassaldare Longhena. The two storied facade is of marble; a point of interest are two obelisks on the roof whose function is to hide the chimneys.

Ca' Foscari

Canal Grande/Rio Foscari
Line 1, Stop: San Tomá Ca' Rezzonico.
The University of Venice is housed in the former palace of Doge Francesco Foscari (1423-57). He had the longest term as Doge in the history of the republic but in the year of his death 1457 he was put aside by the Loredan family, while his son Jacopo was sent into banishment. He was said to have conspired with the Sforzas of Milan.

In 1574 the French King Henry III stayed in this palace during his trip to Venice.

Ca' da Mosto

Canal Grande
Line 1, Stop: Ca'd' Oro.
This 12th-century Venetian-Byzantine palace was the birthplace in 1432 of the explorer Alvise da Mostos. He was the first European to round Cape Verde on the west African coast and he discovered the Canary Islands.

From the 16th-18th centuries, the palace was a famous hotel known as **Leon Bianco**. Emperor Joseph II, son of Maria Theresa stayed here.

Ca'd' Oro

See "Museums".

Ca' Rezzonico

See "Museums".

Palazzo Camerlenghi

Canal Grande/Ponte di Rialto
Line 1, Stop: Rialto.
The present building was erected between 1525 and 1528 to replace an older building completely destroyed in the Rialto fire of 1513. The palace was the seat of the Camerlenghi, the three highest financial officials of the Republic; in the ground floor was the Debtors' Prison.

Financial offences were harshly punished in 16th-century Venice. The costly interior, including paintings by Bonifazio Pitati, can be admired in the Accademia and in the Fondazion Cini on San Giorgio Maggiore.

Palazzo Contarini del Bovolo

Calleta Contarini del Bovolo
Line 1, Stop: Santa Maria del Giglio.
This palace is named after its spiral staircase (*Bovolo* = snail) designed by Giovanni Candi in 1500; it ascends inside a round tower in the courtyard. The decorative staircase is one of the most photographed sights in Venice.

Palazza Contarini-Spinelli

Rio Ca' Corner/Canal Grande
Line 1, Stop: Sant' Angelo.
16th-century palace by Mauro Codussi. The oldest palace in Venice with a complete stone facade. Next to the Palazzo Vendramin-Calergi is one of the most beautiful examples of a renaissance palace.

Palazzo Contarini-Fasan

Riodell Albero/Canal Grande
Line 1, Stop: Santa Maria del Giglio.
Also called **Casa della Desdemona** by the Venetians; the daughter of a Venetian Senator was supposed to have lived here before her marriage to Othello, the Moor. A must for Shakespeare and Verdi fans.

Palazzo Corner-Ca' Grande

Canal Grande
Line 1, Stop: Santa Maria del Giglio.
Jacopo Sansovino designed this palace in 1537; today it houses the **Prefettura**, the Provincial Government. The name **Casa Grande** refers to the enormous dimensions of the building, made for Jacopo Cornaro (Venetian Corner), the nephew of Caterina Cornaro (1454-1510) who was Queen of Cyprus from 1473-89.

Palazzo Corner della Regina

Cale Corner/Canal Grande
Line 1, Stop: San Staé.
Queen Caterina Cornaro was born in the predecessor of this present building in 1454. The old Venetian noble family of the Cornaro was so wealthy, through the sugar plantations on Cyprus, that the King of the island Jacopo II married the young Caterina in

1472. After the King's death the Republic, who had an eye on the rich and strategic island, forced the Queen to abdicate. Today the Venetian state pawnshop is housed in the Palazzo Corner.

Palazzo Dandolo
Riva degli Schiavoni 4191, Castello.
This was formerly the house of Doge Enrico Dandol (1192-1205), the conqueror of Constantinople. Today it is the luxury Hotel Danieli. (see "Where to Stay".)

Palazzo Dario
Canal Grande
Line 1, Stop: Salute.
Giovanni Dario, for whom the palace was built in 1487, was Ambassador of the Venetian Republic at the court of Sultan Mehmet II in Constantinople in 1479. The building has beautiful marble incrustations on the Facade; the rosettes and ornaments recall the decoration of the Church of Santa Maria dei Miracoli. (see "Churches".)

Palazzo Duodo
Campo Sant' Angelo, San Marco
Line 1, Stop: Sant' Angelo.
In this gothic palace from the 15th century which is in the city and not on the Canal Grande, there was once an inn, the **Tre Stelle**. Here the musician, Domenico Cimarosa, one of the most important composers of Italian comic opera, died in 1801. Goethe, who admired his work very much said of him: "The Comedy and humor of his music make nonsense itself into great art."

Palazzo Ducale
(The Doge's Palace: see "Museums".)

Palazzo Giustinian
Calle Giustinian/Canal Grande
Line 1, Stop: Ca' Rezzonico.
The palace next door to the Palazzo Foscari is really two buildings in one, with a narrow alley between the two. In 1858-59 Richard Wagner composed the second act of *Tristan and Isolde* here.

Palazzo Grassi
Campo San Samuele/Canal Grande
Line 1, Stop: San Samuele.
Erected in 1718 by Giorgio Massari for the Grassi family from Bologna, who lived here

until the beginning of this century.
The layout of the palace is interesting because it is built around a large square inner courtyard. In 1985 the Fiat company purchased the palace and had it restored to serve as a Culture Center. It was opened in 1986 with a striking exhibition entitled "Future World". Other exhibitions are planned annually together with concerts and theater productions.

Palazzi Grimani
Rio di San Luca/Canal Grande
Line 1, Stop: Sant' Angelo.
This palace near Sant' Angelo was built by Michele Sammicheli about 1540 for the Procurator Girolamo Grimani. It looks heavy and massive in a very un-Venetian way; today it houses the Court of Appeal.

The second Palazzo Grimani on the Rio San Polo comes from the early 16th century and had beautiful polychrome marble incrustations that recall the Doge's Palace.

Palazzo Gritti
(See "Where to Stay")

Palazzio Labia
Fondamenta Labia, near the Church of San Geremia
Line 5, Stop: Ponte delle Guglie.
In the ballroom on the first floor are the Tiepolo frescoes, showing scenes from the life of Antony and Cleopatra. The Labia family were famous for their wealth and their extravagance. (See chapter on "The Other Venice"). Today this is the home of RAI, Italian radio and television.

Palazzi Loredan-Farsetti
Riva del Carbon/Canal Grande
Line 1, Stop: Rialto.
Here is the city hall and the administration of Venice. In the 18th century this palace housed the Austrian Ambassador – Venetians still call it **Palazzi del Ambasciatore**.

Palazzo Manin
Riva del Carbon/Canal Grande
Line 1, Stop: Rialto.
Jacopo Sansovino built this palace between 1532 and 1560; today it houses the **Banca d'Italia**. The architect Giovanni Antonio Selva who also built the Teatro La Fenice, did the interior in classical style in the 18th

century for Ludovico Manin (Doge, 1789-97). Manin, the last Doge, abdicated when Napoleon entered the city.

Palazzo Mocenigo
Canal Grande, Stop: Sant' Angelo.
The rich and powerful Mocenigo family, who produced seven Doges, possessed four city palaces, joined together into a building complex. In the palazzo erected in 1579 the natural philosopher and Dominican monk Giordani Bruno was a guest. His host, Giovanni Mocenigo, denounced him to the Inquisition for heresy and Bruno was later burnt at the stake. Bruno believed in the infinity of space, which he deduced from the infinite qualities of God. He reasoned further that God could produce nothing finite.

The three other palaces are from the 17th and 18th centuries. In the last palace, concerts with 18th-century Venetian music are held every Tuesday and Saturday from November to March. Afternoon tea is served between 1630-1830 hrs.

Palazzo Pesaro
Bassaldare Longhena began this palace in 1676 for the Procurator Leonardo Pesaro; it was finished in 1710 by Antonio Gaspari. Today it contains the Gallery of Modern Art and the Oriental Museum (See "Museums".)

Palazzo Pisani
Canal Grande/Rio di Santissimo Stefano
Line 1, Stop: Accademia.
An enormous baroque building, like a castle, begun in 1614/15 but not completed until the 18th century. It contains many trophies, ships' lanterns and mementos of Admirale Pisani. There are paintings by Ricci, Domenico, Tiepolo and others.

Since 1897 the palace has housed the State Conservatorium; its most famous director was the composer Ermanno Wolf-Ferrari (1876-48). His best known opera is *I Quatro Eusteghi*, The Four Boorish Husbands, after Goldoni.

The Conservatorium has a small museum in the palace with mementoes of famous composers (Richard Wagner etc.) and a collection of old musical instruments.

Palazzo Vendramin-Calergi
Calle Larga Vendramin/Canal Grande
Line 1, Stop: San Marcuola.

The palace is one of the finest examples of Venetian renaissance architecture, built in the years 1504-09 by Mauro Codussi and Tullio Lombardi. The Calergi first owned the palace, then the Grimani (16th century) and finally the Vendramin in the 18th century. On February 13, 1883, Richard Wagner died here; he had been living in Venice with his family since the summer of 1882. In winter there is a Casino in the Palace.

Palazzo Venier dei Leone
Canal Grande/Fondamenta Venier
Line 1, Stop: Accademia or Salute.
This unfinished palace from the 18th century is near the Church of Santa Maria della Salute. The name "dei Leone" comes from the fact that the Venier family kept lions in their large garden.

After the Second World War, the American Peggy Guggenheim (1898-1979) purchased the building and it still contains her collection of Modern Art. (see "Museums".)

THEATERS

Teatro all' Avogaria
Campo San Sebastian, 1617 Dorsoduro.
Mainly productions in Venetian dialect.

Teatro al Frari
Compagnia Cittádi Venezia Serenissima, Ramo delle Chiovere, 3089 San Polo.

Teatro Goldoni
Calle Goldoni, San Marco.
Built in 1678.

Teatro La Fenice
Campo San Fantin, 1965, San Marco.
Tel: 5210161.
Venice's most famous Opera House. The Festival of Contemporary Music is also held here. The theater is open from November to July. Box office times: 0930-1230 and 1600-1800 hrs.

Teatro Malibran
Corte del Teatro Malibran, Cannaregio.
Named for the famous Spanish singer Maria Malibran (1808-1836) who often performed in Venice. Today mostly ballet is offered in Teatro Malibran, which was built in 1678.

Teatro di Palazzo Grassi
Salizzada San Samuele, 3213, San Marco.

Teatro del Ridotto
Calle Vallareso, San Marco.
Tel: 5222939.
In the 18th century there was a famous casino here for Venetian and foreign aristocracy. The Ridotto is seen on pictures by Guardi and Longi.

LIBRARIES

Biblioteca Mariana
Piazzale San Marco, 1-13A
Open Monday to Friday 0900-1900 hrs; Saturday 0900-1300 hrs. Closed Sunday.
The Biblioteca Mariana is an architectural masterpiece, built between 1536 and 1553 by Sansovino and completed after his death by Vincenzo Scamozzi.

Today it houses the display rooms of the St. Mark's Library, with old manuscripts, book illustrations, gems, calligraphy and a precious collection of over 831 Flemish miniatures, (Brevarium Grimani) from the 16th century.

In the vestible there is a ceiling painting by Titian (Wisdom) and on the ceiling of the Golden Chamber there are 21 allegorical figures, 3 by Veronese (Arithmetic, Music, Geometry) and 12 portraits of philosophers around the walls, including some by Tintoretto. The reading rooms can be used by appointment, Tel: 5208788.

Biblioteca Fondazione Cini
San Giorgio Maggiore
Tel: 5289900.
Open Monday-Friday 0900-1200 hrs and 1530-1830 hrs, by appointment only. Closed Saturdays and Sundays.

Biblioteca Querini-Stampalia
Near Santa Maria Formosa,
Calle Querini-Stampalia 4778
Tel: 5225235.
Open 1000-1900 hrs, closed Mondays. Entry fee: 1,000 lire.
The library possesses a collection of 120,000 volumes and manuscripts, mainly from Venice and its environs. Next to the library in the Palazzo Querini-Stampalia is a collection of paintings with works from the 14th to the 18th centuries.

State Archives
Next to Frari Church on the Campo dei Frari
Open Tuesday, Thursday 0830-1400 hrs and 1500-1800 hrs; other days 0830 to 1400 hrs.

University Library
In the Ca' Foscari, Calle Barnardo 3199
Open from Monday to Friday 0900-2000 hrs; Saturday 0900-1400 hrs.

Library and Archives of the Biennale
Palazzo della Regina, Calle della Rosa, 2214
Open Monday-Saturday 0900-1400 hrs.

Biblioteca Correr
Piazza San Marco 52
Open Monday to Saturday 0900-1300 hrs. Closed Sundays.

Theater Library
In the Casa Goldoni,
Calle dei Nomboli 2798
Open Monday to Saturday 0830-1330 hrs.

NIGHTLIFE

BARS & NIGHTCLUBS

The Venetians do not like to stay out late at night. Bars and restaurants mostly close early. The nightclubs and bars that stay open late contain mostly tourists. The Venetians themselves prefer a *bacaro*, a simple, cosy establishment where one can have a glass of wine, a *cicchetti* or savory, and a chat. This entertainment seldom lasts past midnight. Here are a few popular meeting places:

Ai do' Draghi
Campo Sante Margherita
A popular students' meeting place.

Ai Musicanti
Ponte della Canonica, Castello
Daily 2100-2400 hrs, April to October.
Gondeliers sing here every night but few

Venetians come to hear them. The majority of the audience are tourists.

Ai Postali
Fondamenta Rio Mario
Jazz and Reggae played here; in summer one can sit on the canal bank. Many young Venetians come here.

Casanova
Calle Larga Vendramin, in the Palazzo Vendramin which houses the Casino during winter.
Daily 1500-0300 hrs, October to March.
Expensive and traditional.

La Mansarde
Campo San Fantin, near the Teatro La Fenice, above the restaurant "Al Teatro".
Bar with piano and roof garden. Reservations necessary. Closed Mondays.

There are bars with good piano music in some luxury hotels such as the Gritti, Danieli, Excelsior, Des Bains and Cipriani. From the Bar of the Hotel Monaco one has a wonderful view of Santa Maria della Salute in the evenings.

La Perla
Lungomare Marconi 4, Lido
Open daily 1500-0300 hrs from April to September.
Elegant nightclub on the Lido where the Casino is held in summer. A program of music and variety, elegant and expensive.

La Vedova
Via 22 Aprile.
Traditional, simple but friendly establishment, open until midnight.

Linea d' Ombra
Open from 0800-0200 hrs, closed on Wednesdays.
Jazz Club with wine and piano music, near the Salute church in Dorsoduro 19. Every Friday and Sunday there is a jazz concert here from 2200-2400 hrs.

Martini Scala
Calle del Cafetier, 2007, San Marco
Daily except Tuesday 2100-0300 hrs.
Belongs to the fine restaurant "Antico Martini"...a bar with a pleasant atmosphere and piano music. Hot meals are served until late at night.

DISCOS

Club 22
Lungomare Marconi 22, Lido.

Il Souk
Calle Contarini Corfé 1056 a, Dorsoduro.

Parco delle Rose
Gran Viale S, M Elizabetta 56, Lido.

Piper
Lista di Spagna 124 (near Railway station).

Teens' Club
Fondamenta Morosini della Regina, 4890, San Marco.

GAMBLING

Casino
The Casino Municipals is on the Lido in Summer, at the Palazzo del Casino, Lungomare 4; in winter, it is in the city at the Palazzo Vendramin-Calergi. The summer season lasts from April to September, the winter season from October to March.

SHOPPING

SHOPPING AREAS

The main shopping streets of Venice are the Mercerie between San Marco and the Rialto, the Calle Vallareso, Calle Frezzeria and Calle Largo 22 Marzo: here one finds the most expensive antiques, jewelry, fashions and shoes. The further one gets from Piazza San Marco the more reasonable the prices. This also applies to food in shops and restaurants.

VAT

The Value Added Tax in Italy is 27.5 percent. Tourists can have this VAT refunded if they make an application and present it with the original bill. Since this is a nuisance at the border or when leaving Italy one might prefer to shop at the "Tax Free Shop for Tourists". These shops can be found at border crossings and airports.

WHAT TO BUY

BURANO LACE

Jesurum
Ponte Canonica, San Marco; Piazza San Marco, South Arcade.
The famous traditional emporium for hand-worked lace, hand-printed fabrics, and household linen.

Maria Mazzaron
Fondamenta dell' Osmarin 4970 Castello. One of the most famous lace makers in Venice.

GLASS

Barovier & Toso
Fondamenta dei Vetrai 28, Murano.

Gino Cenedese
Piazza San Marco 139, Fondamenta Venier, Murano.

Ongaro e Fuga
Calle Moschio 13, Murano.
Traditional Venetian mirrors.

Ferro & Lazzarini
Fondamente Navagero, 75 Murano.

Pauly
Piazza dei Leoncini, 316 San Marco.

Salviati
Frezzeria, 1230 San Marco.

Venini
Piazza dei Leoncini 314 San Marco.
Every piece here is a work of art.

GROCERIES

Markets are open from 0700-1330 hrs; most close in the afternoon. The Fish market (Pescheria), built in the traditional way in 1907 on 18,000 larch trunks, is open from 0500-1100 hrs, closed Mondays.

Rialto Market
Fruit, Meat, Pescheria (fish) Cheese, Erberia (Vegetable market). Here are the wharves for the fruit and vegetable boats which moor in the afternoon.

The following market are less expensive and fewer tourists shop there:
Campo Santa Margherita: Fruit and vegetables
Rio Terra San Leonardo: Fish and vegetables
Campo Santa Maria Formosa: Vegetables and fruit
Campo Santi Apostoli: Confectionery.

CHEESE (FORMAGGIO)

Casa del Parmigiano
San Polo 214

Allani
Ruga Rialto 654 San Polo

Oil (olio)
La Fonte dell' olio
Calle San Provolo 4963

Pasta
Il Fornaio
Calle San Luca, San Marco
(pasta specialities from all over Italy)

Rizzo
Salizzada San Giovanni 5578, Cannaregio (pasta specialities with paprika, coffee, garlic, cocoa and artichokes).

WINE (VINO)

Enoteca al Volto
Calle Casalli 4081 San Marco.

MARBLED PAPER

A wonderful old craft which has remained very much alive in Venice and which still has many admirers.

Legatoria Piazzesi
Ponte della Feltrina 2511 (near the church of Santa Maria del Giglio).
One can see how it is done.

MASKS

Gabi Lechner
Salizzada San Lio

Laboratoria Artigiano Maschere
Barbarie delle Tole 6657, Castello.

Mondonova
Rio Terra Canal 3063 Dorsoduro.

In all these shops one can buy the best and most artistic Commedia dell' Arte masks in Venice. They are mostly leather, hand-made. Mondonova also creates fantasy masks.

BOOKS

Santa Giovanni e Paolo
Campo SS Giovanni e Paolo 6358 Castello. A good selection of books about Venice in English and French. Also Italian art books and new publications.

Filippi
Calle del Paradiso 5763 Castello.
The best selection of literature on Venice.

Fantoni
Salizzada San Luca 4119 San Marco.
Excellent selection of art books, books on ballet, photography and music.

Sansovino
Bacino Orseolo 84, San Marco.
Valuable art books, prints and old engravings

SUPERMARKETS

Supermercato Full
Strada Nuova, 4237 A Cannaregio.

Supermercato
Via Garibaldi 1133 Castello
Campiello Melani 1338 San Polo;
Via Michieli 16 Lido;
Salizzada San Lio.

Standa
Strada Nuova 3360 Cannaregio.

EXPORT

Up to $500 worth of goods purchased in Italy may be taken out without any duty. Antiques and works of art require a license from the Art Board.

About $350 worth of goods such as tobacco, coffee, tea may be taken out duty free.

SPORTS

PARTICIPANT

Information about all the sporting activities offered in the city can be obtained from **Centro Sportivo Turistico**, Piazzale Santa Maria Elisabetta on the Lido.

• Swimming
The nearest bathing beach is of course the 7-mile (12-km) **Lido**. Most of it, however, belongs to the hotels. Bathing cabins can be rented even if one is not a hotel guest.

There is a public beach at Lungomare d'Annunzio and unrestricted bathing on the island of Pellestrina.

Bathing huts can be rented from: Direzione Attivitá Balneari, Gran Viale Santa Maria Elisabetta 2, Lido.

Another popular bathing resort is **Sottomarina** on the island of Chioggia, 37 miles (50 km) from Venice. There are many other resorts on the north Adriatic coast: Jesolo and Punta Sabbioni, Caorle, Bibione, Eraclea Mare, Lignano Sabbadioro.

• Fencing
Circolo Scherma, Cannaregio 47.

• Golf
Courses on the Lido near the hotels "des Bains" and Excelsior. There is an 18-hole course at the Campo Alberoni on the Lido.

• Riding
Circolo Ippico Veneziano, Ca' Bianca, Lido.

- **Trap Shooting**
Tiro e Segno Nazionale, San Niccoló 23, Lido.

- **Sailing**
Compagnia della Vela, San Marco, Giardinetti (Management)
Tel: 5222593.

Marina: Isola San Giorgio Maggiore
Tel: 5289287.

- **Tennis**
Tennis Club Lido
Via San Gallo 163, Lido
Tel: 5260954.

Tennis Club Marina di Punta Sabbioni
Via Montello/Punta Sabbioni.

Tennis Club Venezia
Lungomare Marconi 41, Lido
Tel: 5260335.

One can also play on the hotel tennis courts at the Lido.

- **Windsurfing**
Hotel Excelsior, Lungomare Marconi 41, Lido.

SPECIAL INFORMATION

STUDENTS

Study in Venice: General information should be obtained from foreign programs found in one's own country.

The student organization *L'Ufficio Assistenza del' ESU* Ca' Foscari, Calle Giustinian 3246 Dorsoduro, gives out a brochure *Universittá*, full of important information on how to proceed.

FACULTIES IN VENICE

Architecture, Chemistry, Literature, Philosophy, Languages, Political Economy, and Art History.

Accademia di Belle Arti
Campo della Caritá 1050, Dorsoduro (Art History).

Universitádi Ca' Foscari
Calle Giustinian 3246 Dordoduro (Languages).

Instituto di Architectura
Campazzi di Tolentini 191 Santa Croce (Architecture, Urban Studies.)

PHOTOGRAPHY

Film and photographic supplies are available in the photographic supply shops of Venice – the quality is good but the prices are high. Slides can be developed and there are very good series of slides with sights of Venice on sale. One can take photographs just about everywhere in Venice. Flashlights are not permitted in the churches as they harm the oil paintings. Look for directions about taking photographs on the spot.

LANGUAGE

SPEECH

"The Venetian dialect is softer, gentler and more flowing than the written speech and endlessly rich in words of flattery and endearment, which shows the sweet nature of the people."

Georg von Martens described the Venetian dialect in this way in 1838 and Lord Byron and Madame de Sael both expressed their admiration for it in expressions such as "sweet bastard latin" and "charming burr". Everyone who hears Venetians speaking together, even a listener whose Italian is not perfect, can recognize a distinct difference from the general speech.

In *Venessian* - as Venetians call their speech with loving pride – tradition, self-confidence and the memory of a people's proud history are all kept alive. The trade relationship of the Venetian maritime republic are shown in the many borrowings from Hebrew, Spanish, Turkish and Arabic.

The use of the dialect is not a sign of lack of education or an inability to speak correctly as it is in some countries. The lovable character of the Venetians seems to be best expressed in their dialect so that it was used even in the best circles as part of the Venetian culture: all of Goldoni's comedies are written in the Venetian dialect. That this dialect today has no importance beyond Venice and did not become the general written speech of Italy has an historical explanation. In the 15th and 16th century, at the height of Venice's political power, the Venetian speech was not a dialect but the general means of expression, spoken and written everywhere. There were other Italian dialects and finally the Tuscan dialect triumphed as a result of the literary works of the Florentine writers such as Dante, Petrarch and Boccaccio. Venetian list its supremacy and today the Tuscan speech is regarded as the purest and clearest form of Italian.

This didn't impress the Venetians in the least. They showed their pride in their dialect not only in the way they went on speaking it but especially in the way that they give their streets, alleys, squares and churches names in *Venessian*: San Vidal instead of San Vitale, San Salvador instead of San Salvatore, San Lio instead of San Leone, Sant' Aponal instead of San' Apollinaire.

Of course the visitor will not be able to make much of these special Venetian creations at first. Who could tell that San Zanipolo is the altered name for the Church of Santissimi Giovanni e Paolo! *Zani* is the diminutive of Giovanni and *Polo* the dialect form of Paolo. Other combinations include *San Staé* for Sant' Eustachio, *San Marcuola* for SS Ermargora e Fortunato, *San Trovaso* for SS Gervasio e Protasio and *San Zan Degola* for San Giovanni Decollato (St. John the Decapitated).

But even everyday words are not left alone. It is as if one letter must be changed at least, to give the word the true "Venessian" ring. So *pesce* (fish) becomes psees, *cicisbeo* (lover) sigisbeo, *aneglo* becomes anzelo and Giuliano *Zulian*.

The Venetians love shortening words, as shown by the names of the churches; the write *Ca'* for *Casa*, meaning a patrician house or a palazzo. *Frari* stands for *frati* (brother, monk, friar) and in some family names the ending is left off giving Corner for Coenaro, Venier for Veniero, Falier for Faliero, Loredan for Loredano.

The names of various occupations show the Venetian humor and inventiveness and have no equivalent in Italian. An *Erbaröl* is a seller of vegetables and herbs (from "erba" = herb) a *Pistór* is a baker or a pastrycook, a *Luganegher* a sausage maker and a *Saonér* a seller of soap.

A last typically Venetian expression is the name for a gondoliere. Perhaps the Venetians found this word too long for everyday use…they simply call *"Pope"* when they want to cross the Grand Canal quickly with the Traghetto.

FURTHER READING

FICTION & BIOGRAPHY

Andersch, Alfred. *Die Rote*. Zürich: 1974.

D'Annuncio, Gabriele. *Il Fuoco*. 1925. Translated as the *Flame of Life*.

Calvino, Italo. *Le Citta Invisibili*. Translated as *Invisible Cities*, 1972.

Casanova, Giacomo. *Memoirs*. Translated into many languages.

Fruttero, Carlo & Franco Lucentini. *L' Amante Sense Fissa Dimora*. 1987.

Habe, Hans. *Palazzo*. München: 1978.

Hemingway, Ernest. *Across the River and into the Trees*. 1950.

Highsmith, Patricia. *Those Who Walk Away*. Pan Books: 1968; Hamlyn Paperbacks: 1979.

James, Henry. *The Wings of the Dove*. 1902.
———. *The Aspern Papers*. 1888.

Jong, Erica. *Serenissima*. Dell: 1987.

Mann, Thomas. *Der Tod in Venedig*. 1912. Translated as *Death in Venice*.

Palazzeschi, A. *The Doge*.

Passinetti, P.M. *Venetian Red*.

Proust, Marcel. *Albertine Disparue*. 1925. aka *La Fugitive*. (Part six of the long novel *A la recherche du temps perdu* 1913-27. Translated by C.K. Scott-Moncrieff as *The Sweet Cheat Gone*, part six of *Remembrance of Things Past*.)

Roché, H.P. *Jules et Jim*.

Rolfe, Frederick W. (alias Baron Corvo) *The Desire and Pursuit of the Whole*. Published posthumously in 1934. A Romance of Modern Venice.

Symona, A.J.A. *The Quest for Corvo*. 1934. An Experiment in Biography.

Toddi, Silvio. *Valid for ten days*.

Vesper, Bernward. *Der Reise*. Jossa: 1977. Translated as *The Journey*.

Von Hoffmannsthal, Hugo. *Andreas*. 1930.

HISTORY, ART & TRAVEL

Gasparetto, Astone. *Il vetro di Murano delle orignai ad oggi* (Murano glass from its origins to the present day). Venice: 1958. Standard work with text in English, German and French.

Guiton, Shirley. *A World by Itself: Tradition and Change in the Venetian Lagoon*. London: 1970.

Hale, J.R. (ed.) *Renaissance Venice*. London: 1973.

Howells, William Dean. *Venetian Life*. 1866.

Italian Journeys. 1867. (The distinguished American man of letters was consul in Venice 1861-65).

Kretschmayr, Heinrich. *Geschichte von Venedig*.

Lauritzen, Peter. *Venice. A Thousand years of culture and civilisation*. New York: 1981.

Lebe, R. *Als Markus nach Venedig kam*. München: 1987. Well-founded, readable account of Venetian history and the cult of St. Mark.

Links, J.G. *Venice for Pleasure*. London: 1966.

Lorenzetti, Giulio. *Venice and its lagoon*. Triest: 1980.

McCarthy, Mary. *Venice Observed*. U.K.: Heinemann, 1961. The distinguished American novelist gives a brilliant, loving and witty account of Venice, its atmosphere and its legends.

Morris, Jan. *Venice*. Faber & Faber: London, 1979. *A Venetian Bestiary*. London: 1979. Stylish readable books of history, essays and anecdotes.

Norwich, J.J. *Venice, The Rise to Empire*. London: 1977

Ruskin, John. *The Stones of Venice (1851-53)*. Classic volume of art history and criticism.

Standard German history of Venice. Aalen: 1964. 3 volumes.

Twain, Mark. *A Tramp Abroad*. 1880.

Venice, The Greatness and the Fall. 1981.

Von Goethe, Johann Wolfgang. *Italienische Reise*. erster Teil 1786 dtv Gesemtausgabe, Bd 25, München 1962 (translated as *Italian Journeys*).

Worstenhome, Simon T. *Venetian Opera in the 17th century*. Oxford: 1954.

Zorzi, Alvise. *Venice, 1697-1797*. Also *Marco Polo and Venice: History of the*

Lion Republic.

Zorzi, B. (1922) is a popular Venetian historian and contributor to the *Mondo* and *La Stampa*.

PICTURE BOOKS

de Osma, Guillermo. *Fortuny, His Life and his work.* London: 1980.

Faure, Gabriel. *Venice.* Würzburg: 1964.

Lauritzen, Pater & Alexander Zielke. *Venezianische Paläste.* München: 1979.

Pignatti, Terisio. *Piazza San Marco.* Novara: 1957.

Santagiuliana, Fabio. *Carnival in Venice.* 1981.

Siegert, Dietmar. *Venedig in frühen Photographien (1848-1905).* A beautiful book of early photographers and poems by travelers of the period.

USEFUL ADDRESSES

TOURIST INFORMATION

Helpful Information from A-Z: The helpful brochure *Un ospite di Venezia* is put out by the Hotel Porters' Association and is obtainable at information desks. It contains information on cultural events, hotels, the going rate for gondolas and *motoscafi*, important telephone numbers, coming events, the vaporetti timetable, church services, opening times of museums, travel agents and the address of the all-night pharmacy.

Other tourist information may be gotten from the following:

Ente Provinciale Turismo (E.P.T.)
Piazza San Marco 71/C (near the passage through the Napoleonic Wing)
Open Monday to Saturday 0900-1300 hrs.

Ente Provinciale Turismo (E.P.T.)
Piazzale Roma
Open 0830-1830 hrs.

Here the visitor receives a city plan, free of charge, and the brochure *Un ospite di Venezia* in Italian and English.

Assessorato al Turismo (The Tourist Department of the city)
Ca' Giustinian, Salizzade San Moisé 1364/A
Tel: 5209955.
Open 0830-1830 hrs
For a small price one can obtain an information folder with a plan of the city, a calendar of events, and an up-to-date information in English, French and German. In the Ca' Giustinian one can obtain posters of Venice and its festivals such as the *Regatta Storica*.

Sometimes young people can receive a pass which entitles them to reductions in museums or restaurants. Ask for information about this scheme.

From the first floor of the building there is a fine view of the island of San Giorgio Maggiore and the Dogana.

Azienda Autonoma Turismo
Information office of the A.A.T. at the Railway Station.
Open Monday to Saturday 0800-2000 hrs; Sunday 1200-2000 hrs.

Ente Nazionale per il Turismo
ENIT has branches in all major European cities, as well as overseas.

Goethestr 20
8000 München 2
West Germany
Tel: Germany 089/530369.

Kaiserstr 65
6000 Frankfurt Am Main
West Germany
Tel: Germany 089/530369.

Kärntnerring 4
1010 Vienna
Austria
Tel: Austria 1222/654374.

Rue du Marché 3
1204 Geneva
Switzerland
Tel: Switzerland 022/282922.

Under the number 111 in Venice, you can get information and advice at any time. The assistants here speak many languages.

Handicapped persons who visit Venice receive a free plan at the Health Department.

CONSULATES

Bundersrepublik Deutschland
Sottoportico Giustinian (opposite the Accademia)
Tel: 5225100.

Great Britain
Dorsoduro 1065
Tel: 5227207.

USA
Largo Donegani 1, Milan
Tel: 02/652841.

ART/PHOTO CREDITS

INDEX

A
B
C
D
F
G
H
I
J
a
b
c
d
e
f
g
h
i
j
.
l